# JOHN SAYLES

## INTERVIEWS

CONVERSATIONS WITH FILMMAKERS SERIES
PETER BRUNETTE, GENERAL EDITOR

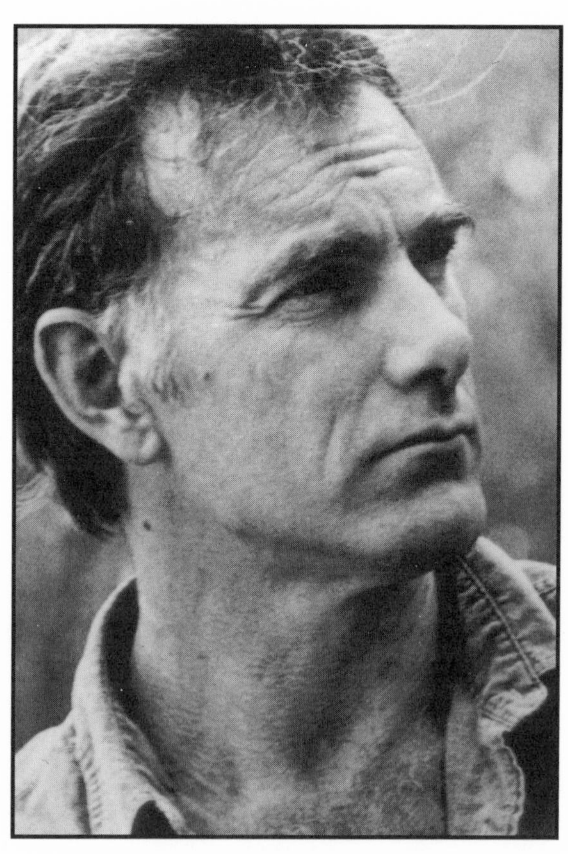

# JOHN SAYLES

# INTERVIEWS

EDITED BY DIANE CARSON

UNIVERSITY PRESS OF MISSISSIPPI / JACKSON

http://www.upress.state.ms.us


Manufactured in the United States of America

02 01 00 99 4 3 2 1

The paper in this book meets the guidelines for permanence and durability of the Committee on Production Guidelines for Book Longevity of the Council on Library Resources.

Insert photographs courtesy Museum of Modern Art, Film Stills Archives

Library of Congress Cataloging-in-Publication Data

Sayles, John, 1950–
John Sayles : interviews / edited by Diane Carson.
p. cm. — (Conversations with filmmakers series)
Filmography: p.
Includes index.
ISBN 1-57806-137-7 (cloth : alk. paper). — ISBN 1-57806-138-5 (pbk. : alk. paper)
1. Sayles, John, 1950– —Interviews. 2. Motion picture producers and directors—United States—Interviews. I. Carson, Diane. II. Title. III. Series.
PN1998.3.S3A5 1999
791.43'0233'092—dc21
[b] 99-17283
CIP

British Library Cataloging-in-Publication Data available

# CONTENTS

# INTRODUCTION

NO OTHER INDEPENDENT FILMMAKER can boast the diversity, longevity, and genius of John Sayles. Though we think first of his exceptional film work, his career for over two decades has encompassed much more. He has won two O. Henry Best Short Story awards: in 1975 for his first published short story, "I-80 Nebraska, M.490–M.205," appearing in *The Atlantic* and in 1977 for "Breed." In that same year, his second novel, *Union Dues,* was nominated for both the National Book Award and the National Book Critics' Circle Award, the only book that year to receive such dual recognition. I cite this early recognition of his writing talent because Sayles continues to help finance his films by working as a "script doctor" for a who's who in Hollywood with contributions (credited and uncredited, some substantive and some minimal) to over two dozen feature films. In addition, Sayles has received two Academy Award nominations for his original screenplays for *Passion Fish* (1992) and *Lone Star* (1996). Quite logically, then, interviewers ask frequently about Sayles's writing—when, how, with what degree of difficulty and enjoyment, for whom, why, with what emphasis—on dialogue or images—and with what influences.

As the interviews collected here show, Sayles enjoys the variety of his writing opportunities, which have included horror films, television series, serious dramatic features, two plays, a couple dozen short stories, and three novels to date. He considers the variety of substance and style complementary and stimulating. His pay also makes possible the fierce independence he adamantly demands for his own cinematic works. As he told Cheryl

Kushner, "It's important to try to make the movies you want to make, the way you want to make them."

From the time Sayles found his creative writing classes at Williams College a breeze to his quick production of scripts for himself and others, he has excelled in writing. The authenticity and multi-dimensionality of central and supporting characters as well as the genuineness of their dialogue, have been enhanced by Sayles's ability to remember long conversations verbatim—conversations sometimes committed to paper for future use. But while writing everything from suspenseful horror films to serious social drama comes relatively effortlessly to Sayles, securing financing has always proved difficult. In many instances in this collection, Sayles notes the contrast between mainstream, studio-desirable fare and the more complex, challenging topics he has chosen to dramatize in his films. Sayles shows himself to be a realist about the financing/exhibition situation. But despite the uphill battle to secure financing, he and longtime partner Maggie Renzi have completed eleven feature films since 1980 and, as this goes to press, are in postproduction on their twelfth.

Because of their extraordinary quality of low budget, high content films, these works have garnered most attention in the interviews collected here. With Sayles's experience as a day laborer, a nursing home orderly, a meat packer in a sausage plant, and a factory worker, among other odd jobs; with his avid interest in and knowledge of various cultures; with his tangential involvement in mainstream cinema productions; and with his distinct and dissimilar films (topics, time periods, hybrid genres, and styles), these discussions encompass a continuum of issues involved in the creative and technical aspects of filmmaking.

Inevitably, since the release of a new film provides the catalyst for most of these newspaper and magazine articles, interviewers cover similar territory. This is unavoidable in such a collection. But, quite remarkably at times, the context for the question places Sayles's response into different relief. To preserve the integrity of each interview and for the revealing, sometimes subtle shifts in approach and in Sayles's responses, every interview is reprinted verbatim. At the very least, similar questions reveal interviewers' common concerns and shared assumptions about readers' interests. Though not the impetus for this project, it is an unanticipated and secondary revelation that I would not want to gloss over.

But the purpose of this collection is to make Sayles's insightful commentary available in one book. Along with many other avid filmgoers, I made a mental note to watch for Sayles's work after seeing *The Return of the Secaucus Seven*. In 1980, his first film struck a singular chord of response in babyboomers and contained a commanding authenticity and intelligence. Like every one of his subsequent films, it challenged us to think more profoundly about our lives and more critically about those other, glossier but more superficial, film experiences. It challenged us to consider the profound connections and the perplexing problems we share. As he told Kent Black in 1995, "In all my films, I've explored questions of identity and community," and as Sayles anchored film after film in these most basic human constructs, journalist after journalist has pursued the nature and implications of his observations, of everyone "tied up together" (Baron).

Since important principles must be lived ones, the application of his beliefs extends to Sayles's working style. "We try to get rid of rank as much as we can on a movie set," Sayles said to Nancy Scott. Echoing this conviction, he commented to Kathy Huffhines, "I do see the social and political in everything." This certainly describes the rallying cry of all of Sayles's films from his earliest in 1980 to his current effort.

With *The Return of the Secaucus Seven,* Sayles hit the cinema world's radar screens with an impressive debut effort. Journalists' attention followed and increased with each film. As the interviews from this early period show, Sayles had already given serious thought to, understood well, and articulated clearly his values and agenda. Remarkably, neither has been compromised or diminished since 1980. As Sayles told David Chute in 1981 in the interview which begins this collection, "Very few people get to make more than a couple of independent films without either starting to work for the studios, or giving up, turning into an underground filmmaker. . . . It would be great if I could pull it off." The interviews that follow provide insight into exactly how and why he did succeed at this nearly impossible feat.

Through all of the interviews, certain themes recur: his rejection of pretentious exploitation films, his disinterest in directing high-priced "schlock," his indifference to studio lures, the need to scramble for production money, his inventive strategies for production on a shoestring budget, the lack of appeal of his projects to Hollywood, his influences from favorite films and filmmakers, the integral interrelationship of personal and sociopolitical problems, the cautious belief in constructive change tempered by a realistic recognition of deep-seated, inherited problems, and the joy of good hard work. The interviews are arranged chronologically beginning with his first film. Because Sayles had a distinguished record of awards for his writing, many interviewers pursued his writing angle on *Return of the Secaucus Seven.* Sayles obligingly details the way he outlines, how he develops fully rounded characters in minimal screen time, where and how he writes, how he compensates for lack of camera movement, and his non-negotiable priority—"I get the final cut and casting control" (Lyman), for which he will always sacrifice a larger budget.

Fortuitously, then, he received a MacArthur Foundation Award in 1983. The tax-free, $30,000 grant for each of five years helped Sayles's efforts. But the best story here is Sayles's learning of the "genius grant" (not surprisingly, Sayles dislikes the "genius" label) while editing *Baby, It's You.* As Sayles told John Hartl, after receiving the phone call informing him of the award, Sayles said, "That's great. I really have to go back to work now."[1]

As Sayles moved on to *Lianna* and *Baby, It's You,* he emphasized his focus on exploring characters' behavior—the prejudices they encounter, the stereotypes they contest, and the class divisions they challenge. Interviews from this period reveal the impassioned integrity of his social conscience and of his filmmaking process as well. As he reveals in many comments and asserts to Judy Stone, "I don't believe in tricking people. . . . I don't think you can make a movie with principles about the way people treat each other and treat actors terribly." His principled approach extends to researching his subject matter in depth and to listening and talking to many sources. As a man writing and directing a film about a lesbian and as a white person setting a film in Harlem, crossing gender and racial boundaries, such sensitivity is not only admirable but necessary to assure veracity. But Sayles carefully qualifies his efforts, asserting the modest claims of his films. *Lianna* is *ONE* woman's story; *Brother From Another Planet* is an imaginative, outsider's take on certain cultural peculiarities and problems. Because of the specificity and individuality of his characters, no claims to universality ever apply, despite the far-reaching implications of emblematic events.

Sayles's emphasis on maintaining momentum through character development not action scenes figures prominently in the interviews clustering around *Lianna, Baby, It's You,* and *The Brother From Another Planet.* Sayles explicitly and implicitly reveals his concern for veracity, achieved through the precision of dialogue and refusal to capitulate to facile resolutions. As he told *American Cinematographer,* "My first priority is always with the acting and the believability of the characters."

In the late '70s and early '80s, Sayles also wrote and revised scripts for several horror and science fiction films, most infamously Roger Corman's *Piranha.* His desire to write a good script, whether about werewolves or piranhas or alligators, and to respect his audience comes through in his interview with Robert Seidenberg. As Sayles said, "[I'm] careful not to condescend to what you're writing or to the viewer... they can sense that." Such an attitude is as refreshing as it is rare. Moreover, this does not make such work somber. In fact, Sayles's playful sense of humor and love of sci-fi classics surface best in Gerald Peary's article from *The Twilight Zone Magazine.* Talking about *Alligator,* Sayles said, "I liked the idea of the alligator walking around on fire. They said no, because the alligator was booked for a personal appearance in a flatbed truck for publicity. We couldn't destroy it." But in the midst of his "scriptwriter-for-hire" work, he also writes scripts for television about matters of great importance. For example, he wrote *Unnatural Causes* for television "on Agent Orange because I want the story to get out while the veterans' class action suit is still going. TV can move so much faster and is seen by more people."[2]

In the late '80s, Sayles made two films set one year apart. *Matewan* tells the story of the 1920 Matewan, West Virginia, coal miners' massacre and *Eight Men Out* takes us inside the 1919 Chicago "Black Sox" Scandal. Sayles had worked on both projects for years before they came to fruition—a history detailed in several interviews given at the time of these two films' releases. As Kathy Huffhines relates, Sayles's strong social and political beliefs come through in all his films, but especially in *Matewan.* In addition, during production, Sayles put his money where his mouth is. Shooting in Thurmond, West Virginia, he notes, "We wound up hiring about half the town" (Huffhines).

In interviews given to publicize these films, Sayles comments on his choice of topics, his production methods, and the contrast between his work and Hollywood's. Discussing *Eight Men Out,* he says, "It's important to try to make the movies you want to make" (Kushner). Or, as he knows, "Union-war films are probably not the hottest topic at Hollywood power breakfasts these days, probably not trendy vehicles for trendy young stars who are being rushed into yet more movies about trendy young subjects for trendy young audiences" (Vecsey). By contrast, Sayles wants his films to be about something that matters: a Union and union. Speaking about *Matewan,* he makes an observation equally appropo of all his work, "I can take a lot of risks that studios won't talk about. I can talk about things in depth. I can make the audience uneasy" (Vecsey).

With *Matewan,* Sayles harnesses the full force of his adaptable style and searing substance. It and *Eight Men Out* form strong companion pieces as Sayles acknowledges to Dan Smith: "*Matewan* is about a whole town . . . *Eight Men Out* is not just about eight people but a lot of others, different strata of society. It's about how people can corrupt each other, how they lose an ideal or a spirit." And in both, Sayles integrates morality, history, and allegory, as he will in future films. Ironically but in his characteristically nonconformist way, Sayles "can't think of a better time to make a movie like [*Matewan*]—when unions are kind of on the ropes."[3] And while the subject of baseball remains, through good and bad times, dear to American hearts, a film about the reprehensible 1919 baseball scandal is not an audience draw. Both films were spurned by studios for their political content. Even more problematic by studio standards, Sayles probes the complicated motivations for the players' sell out rather than exploiting the titillating aspects or simplifying the ethical (or unethical) decisions.

Sayles is realistic about his appeal and lack thereof to those who make what he calls "the cinema of affluence. . . . The idea in most contemporary movies is to basically pay attention to yourself and that basically you can run your life without having anything upsetting come into your path if you work things right . . . that's a very political statement . . . [but] I want to go beyond the two-dimensional feel of most contemporary movies" (O'Sullivan). He knows that neither *Matewan* nor *Eight Men Out* would appeal to studios. How could they? *Matewan* resists the satisfying, triumphant shootout and, though America loves inspiring, rabble-rousing athletes, "who wants a sports movie about people who lose?" (Kushner). Almost as though answering his own question, Sayles asserts, "Movies can be entertaining without happy endings . . . involvement is what I'm after, more than people coming out feeling they've solved the problems of the world."[4] Or, to put it another way, Sayles says, "I think what marginalizes my movies is their complexity. The bad people. The good people. The girl.

The hero. That's not what I do and the minute you start to do something more complex, they [the studios] start to get nervous."[5] Continuing, it almost seems, to think through and pursue his ideas on this, Sayles told Claudia Dreifus of *The Progressive,* "I find that in this country there's a real suspicion of content. Sometimes, a real resentment of content. . . . I'm *not* nonchalant. I'm interested in the stuff I do being seen as widely as possible—but I'm not interested enough to lie."

As several journalists in this section note, Sayles breaks filmmaking conventions thematically and stylistically. As Sayles replies to Linda Billington, "It may not look the way we'd like it to look or sound the way we'd like it to sound or get seen by as many people as we'd like to have see it—but at least it will say the stuff we want it to say." With at least 52 speaking roles in *City of Hope,* he "wanted people to be able to tell—in part by the way it is shot—that there's no way these people can avoid affecting each other, even if they've never met" (Baron). And whether focused on a large urban environment or an isolated community in Ireland, as he told Philip Wuntch in their discussion of *The Secret of Roan Inish,* "Community—or the lack of it—is very important."

During the 90s and Sayles's movement from *City of Hope* to *Passion Fish* to *The Secret of Roan Inish* to *Lone Star* and *Men with Guns,* journalistic interest in his films and his political opinions tangential to them have increased. Perhaps we finally acknowledged (after the '80s "me decade") that personal problems reflect and in turn affect group dynamics. Among the highlights of the many good interviews on this handful of exceptional films are the following. In his lengthy *Cineaste* interview, Sayles discusses the "tribalism" that quickly surfaces in city and national politics, the economic and family variables that must be factored in, and the bewildering dilemmas that force difficult choices. And in his substantive exchange with Trevor Johnston for *Sight and Sound,* Sayles elaborates on mass culture and its limitations, his approach and longevity. "First of all, I'm not afraid of failure," a comment that could serve as Sayles's mantra for his distinguished but not always profitable films.

Thanks to recent, modest box office success, Sayles could come closer to achieving his visual objectives, and the interviews from this time period appropriately highlight that possibility. His and cinematographer Haskell Wexler's "Q&A" with *American Cinematographer* adds important information about the technical details, including the quality of light and the choice of palette and how both express what should be the complementary relationship between emotional and stylistic elements. As David Kipen notes on this subject, Sayles talks knowledgeably about visual aspects, to the surprise of some critics. Sayles comments to Kipen, for example, that "*Roan Inish* may be the least green movie ever filmed in Ireland [because] green is a tough color to control," causing particular problems maintaining skin tones.

Similarly, Megan Ratner's interview for *FILMMAKER* includes Sayles's reasons for the theatrical transitions, musical choices, and editing rhythms on *Lone Star* as well as the thematic emphasis. Responding to one question, Sayles connects the presence or absence of borders (literal and figurative ones that dominate *Lone Star*) with his technical choices—the soft cuts instead of the dissolves and hard cuts usually used between scenes. In addition, his choice of the widescreen format, keeping several characters in the frame together (important also in *City of Hope*) reinforces his insistence on the connectedness of individuals. He pursues this idea even further with Tim Miller of the *Cape Cod Times*. "I didn't want there to be a border, to be a line, between the present and the past, because *Lone Star,* to me, so much is about the burden of history."

As Sayles told me at the 1997 Toronto Film Festival, when he wrote *Lone Star,* as with his next film *Men with Guns,* he had in mind many such border battles from Bosnia to the former Soviet Union to Africa as well as Latin America and the American-Mexican boundary. Leaving the country unnamed in *Men with Guns* encourages our associating this type of conflict with multiple, as opposed to one specific, country, he explained.

Perhaps the title of his latest film, *Limbo,* says it best. Though he calls it "a very broad metaphor for what's happening in the economy of the United States" (Woodford), his sharply drawn characters reside in, or move through, transitional stages as well. Ironically, in the first interview in this collection, Sayles says, "All my movie projects are in limbo. My whole life is in limbo." Nevertheless, "We have to all hold ourselves responsible," however complex the problems we address.

For the issues raised in all of the interviews, as in all Sayles's films, there are no easy answers. Throughout his career, Sayles has addressed equally complex and, at times, maddeningly insoluble issues without offering happy endings or simplistic resolutions. With the heightened attention accorded independent filmmakers over the last few years, Sayles truly seemed ahead of his time when he began in 1980. Today, for many, the concept of "independence" in film circles no longer includes an integrity of challenging ideas or a financial separation from the studio machines. This lack of ideological and economic independence threatens to compromise, and often does compromise, less determined filmmakers. Sayles knows, and knew two decades ago, studios don't give huge checks and artistic independence. He chose and has remained true to his vision.

Additionally, with the recent increased attention accorded independent filmmakers, general audiences have noticed Sayles. As he said to me, *Lone Star,* in particular, drew audiences because of its inclusion of familiar icons, albeit in unfamiliar contexts. He has also achieved more "popular" recognition as a result of his fellow writers' nominating him twice for an Academy Award for best screenplay. And as talented actors search for good material and find it increasingly wanting, recognizable names eagerly work with him for scale. Because of Sayles's recognition of good, often unknown, talent (brought to the attention of other casting directors, in several instances), the avid filmgoing public increasingly recognizes Sayles's consistent excellence. Nevertheless, with his fierce refusal to capitulate or negotiate his artistic vision, Sayles will never be mainstream.

Sayles remains as much an exemplary maverick today as he was when he began hitchhiking from place to place and telling stories to those who gave him a lift in a beat up pickup or a rattling roadster. He continues to tell his stories to those who give him a chance and to compel our interest as his chameleon-like changes from urban life to Irish myth to border battles pull us in. His accomplishments are even more impressive than we realized at first glance in the early and mid 80s. To have maintained his principles, to have refused the easy paths, to have challenged himself and us repeatedly, to have avoided the limelight when it was offered, to have moved from one demanding project to another, Sayles has claimed his artistic independence.

In Toronto in 1997, I told him about my hope to pull together a collection of interviews. He said, "Good luck, I've done a zillion interviews." I didn't find quite that many, but he has obliged newspapers and periodicals, large and small, exactly as one would expect from a person so committed to telling his stories to all of us who want to listen. I close expecting that everyone who reads this will find meaningful technical suggestions and philosophical ideas. I continue to think about many of his remarks and

I hope from this collection you get to know John Sayles better and to enjoy thinking about and discussing his insights.

I want to thank all those at University Press of Mississippi for their support and patience with the daunting process of securing interviews and permissions to use them. I am particularly grateful to Seetha Srinivasan, Anne Stascavage, Elizabeth Young, and Shane Gong. They answered numerous questions, encouraged and helped me through the completion of this project. I am also grateful to the many authors with whom I spoke and the permissions editors across the United States. Without exception, everyone was polite, helpful, and responsive. To my always positive, incredibly able assistant, Deb Watson, my heartfelt thanks for hours of help. Finally I must express my appreciation to my husband and best friend, Willis Loy, without whom none of this would make sense.

## Endnotes

1. John Hartl, "Counterculture Producer Is Building a Reputation," *The Seattle Times,* 11 February 1983.

2. Dale Pollock, "*Brother* Director Is an Alien to Hollywood," *Los Angeles Times,* 20 October 1984.

3. Jim DeBrosse, "Sayles Bows to No One," *The Cincinnati Enquirer,* 13 September 1987.

4. Robert W. Butler, "A Montage of Inexorable Urban Decay," *Kansas City Star,* 20 October 1991.

5. Susan Stark, ". . . But Director Sayles's Scenario Isn't Completely Grim," *Detroit News,* 25 October 1991.

# JOHN SAYLES: CHRONOLOGY

1950 John Thomas Sayles is born on September 28, 1950, in Schenectady, New York, to Donald John Sayles, school administrator, and Mary Rausch Sayles, a schoolteacher. Sayles is of German-Irish descent. Both grandfathers were policemen.

Attended Mount Pleasant High School in Schenectady and earned letters in basketball, baseball, track, and football.

1968 Rejected by the U.S. Army because of a missing vertebra. Enters Williams College (Massachusetts) where he majors in psychology, plays intramural basketball and baseball, enrolls in creative writing classes, begins to take writing seriously, and acts in plays.

1972 Sayles graduates from Williams College, Williamstown, Massachusetts, with a B.S. in psychology. Over the next couple years, Sayles works as an orderly in a nursing home in Albany, as a day laborer in Atlanta, as a meat packer in Boston, and hitchhikes hundreds of miles.

1975 Sayles's first novel, *The Pride of the Bimbos* is published by Little Brown. Sayles's short story, "I-80 Nebraska, M.490–M.205," published in *The Atlantic,* wins his first O. Henry short-story award.

1977 Sayles begins writing for Roger Corman's New World Pictures. *Union Dues,* his second novel, is published and nominated for both the National Book Award and the National Book Critics' Circle Award (the only book to receive both these nominations in 1977.) Sayles short story, "Breed," wins his second O. Henry award as one of the year's best short stories.

1978 *Piranha,* for which Sayles wrote the screenplay, is released.

1979 Sayles writes, directs, and edits *The Return of the Secaucus Seven,* his first feature film. It costs $60,000 and is shot in 22 days. He plays the supporting role of Howie. His script wins the Los Angeles Film Critics' Award for Best Screenplay and is included on the year's top 10 by *Time, The Boston Globe,* and *The Los Angeles Times,* among others. Called by some a precursor of *The Big Chill* (1983), Sayles's film makes $2 million.

*The Lady in Red,* for which Sayles wrote the screenplay, is released. Sayles collection of 15 short stories, *The Anarchists' Convention* is published by Little Brown.

1980 *Alligator,* is released, from an original story by Sayles and from a Sayles screenplay. *Battle Beyond the Stars,* for which Sayles wrote the screenplay, is released. *The Howling,* for which Sayles is credited as a co-screenplay writer, is released. The made-for-television film, *A Perfect Match,* with a teleplay by Sayles, airs.

1981 Sayles directs his own one-act plays *New Hope for the Dead* and *Turnbuckle* at the Boat Basin Theater in New York City, a place considered Off-Off Broadway, with little success.

1983 *Lianna* is released and costs $300,000, which took one and a half years to raise. It is shot in 36 days. Sayles writes, directs and edits and plays the role of Jerry.

*The Challenge,* with Sayles credited as one of three writers, is released.

*Baby, It's You* is released, costing $3 million. Sayles writes and directs.

Sayles receives a John D. and Catherine T. MacArthur Foundation ("genius") Award, a grant of $30,000 a year for five years, tax free.

1984 *Hard Choices,* in which Sayles plays the role of Don, is released.

*The Brother From Another Planet* is released. Sayles writes, directs, edits, and plays the role of one of the alien bounty hunters. He wrote it in six days, it cost $350,000 to make and is shot in four weeks.

He also directs "Born in the U.S.A.," "I'm on Fire," and "Glory Days," all three music videos featuring Bruce Springsteen.

*The Clan of the Cave Bear,* with a screenplay by Sayles, and *Enormous Changes at the Last Minute,* with Sayles credited as the primary writer, are released.

1987 *Matewan* is released. Sayles writes, directs and plays the role of the preacher. Sayles's book, *Thinking in Pictures: The Making of the Movie 'Matewan,'* is released by the Houghton Mifflin Company. Budgeted at $4 million, it took 44 days to shoot. Sayles began working on the screenplay in 1979. Cinematographer Haskell Wexler received an Academy Award nomination for his work on the film.

*Wild Thing,* based on a Sayles's story and with a screenplay co-written by Sayles, is released. Sayles plays the motorcycle policeman.

1988 *Eight Men Out* is released. Sayles writes, directs and plays the role of Ring Lardner. Also budgeted at $6.5 million, it takes 9 weeks to shoot. Sayles wrote the first draft of the screenplay 11 years ago.

1989 *Mountain View* is released. It is directed by longtime partner and producer Maggie Renzi in collaboration with Sayles. *Breaking In* is released; screenplay by Sayles. The pilot of "Shannon's Deal," teleplay by Sayles, airs on television beginning the 13 episode series.

1990 *City of Hope* is released. Sayles writes, directs and edits and plays the role of garage owner Carl. The film includes over 52 speaking parts.

"Shannon's Deal" continues to run as a television series with Sayles as a creative consultant. He writes and appears in several of the episodes.

1991 Sayles's novel, *Los Gusanos (The Worms),* is published. The story is set in a Miami community and Sayles visits Miami several times to learn about the culture he depicts and teaches himself Spanish.

1992 *Passion Fish* is released. Sayles writes, directs and edits. The film, budgeted at $3.1 million, is shot in six weeks. Sayles draws on his work as a hospital orderly and in nursing homes to dramatize the dynamics of patient and caretaker. His screenplay receives an Academy Award nomination (*The Crying Game* wins) and Mary

McDonnell receives a best actress nomination. (Emma Thompson wins for *Howards End*.)

*Straight Talk* is released with Sayles in the role of Guy Girardi. *Malcolm X* is released with Sayles playing an FBI agent. *Matinee* is released with Sayles as a moral crusader.

1993 *A Safe Place* is released, script by Sayles. *My Life's in Turnaround* is released with Sayles playing a film producer.

1994 *The Secret of Roan Inish* is released. Sayles writes, directs and edits.

*Men of War* and *Bedlam* are released, both with screenplay collaboration by Sayles.

1996 *Lone Star* is released. Sayles writes, directs and edits. Sayles is nominated for an Academy Award for the screenplay. (*Fargo* wins.)

*Apollo* 13 is released with script credit to Sayles.

1997 *Men with Guns/Hombres Armados* is released, in Spanish, English, Nahuatl, Tzotzil, Maya and Kuna. Sayles writes directs and edits.

1998 *Sayles on Sayles* by Sayles and Gavin Smith is released by Faber and Faber. In it Sayles discusses his career and films.

Sayles writes and goes into production on his twelfth feature film, *Limbo*. Summer 1998, shooting takes place in Alaska.

# FILMOGRAPHY

## As Director

1980
THE RETURN OF THE SECAUCUS SEVEN
Production Company: Salsipuedes Productions, Inc.
Producers: Jeffrey Nelson, William Aydelott
Director/Screenplay/Editing: **Sayles**
Cinematography: Austin de Besche
Music: Mason Daring
Cast: Bruce MacDonald (Mike Donnelly), Adam LeFevre (J. T.), Gordon Clapp (Chip Hollister), Karen Trott (Maura Tolliver), David Strathairn (Ron Desjardins), Marisa Smith (Carol), Carolyn Brooks (Meg), Nancy Mette (Lee), Brian Johnston (Norman), Ernie Bashaw (Officer), Jessica MacDonald (Stacey), Jeffrey Nelson (Man), Maggie Renzi (Katie), Maggie Cousineau (Frances), Jean Passanante (Irene Rosenblum), Mark Arnott (Jeff), **Sayles** (Howie), Amy Schewel (Lacey Summers), Eric Forsythe (captain), Betsy Julia Robinson (Amy), John Mendillo (bartender), Jack Lavalle (booking officer), Benjamin Zaitz (Benjamin)
16 mm, Color
110 minutes

1983
LIANNA
Production Company: Winwood Company
Producers: Jeffrey Nelson and Maggie Renzi

Director/Screenplay/Editing: **Sayles**
Cinematography: Austin DeBesche
Music: Mason Daring
Cast: Linda Griffiths (Lianna), Jane Hallaren (Ruth), Jon De Vries (Dick), Jo Henderson (Sandy), Jessica Wight MacDonald (Theda), Jesse Solomon (Spencer), **Sayles** (Jerry), Stephen Mendillo (Bob), Betsy Julia Robinson (Cindy), Nancy Mette (Kim), Maggie Renzi (Sheila), Madelyn Coleman (Mrs. Hennessy), Robyn Reeves (job applicant), Marta Renzi (dancer)
16 mm. Color
112 minutes

1983
BABY, IT'S YOU
Production Company: Double Play Productions and Paramount Pictures Corporation
Producers: Griffin Dunne and Amy Robinson
Director/Screenplay: **Sayles**
Original Story: Amy Robinson
Cinematography: Michael Ballhaus
Production Design: Jeffrey Townsend
Editing: Sonya Polonsky
Cast: Rosanna Arquette (Jill Rosen), Vincent Spano ("Sheik" Capadilupo), Joanna Merlin (Mrs. Rosen), Jack Davidson (Dr. Rosen), Nick Ferrari (Mr. Capadilupo), Dolores Messina (Mrs. Capadilupo), Leora Dana (Miss Vernon), William Joseph Raymond (Mr. Ripeppi), Sam McMurray (Mr. McManus), Liane Curtis (Jody), Claudia Sherman (Beth), Marta Kober (Debra), Tracy Pollan (Leslie), Rachel Dretzin (Shelly), Susan Derendorf (Chris), Frank Vincent (Vinnie), Robin Johnson (Joann), Gary McCleery (Rat), Matthew Modine (Steve), John Ferraro (Plasky), Phil Brock (Biff), Robert Downey Jr. (Stewart), Fisher Stevens (stage manager)
35 mm, Color
104 minutes

1984
THE BROTHER FROM ANOTHER PLANET
Production Company: A-Train Films
Released by: Cinecom International Films

Producers: Peggy Rajski and Maggie Renzi
Director/Screenplay/Editing: **Sayles**
Cinematography: Ernest Dickerson
Production Design: Nora Chavooshian
Music: Mason Daring
Cast: Joe Morton (The Brother), Tom Wright (Sam Prescott), Caroline Aaron (Randy Sue Carter), Herbert Newsome (Little Earl), Dee Dee Bridgewater (Malverne Davis), Daryl Edwards (Fly), Leonard Jackson (Smokey), Bill Cobbs (Walter), Steve James (Odell), Edward Baran (Mr. Vance), **Sayles** and David Strathairn (Men in Black), Maggie Renzi (Noreen), Olga Merediz (Noreen's Client), Minnie Gentry (Mrs. Brown), Ren Woods (Bernice), Reggie Rock Bythewood (Rickey), Alvin Alexis (Willis), Rosetta Le Noire (Mama), Michael Albert Mantel (Mr. Lowe), Jaime Tirelli (Hector), Liane Curtis (Ace), Chip Mitchell (Ed), David Babcock (Phil), Sidney Sheriff Jr (Virgil), Carl Gordon (Mr. Price), Fisher Stevens (card trickster), Kim Stauton (teacher), Anthony Thomas (basketball player), Rosanna Carter (West Indian woman), Josh Mostel (Casio vendor)
35 mm, Color
108 minutes

1985
"Born in the U.S.A."
"I'm on Fire"
"Glory Days"
Director: **Sayles**, music videos for Bruce Springsteen

1987
MATEWAN
Production Company: Red Dog Films, Cinecom Entertainment Group, Film Gallery
Producers: Peggy Rajski and Maggie Renzi
Executive Producers: Amir Malin, Mark Balsam, Jerry Silva
Director/Screenplay: **Sayles**
Cinematography: Haskell Wexler
Production Design: Nora Chavooshian
Costumes: Cynthia Flynt
Editing: Sonya Polonsky

Music: Mason Daring
Cast: Chris Cooper (Joe Kenehan), Mary McDonnell (Elma Radnor), Will Oldham (Danny Radnor), David Strathairn (Sid Hatfield), Ken Jenkins (Sephus), Kevin Tighe (Hickey), Gordon Clapp (Griggs), James Earl Jones ("Few Clothes" Johnson), Bob Gunton (C. E. Lively), Jace Alexander (Hillard Elkins), Joe Grifasi (Fausto), Nancy Mette (Bridey Mae), Jo Henderson (Mrs. Elkins), Josh Mostel (Cabell Testerman), Gary McCleery (Ludie), Maggie Renzi (Rosaria), Tom Wright (Tom), Michael Preston (Ellix), Thomas A. Carlin (Turley), **Sayles** (preacher)
35 mm, Color
133 minutes

1988
EIGHT MEN OUT
Production Company: Orion Pictures Corporation
Producers: Sarah Pillsbury and Midge Sanford
Executive Producers: Barbara Boyle, Jerry Offsay
Director/Screenplay: **Sayles**
Based on the Novel by: Eliot Asinof
Cinematography: Robert Richardson
Production Design: Nora Chavooshian
Editing: John Tintori
Music: Mason Daring
Cast: John Cusack (Buck Weaver), Charlie Sheen (Hap Felsch), D. B. Sweeney ("Shoeless" Joe Jackson), Jace Alexander (Dickie Kerr), Gordon Clapp (Ray Schalk), Don Harvey (Swede Risberg), Bill Irwin (Eddie Collins), Perry Lang (Fred McMullin), James Read ("Lefty" Williams), Michael Rooker (Chick Gandil), David Strathairn (Eddie Cicotte), John Mahoney (Kid Gleason), James Desmond (Smitty), **Sayles** (Ring Lardner), Studs Terkel (Hugh Fullerton), Michael Lerner (Arnold Rothstein), Richard Edson (Billy Maharg), Christopher Lloyd (Bill Burns), Michael Mantell (Abe Attell), Kevin Tighe (Sport Sullivan), Clifton James (Charles Comiskey), Barbara Garrick (Helen Weaver), Wendy Makkena (Kate Jackson), Maggie Renzi (Rose Cicotte), Nancy Travis (Lyria Williams), Ken Berry (heckler), Danton Stone (hired killer), Stephen Mendillo (Monk), Jim Stark (reporter), John Anderson (Judge Kenesaw Mountain Landis), Eliot Asinof (Heydler), Clyde Bassett (Ben Johnson), John D. Craig, (Rothstein's Lawyer), Michael Laskin

(Austrian), Randle Mell (Ahearn), Robert Motz (District Attorney), Bill Raymond (Ben Short), Brad Garrett (PeeWee), Tay Strathairn (Bucky), Jesse Vincent (Scooter)
35 mm, Color
120 minutes

1989
MOUNTAIN VIEW
Production Company: Alive From Off Center and WGBH
Producers: Susan Dowling and Maggie Renzi
Executive Producer: Susan Dowling
Director: Marta Renzi in collaboration with **Sayles**
Cinematography: Paul Goldsmith
Production Design: Sandra McLeod
Editing: Susan Dowling and Marta Renzi
Music: Mason Daring
Cast: Thomas Eldred (Old Man), Jane Alexander (Bartender), Jace Alexander (Son), Fred Holland, Mary Schultz (couple on porch), Jim Desmond (Barfly), Marta Jo Miller (Young Mother), Christine Philion and Nathaniel E. Lee (Newlyweds), Cathy Zimmerman and Thomas Grunewald (couple in truck), Marta Renzi (other woman), Joanne Callum and Caroline Grossman (girlfriends), Doug Elkins and Chisa Hidako (son's friends), Sarah Grossman Greene, Irene Krugman, Caitlin Miller, and Amos Wolff (children)
16 mm, Color
25 minutes

1991
CITY OF HOPE
Production Company: Esperanza Inc.
Released by: Samuel Goldwyn Company
Producers: Sarah Green and Maggie Renzi
Executive Producers: John Sloss and Harold Welb
Director/Screenplay/Editing: **Sayles**
Cinematography: Robert Richardson
Production Design: Dan Bishop and Dianna Freas
Music: Mason Daring

Cast: Vincent Spano (Nick Rinaldi), Joe Morton (Wynn), Tony Lo Bianco (Joe Rinaldi), Barbara Williams (Angela), Chris Cooper (Riggs), Charlie Yanko (Stavros), Angela Bassett (Reesha), Jace Alexander (Bobby), Todd Graff (Zip), Scott Tiler (Vinnie), **Sayles** (Carl), Bill Raymond (Les), Maggie Renzi (Connie), Tom Wright (Malik), Frankie Faison (Levonne), David Strathairn (Asteroid), Anthony John Denison (Rizzo), Rose Gregorio (Pina), Kevin Tighe (O'Brien), Josh Mostel (Mad Anthony), Joe Grifasi (Pauly), Gina Gershon (Laurie), Miriam Colon (Mrs. Ramirez), Daryl Edwards (Franklin), Jude Ciccolella (Paddy), Mason Daring (Peter), Lawrence Tierney (Kerrigan), Michael Mantell (Zimmerj), Louis Zorich (Mayor Baci), Stephen Mendillo (YoYo), Gloria Foster (Jeanette), Ray Aranha (former mayor)
35 mm, Color
130 minutes

1992
PASSION FISH
Production Company: Atchafalaya
Released by: Miramax
Producers: Sarah Green and Maggie Renzi
Executive Producer: John Sloss
Director/Screenplay/Editing: **Sayles**
Cinematography: Roger Deakins
Production Design: Dan Bishop and Dianna Freas
Music: Mason Daring
Cast: Mary McDonnell (May-Alice), Alfre Woodard (Chantelle), David Strathairn (Rennie), Vondie Curtis-Hall (Sugar), Leo Burmester (Reeves), Nora Dunn (Ti-Marie), Mary Portser (Precious), Angela Bassett (Dawn/Rhonda), Sheila Kelley (Kim), Nancy Mette (Nina), Lenore Banks (Nurse Quick), William Mahoney (Max), Maggie Renzi (Louise), Tom Wright (Luther), John Henry (Dr. Blades), Marianne Muellerleile (Drushka)
35 mm, Color
135 minutes

1994
THE SECRET OF ROAN INISH
Production Company: Skerry Movies Corporation and Jones Entertainment Group

Producers: Sarah Green and Maggie Renzi
Executive Producers: John Sloss, Glenn R. Jones, Peter Newman
Director/Screenplay/Editing: **Sayles**
Based on the novel *Secret of the Ron Mor Skerry* by Rosalie K. Fry
Cinematography: Haskell Wexler
Production Design: Adrian Smith
Costumes: Consolata Boyle
Music: Mason Daring
Cast: Jeni Courtney (Fiona Coneelly), Mick Lally (Hugh/Grandfather), Eileen Colgan (Tess/Grandmother), John Lynch (Tadhg Coneelly), Richard Sheridan (Cousin Eamon), Cillian Byrne (Jamie), Pat Howey (priest), Dave Duffy (Jim Coneelly), Declan Hannigan (oldest brother), Gerard Rooney (Liam Coneelly), Susan Lynch (Sylkie)
35 mm, Color
103 minutes

1996
LONE STAR
Production Company: Rio Dulce/Castle Rock Entertainment
Producers: R. Paul Miller and Maggie Renzi
Executive Producer: John Sloss
Cinematography: Stuart Dryburgh
Director/Screenplay/Editing: **Sayles**
Production Design: Dan Bishop
Costumes: Shay Cunliffe
Music: Mason Daring
Cast: Chris Cooper (Sam Deed), Elizabeth Peña (Pilar Cruz), Joe Morton (Delmore "Del" Payne), Matthew McConaughey (Buddy Deeds), Kris Kristofferson (Charlie Wade), Clifton James (Mayor Hollis Pogue), Frances McDormand (Bunny), Miriam Colon (Mercedes Cruz), Jesse Borrego (Danny), Tony Plana (Ray), Stephen Mendillo (Cliff), LaTanya Richardson (Priscilla Worth), Stephen J. Lang (Mikey), Ron Canada (Otis Payne), Gabriel Casseus (Young Otis), Leo Burmester (Cody), Chandra Wilson (Athens), Eddie Robinson (Chet), Gordon Tootoosis (Wesley Birdsong), Oni Faida Lampley (Celie), Eleese Lester (Molly), Joe Stevens (Deputy Travis), Gonzalo Castillo (Amado), Richard Coca (Enrique), Tony Frank (Fenton), Jeff Monahan (Young Hollis), Damon Guy (Shadow), Dee Macaluso (Anglo

Mother), Luis Cobo (Mexican American father), Marco Perella (Anglo father), Don Phillips (principal), Tay Strathairn (Young Sam), Vanessa Martinez (Young Pilar)
Film Extract: *Black Mama, White Mama* (1973)
35 mm, Color
135 minutes

1997
MEN WITH GUNS/HOMBRES ARMADOS
Production Company: Lexington Road Productions and Clear Blue Sky Productions in association with The Independent Film Channel and Anarchists' Convention
Released by: Sony Pictures Classics
Producers: R. Paul Miller and Maggie Renzi
Executive Producers: Jody Patton, Lou Gonda, John Sloss
Director/Screenplay/Editor: **Sayles**
Cinematography: Slawomir Idziak
Music: Mason Daring
Production Design: Felipe Fernández del Paso
Costumes: Mayes C. Rubeo
Cast: Federico Luppi (Dr. Fuentes), Damián Delgado (Domingo, the soldier), Dan Rivera González (Conejo, the boy), Tania Cruz (Graciela, the mute girl), Damián Alcázar (Padre Portillo, the priest), Mandy Patinkin (Andrew), Kathryn Grody (Harriet), Iguandili López (mother), Nandi Luna Ramírez (daughter), Rafael De Quevedo (general), Carmen Madrid (Angela, Dr. Fuentes's daughter), Esteban Soberanes (Raúl, Angela's fiance), Iván Arango (Cienfuegos), Lizzie Curry Martínez (Montoya), Roberto Sosa (Bravo), Maggie Renzi and Shari Gray (tourists by pool), Paco Mauri (captain), David Villalpando and Raúl Sánchez (gum people)
35 mm, Color
123 minutes

## As Screenwriter

1978
PIRANHA
Production Company: Piranha Productions/New World Pictures
Executive Producers: Roger Corman, Jeff Schechtman
Producers: Jon Davison, Chako Van Leeuwen

Director: Joe Dante
Screenplay: **Sayles**
Original story: Richard Robinson, **Sayles**
Cinematography: Jamie Anderson (Metrocolor)
Editing: Mark Goldblatt, Joe Dante
Music: Pino Donaggio
Cast: Bradford Dillman (Paul Grogan), Heather Menzies (Maggie McKeown), Kevin McCarthy (Dr. Robert Hoak), Keenan Wynn (Jack), Dick Miller (Buck Gardner), Barbara Steele (Dr. Mengers), Belinda Balaski (Betsy), Melody Thomas (Laura), Bruce Gordon (Colonel Waxman), Barry Brown (trooper), Paul Bartel (Dumont), Shannon Collins (Suzie Grogan), Shawn Nelson (Whitney), Richard Deacon (Earl Lyon), **Sayles** (soldier)
35 mm, Color
94 minutes

1979
THE LADY IN RED
Production Company: New World Pictures
Producer: Julie Corman
Director: Lewis Teague
Screenplay: **Sayles**
Cinematography: Daniel Lacambre (Metrocolor)
Production Design: Jac McAnelly
Editing: Larry Bock, Ron Medico, Lewis Teague
Music: James Horner
Cast: Pamela Sue Martin (Polly Franklin), Robert Conrad (John Dillinger/Jimmy Lawrence), Louise Fletcher (Anna Sage), Robert Hogan (Jake Lingle), Laurie Heineman (Rose Shimkus), Glenn Withrow (Eddie), Rod Gist (Pinetop), Peter Hobbs (Pops Geissler), Christopher Lloyd (Frog-nose), Dick Miller (Patek), Nancy Anne Parsons (Tiny Alice), Alan Vint (Melvin Purvis), Milt Kogan (preacher), Chip Fields (Satin), Buck Young (Hennessey), Phillip R. Allen (Elliot Ness), Ilene Kristen (Wynona), Joseph X. Flaherty (Frank), Terri Taylor (Mae), Peter Miller (Fritz), Mary Woronow (woman bank robber), Jay Rasumny (Bill), Michael Cavanaugh (undercover cop), Arnie Moore (trucker), John Guitz (Momo), Saul Krugman (judge), Blackie Dammett (immigration officer)
35 mm, Color
93 minutes

1980
ALLIGATOR
Production Company: Alligator Associates, Group I Productions
Executive Producer: Robert S. Bremson
Producer: Brandon Chase
Director: Lewis Teague
Screenplay: **Sayles**
Original story: **Sayles** and Frank Ray Perilli
Cinematography: Joe Mangine
Editing: Larry Bock, Ronald Medico
Music: Craig Hundley
Cast: Robert Forster (Det. David Madison), Robin Riker (Marisa Kendall), Michael V. Gazzo (Police Chief Clark), Dean Jagger (Slade), Sydney Lassick (Lou Gutchel), Jack Carter (Mayor Ledoux), Perry Lang (Jim Kelly), Henry Silva (Colonel Brock), Bart Braverman (Thomas Kemp), John Lisbon Wood (mad bomber), James Ingersoll (Helms), Robert Doyle (Bill), Patti Jerome (Madeline), Angel Tompkins (newswoman), Sue Lyon (ABC newswoman)
35 mm, Color
94 minutes

1980
BATTLE BEYOND THE STARS
Production Company: New World Pictures
Executive Producer: Roger Corman
Producer: Ed Carlin
Director: Jimmy Teru Murakami
Screenplay: **Sayles**
Original story: **Sayles** and Anne Dyer
Cinematography: Daniel Lacambre
Additional photography: James Cameron
Editing: Allan Holzman and Robert J. Kizer
Music: James Horner
Cast: Richard Thomas (Shad), Robert Vaughn (Gelt), John Saxon (Sador), George Peppard (Space Cowboy), Darlanne Fluegel (Nanelia), Sybil Danning (St. Exmin), Sam Jaffe (Dr. Hephaestus), Morgan Woodward (Cayman), Carol Boen (First Nestor), John Gowens (Second Nestor), Steve Davis (Quopeg), Larry Meyers (The Kelvin), Lara Cody (The Kelvin), Lynn

Carlin (Nell), Jeff Corey (Zed), Marta Kristen (Lux), Julia Duffy (Mol), Eric Morris (Pen), Doug Carleson (Pok), Ron Ross (Dab), Terrence McNally (Gar)
35 mm, Color
103 minutes

1980
THE HOWLING
Production Company: Avco Embassy Pictures, International Film Investors, Wescom Productions:
Executive Producer: Steven A. Lane
Producers: Michael Finnell and Jack Conrad
Director: Joe Dante
Screenplay: **Sayles** and Terence H. Winkless
Original novel by: Gary Brandner
Cinematography: John Hora
Editing: Mark Goldblatt, Joe Dante
Music: Pino Donaggio
Cast: Dee Wallace (Karen White), Patrick Macnee (Dr. George Waggner), Dennis Dugan (Chris), Christopher Stone (R. William "Bill" Neill), Belinda Balaski (Terry Fisher), Kevin McCarthy (Fred Francis), John Carradine (Erle Kenton), Slim Pickens (Sam Newfield), Elisabeth Brooks (Marsha), Robert Picardo (Eddie), Margie Impert (Donna), Noble Willingham (Charlie Barton), James Murtaugh (Jerry Warren), Jim McKrell (Lew Landers), Kenneth Tobey (older cop), Don McLeod (T. C.), Dick Miller (Walter Paisley), Roger Corman (man in phone booth), **Sayles** (morgue attendant)
35 mm, Color
90 minutes

1980
A PERFECT MATCH (made for TV)
Production Company: Lorimar Productions
Executive Producers: David Jacobs, Lee Rich
Producer: Andre Guttfreund
Director: Mel Damski
Teleplay: **Sayles**
Story by: Andre Guttfreund and Mel Damski
Cinematography: Ric Waite

Editing: John Farrell
Music: Billy Goldenberg
Cast: Linda Kelsey (Miranda McLloyd), Michael Brandon (Steve Triandos), Lisa Lucas (Julie Larson), Charles Durning (Bill Larson), Colleen Dewhurst (Meg Larson), Clyde Kusatsu (Dr. Tommy Chang), Bonnie Barllett (Judge Greenburg), Hildy Brooks (Esther), Alexa Kenin (Angel), Bever-Leigh Banfield (Rhonda)
35 mm, Color
100 minutes

1982
THE CHALLENGE
Production Company: CBS Theatrical Films
Executive Producer: Lyle Poncher
Producers: Robert L. Rosen and Ron Beckman
Director: John Frankenheimer
Screenplay: Richard Maxwell, **Sayles**, and Ivan Moffatt
Cinematography: Kozo Okazaki (Deluxe)
Production Design: Yoshiyuki Oshida
Editing: John W. Wheeler
Music: Jerry Goldsmith
Cast: Scott Glenn (Rick Murphy), Toshiro Mifune (Toru Yoshida), Donna Kei Benz (Akiko Yoshida), Atsuo Nakamura (Hideo Yoshida), Calvin Jung (Ando), Clyde Kusatsu (Go), Sab Shimono (Toshio Yoshida), Kiyoaki Nagai (Kubo), Kenta Fukasaku (Jiro), Shogo Shimada (Takeshi Yoshida), Yoshio Inaba (instructor), Seiji Miyaguchi (old man), Miiko Taka (Sensei's wife)
35 mm, Color
116 minutes

1982
ENORMOUS CHANGES AT THE LAST MINUTE
Production Company: Ordinary Lives Inc.
Producer: Mirra Bank
Directors: Ellen Hovde (Virginia's Story), Mirra Bank and Ellen Hovde ("Faith's Story"), Mirra Bank ("Alexandra's Story")
Screenplay: **Sayles** with Susan Rice
Original stories by: Grace Paley

Cinematography: Tom McDonough
Cast: "Virginia's Story": Ellen Barkin (Virginia), David Strathairn (Jerry), Ron McLarty (John), Sudie Bond (Mrs. Raferty); "Faith's Story": Lynn Milgram (Faith), Jeffrey DeMunn (Ricardo), Zvee Scooler (Pa), Eda Reiss Merin (Ma), Fay Bernardi (Mrs. Hegel-shtein); "Alexandra's Story": Maria Tucci (Alexandra), Kevin Bacon (Dennis), John Wardell (Doc), Lou Criscuolo (George)
35 mm, Color
110 minutes

1986
THE CLAN OF THE CAVE BEAR
Production Company: Jonesfilm, Guber-Peters Company, Jozak Company, Decade Productions
Executive Producers: Mark Damon, John Hyde, Jon Peters, and Peter Guber
Producers: Gerald I. Isenberg and Stan Rogow
Sidney Kimmel
Director: Michael Chapman
Screenplay: **Sayles**
Based on the novel by: Jean M. Auel
Cinematography: Jan de Bont (Technicolor)
Production Design: Tony Masters
Editing: Wendy Greene Bricmont and Paul Hirsch
Music: Alan Silvestri
Cast: Daryl Hannah (Ayla), Pamela Reed (Iza), James Remar (Creb), Thomas G. Waites (Broud), John Doolittle (Brun), Curtis Armstrong (Goov), Martin Doyle (Grod), Adel C. Hammond (Vorn), Tony Montanaro (Zoug), Mike Muscat (Dorv), John Wardlow (Droog), Keith Wardlow (Crug), Karen Austin (Aba), Barbara Duncan (Uka), Gloria Lee (Oga), Janne Mortil (Ovra), Lycia Naff (Uba), Linda Quibell (Aga), Bernadette Sabath (Ebra)
35 mm, Color
98 minutes

1986
UNNATURAL CAUSES (made for TV)
Production Company: Blue Andre Productions, ITC Productions
Executive Producers: Blue Andre and Robert M. Myman

Producer: Blue Andre
Director: Lamont Johnson
Teleplay: **Sayles**
Story by: Martin M. Goldstein, Stephen Doran, and Robert Jacobs
Cinematography: Larry Pizer
Production Design: Anne Pritchard
Editing: Paul LaMastra
Music: Charles Fox
Cast: John Ritter (Frank Coleman), Alfre Woodard (Maude DeVictor), Patti LaBelle (Jeanette Thompson), John Vargas (Fernando "Nando" Sanchez), Frederick Allen (kid), Richard Anthony Crenna (soldier), Frank Pellegrino (Raul), Jonathan Welsh (Dr. Lester), Luba Gay (Rena), **Sayles** (Lloyd), Roger Steffans (Golub)
35 mm, Color
100 minutes

1987
WILD THING
Production Company: Filmline, Atlantic Releasing
Producer: David Callaway
Director: Max Reid
Screenplay: **Sayles**
Based on a story by: **Sayles** and Larry Stamper
Cinematography: Rene Verzier (Sona Color)
Production Design: John Meighen and Jocelyn Joli
Editing: Battle Davis, Steven Rosenblum
Music: George S. Clinton
Cast: Rob Knepper (Wild Thing), Kathleen Quinlan (Jane), Robert Davi (Chopper), Maury Chaykin (Detective Trask), Betty Buckley (Leah), Guillaume Lemay-Thivierge (Wild Thing, age ten), Robert Bednarski (Free/Wild Thing, age three), Clark Johnson (Winston), Sean Hewitt (Father Quinn), Teddy Abner (Rasheed), Cree Summer Francks (Liza), Sawn Levy (Paul), Rod Torchia (Hud), Christine Jones (Laurie), Robert Austern (Wiz), Tom Rock (Braindrain), Alexander Chapman (Shakes), Robert Ozores (El Borracho)
35 mm, Color
92 minutes

1989
BREAKING IN
Production Company: Breaking In Productions, Samuel Goldwyn Company
Producer: Harry Gittes
Director: Bill Forsyth
Screenplay: **Sayles**
Cinematography: Michael Gibbs (Medallion Color)
Editing: Michael Ellis
Production designers: Adrienne Atkinson, John Willett
Music: Michael Gibbs
Cast: Burt Reynolds (Ernie Mullins), Casey Siemaszko (Mike Lefebb), Harry Carey, Jr. (Shoes), Sheila Kelly (Carrie), Lorraine Toussaint (Delphine), Albert Salmi (Johnny Scat), Maury Chaykin (Tucci), Stephen Tobolowsky (district attorney), Richard Key Johnes (Lou), Tom Laswell (Bud), Frank A. Damiani (waiter), David Frishberg (nightclub singer), John Baldwin (Sam the Apostle), Eddie Driscoll (Paul the Apostle), Melanie Moseley (young woman apostle), Galen B. Schrick (choir master), Duggan L. Wendeborn (Faith House member), K. Gordan Scott (counterman), Clifford Nelson, Roy McGillivray (old men), Kim Singer (anchorwoman), Charles E. Compton (real estate agent)
35 mm, Color
94 minutes

1989
"Shannon's Deal" (made for TV series pilot)
Production Company: Stan Rogow Productions, NBC
Producers: Stan Rogow, Gareth Davis, Jim Margellos, and Allan Arkush
Director: Lewis Teague
Teleplay: **Sayles**
Cinematography: Andrew Dintenfass
Production Design: John Vallone
Editing: Neil Travis
Music: Wynton Marsalis
Cast: Jamey Sheridan (Jack Shannon), Elizabeth Peña (Lucy Acosta), Richard Edson (Wilmer), Jenny Lewis (Neala Shannon), Alberta Watson (Teri), Martin Ferrero (Lou Gandolph), Miguel Ferrer (Todd Spurrier),

Claudia Christian (Molly Tempke), Ely Pouget (Gwen), Ron Joseph (Det. Joe Menke), Michael Bowen (Scotty Powell), Eddie Velez (Chuy Vargas), Andrew Lowery (Eric), Stefan Gierasch (Klaus), Danny Trejo (Raul), Kevin Peter Hall (card player), Coco Mendoza, Russell Yip, Jessie Dizon, Brian Smiar
35 mm, Color
120 minutes

1990–91
SHANNON'S DEAL (TV series)
Production Company: Stan Rogow Productions, NBC
Executive Producer: Stan Rogow
Producers: Gareth Davies, Jim Margellos; Allan Arkush (second season)
Created by/creative consultant: **Sayles**
Cinematography: Stevan Larner; Michael Gerschman (second season)
Editing: William B. Strich, Stephen Potter, and Conrad Gonzalez
Music: Wynton Marsalis (theme); Lee Ritenour; Tom Scott
Cast: Jamey Sheridan (Jack Shannon), Elizabeth Peña (Lucy Acosta), Richard Edson (Wilmer), Jenny Lewis (Neala), Martin Ferrero (Lou Gandolph)
First season, April 1990–May 1990

"Words to Music"
Writer: **Sayles**
Director: Allan Arkush
Cast: Michelle Joiner, Tanya Tucker, **Sayles**, Iggy Pop, David Crosby, Stanley Brock, Joe Bratcher, Julius Harris

"Inside Straight"
Writer: Mark Rossner
Director: Allan Arkush
Cast: Dick Anthony Williams, Ron Joseph, Michael Beach, Tisha Campbell, D. Scott Hoxby, Miguel Ferrer

"Art"
Writer: David Greenwalt
Director: David Greenwalt
Cast: Nicholas Miscusi, Marc Lawrence, Larry Hankin, John Michael Bolger, Mimi Craven

"Custody"
Writer: **Sayles**
Director: Joel Oliansky
Cast: Lucinsa Jenney, Jeff Perry, Bob Delgall, Frank Birney, Julianna McCarthy

"Hitting Home"
Writer: Tom Rickman
Director: Aaron Lipstadt
Cast: Ralph Waite, George Murdock, Ron Joseph, Nick Cassavetes, David Arnott

"Sanctuary"
Writer: John Byrum
Director: John Byrum
Cast: Robert Covarrubias, John Anderson, John Shepherd, Frank McCarthy, Monty Hoffman

"Bad Beat" (Second Season, March 1991–May 1991)
Writers: Eugene Corr, Ruth Shapiro
Director: Eugene Corr
Cast: Darrell Larson, Mary Jo Keenan

"Greed"
Writer: David Greenwalt
Director: Allan Arkush
Cast: Whitman Mayo, Charles Lane, Stephen Tobolowsky, Juanin Clay, Tom Towles, Kurt Fuller, Ron Joseph

"Strangers in the Night"
Writer: Tom Rickman
Director: Tom Rickman
Cast: B. D. Wong, Victor Love, Clark Gregg, Steve Vinovich, Randle Mell, Dee Dee Rescher, Ron Joseph

"First Amendment"
Writer: Barry Pullman
Director: Allan Arkush
Cast: John Kapelos, Brent Hinkley, Stuart Pankin, Kimberly Scott, Sonny Carl Davis

"The Inside Man"
Writer: Corey Blechman
Director: Corey Blechman
Cast: Paul Whitthorne, Mark McManus, Julie Garfield, Michelle Forbes, James Lashly, Richard Roat, David Spielberg, Kimberly Scott

"Matrimony"
Writer: Kathy McCormick
Director: Betty Thomas
Cast: Michele Park, Barry Cullison, Cecile Callan

"Trouble"
Writer: Joan Tewkesbury
Director: Joan Tewkesbury
Cast: Michele Park, Barry Cullison, Cecile Callan

1994
MEN OF WAR
Production Company: MDP Worldwide, Pomarance Corporation, Grandview Avenue Pictures
Executive Producers: Moshe Diamant, Stan Rogow
Producers: Arthur Goldblatt, Andrew Pfeffer
Director: Perry Lang
Screenplay: **Sayles**, Ethan Reigg, and Cyrus Voris
Story: Stan Rogow
Cinematography: Ron Schmidt (Deluxe)
Production Design: Steve Spence and Jim Newport
Editing: Jeffrey Reiner
Music: Gerlad Gouriet
Cast: Dolph Lundgren (Nick Gunnar), Charlotte Lewis (Loki), B. D. Wong (Po), Anthony Denison (Jimmy G), Don Harvey (Nolan), Catherine Bell (Grace), Tiny "Zeus" Lister (Blades), Tom Wright (Jamaal), Tim Guinee (Ocker), Trevor Goddard (Keefer), Kevin Tighe (Merrick), Thomas Gibson (Warren), Perry Lang (Lyle), Aldo Sambrell (Goldmouth), Juan Pedro Tudela (Kalfo)
35 mm, Color
103 minutes

# JOHN SAYLES

## INTERVIEWS

# John Sayles: Designated Writer

DAVID CHUTE/1981

LOW-COST INDEPENDENT MOVIEMAKING is such a terrific idea—maybe the industry's only hope of re-establishing connections, a segment at a time, with an increasingly fragmented audience—that the tendency, in practice, to view independent production, not as a strategy, but as a Cause in its own right, is a dreary spectacle indeed. Dreary is certainly the word for those filmmakers whose independence seems as much an ideological badge of honor as a bid for creative self-sufficiency. Many filmgoers, myself among them, have struggled to hold their eyelids aloft during evenings of "committed cinema." Films like *Northern Lights, The War at Home,* or *Joe and Maxi* wield their high-mindedness like a blunt instrument.

So who can blame us for the foreboding that lay heavy in our hearts as we trudged off last year to see *Return of the Secaucus 7,* a $60,000 first feature, written, directed, and even edited by the highly regarded 29-year-old novelist John Sayles? After all, this guy had written a novel about organized labor and radical activism (the National Book Award nominee *Union Dues*), and his *Secaucus 7* was reputed to be an elegy to the wilted counterculture of the Sixties, the story of seven friends, lapsed activists all, whose weekend reunion in New Hampshire ten years later provides an occasion for reminiscence and recrimination on the dire consequences of turning 30. I was turning 30 myself at the time, it was a gray October in Boston, and *Return of the Secaucus 7* sounded like the very last thing I needed.

---

From *Film Comment,* May/June 1981. Reprinted by permission of *Film Comment* and David Chute.

Well, it's common knowledge now that *Secaucus 7* is anything but a drearily earnest wallow in Radiclib nostalgia. An elegantly plotted, beautifully observed comedy of modern manners, it doesn't quite make one forget that it was cheaply and independently made. The 35mm release prints were blown up from 16mm, and look it, and many of the unknown actors in the cast cannot do justice to the layered ironies of Sayles' pitch-perfect dialogue. But *Secaucus 7* has a skeptical sense of humor about its endlessly self-analytical characters, and it's so deftly structured that one can take pleasure in it simply as a narrative mechanism. *Return of the Secaucus 7* is a film that, in John Sayles' words, "the studios would never make." Yet it has connected as an entertainment—a film you go to for pleasure, not out of duty—with sizable art-house audiences in Boston, Los Angeles and Washington, D.C.—and finally in New York as well, where a second run this March played to sell-out crowds.

*Return of the Secaucus 7* fulfills the abundant promise of independent moviemaking, both creatively and financially, as few recent pictures have. Clearly, a special mixture of talent, common sense, and phenomenal persistence must lie behind Sayles' success. He had, after all, published two novels (*Pride of the Bimbos* and *Union Dues*) and a story collection (*The Anarchists' Convention*) before his 29th birthday. And in just the past three years he has written (or extensively rewritten) the screenplays for three drive-in schlockers produced by Roger Corman's New World Pictures (*Piranha, Battle Beyond the Stars, The Lady in Red*); penned a sniffly TV movie (*A Perfect Match*); scripted an abortive sci-fi project for Steven Spielberg (*Night Skies*); worked at rewriting two more horror films (*Alligator* and *The Howling*); and turned out seven original screenplays as yet unsold. What's more, in the wake of *Secaucus 7*'s triumph Sayles has deals in the works to write and direct three modestly budgeted films for major studios.

A self-motivated fellow, at the very least, John Sayles has combined the traditional career-advancement strategies of the commercial and independent cinemas, banking the money he earned doing hack work to finance his dirt-cheap directorial debut. For me, however, the full extent to which shrewd calculation was involved emerged only when I spoke with Sayles, in early March, at the spacious Hoboken, N.J., home he shares with long-time spouse-equivalent (and *Secaucus 7* co-star) Maggie Renzi.

"After I had done the Corman things," Sayles told me, "I realized that it was going to take me a long time to break into directing by the usual route, which is to write a hit for a studio and then say, 'I want to direct the next one.' For one thing, I knew that I didn't want to direct a horror movie, which is what I would have been offered. Horror films are interesting to write for other people, but spending the time and effort it would take to write and direct one is nothing that would occur to me. I don't think I'd be particularly good at it. So I figured whatever I did or learned about directing I would have to finance myself. I had the Corman money, and I sold *The Anarchists' Convention,* and I got $40,000 together. I knew I could make a 16mm feature for that amount.

"After that I thought, 'Why make a $40,000 version of something the studios would make?' But I needed an audition piece, too, so I wanted to walk a tightrope between making something they'd never make, but having production, writing, and directing values that they would recognize as good for their purposes, too. The basketball scene, where the guys act out their conflicts on the court, is there because I wanted to have a scene in which a point is gotten across by action, without any dialogue. That kind of thing.

"I knew, however, I couldn't afford to make a very visual movie. It was going to have to be dialogue-bound. So I was thinking about ways to keep the movie moving. I thought, 'Well, I can cut a lot.' That's how I got the idea of doing something like *Nashville,* where there are a lot of characters, and you can cut from one to another, and there's a reason to cut, and none of the scenes will be too long.

"From there I thought, 'It's going to be about people turning 30, 'cause the good actors I can afford, the ones that aren't in the Screen Actors Guild yet, are turning 30. It's going to be about a group of people, so I can keep cutting, and it's going to be in a very finite location and time, for budget reasons. I want to have different things to look at, so there'll be day scenes and night scenes, indoor scenes and outdoor scenes.'

"Now I had an idea of just the physical things of the movie, and could almost forget them when I wrote the characters. I said, 'How do I create the most believable people I can, and give them at least one thing that is happening in their lives?' It may be very subtle, but each of these characters starts at one point and gets to another. Like, Katie [Maggie Renzi] is worrying about her relationship with Mike [Bruce MacDonald] and seeing everybody else breaking up, and she's wondering where she's going to put them all in her house. Chip [Gordon Clapp] is worried about being accepted by the group. Jeff [Mark Arnott] and Maura [Karen Trott] are breaking up. And so on.

"Anyway, given those characters and what's happening to them over the weekend, I tried to just let them flow. I'd have a list of locations, the places we'd found to use in North Conway, New Hampshire, and I'd think, 'What can I do at this location that will reinforce all or some of these developments?' At the theater, say, we get to see that Katie, who is worried about her relationship, is very nasty about this actress her boyfriend used to live with. And we see that J.T. [Adam LeFevre] and Maura are sitting together, and that Frances [Maggie Cousineau Arndt] is bummed out about it.

"And so, it just sort of got together. It took me two weeks to write it. I write really fast, usually, and I didn't have to do any research in this case, because the people were composites of people I knew. I even used some true stories that people had told me, that happened to them or to friends of theirs.

"Shooting it, I had to say that the first priority was that the people come across very real, that you don't feel you're watching actors. In fact, I had unknowns, with the advantage that people would think they must all be playing themselves, even though none of them are. I could go a little further in the direction of documentary than you can with known actors. That kind of thing I could do *very* well in my situation, which helped to compensate for some of the things I couldn't do. Like, because of time—we shot it in twenty-two days—and budget, it's a much more proscenium-looking movie than I would like it to be. We didn't have time to light for depth, and there isn't much camera movement. A glaring example is the very first scene, with Mike and Katie yelling from room to room, and they're getting the house ready. As written, that was one shot, with Katie getting some linen and going out into a hallway, and we follow her for a while, and then we pick up Mike and follow him for a while, and we see the entire house as they talk. But we weren't able to do that, because we were shooting in this empty ski lodge in North Conway, not in a real house.

"But you're never going to be able to shoot everything exactly the way you want. I would have liked to have had more time in certain places to cover things more. But it's the first movie I shot, so I didn't even know *how* to cover things. I made some pretty basic mistakes, but I salvaged most of them OK. A lot of the cutting of the non-action scenes was done in the writing rather than in the editing, and that saved us a lot of film stock.

"Of course, doing that limits your flexibility, but this particular script was good in that I didn't need much flexibility, partly because I had so many characters. In the bar scene, where they split up into smaller groups, I would have liked to have had a lot of extras around, so that we could have moved from one conversation to the other, and had them overlap. But I had to cut, cut, cut, because we only had the extras for about twenty minutes, to get one shot. The two-shots were done in an empty bar room, with a lot of noise from Ken's Pub in Boston, that we picked up later."

Obviously, not every moviemaker would be capable of such minute and clearheaded planning. Fewer still could have mapped out a project with so much rigor, and come up with a film displaying the ease and naturalness that distinguish *Return of the Secaucus 7*. John Sayles, however, appears to be one of those rare artists for whom formal restrictions act not as hinderances, but as stimulants to invention.

"It's true," he told me, "that a lot of the specifics of *Secaucus 7* arose out of financial constraints. But almost everything I've done in movie writing has come with givens. We want to have a piranha attack every fifteen minutes. We can't kill the alligator by setting it on fire at the end because we need it in one piece for the publicity tour. But once you start writing, with those givens, it's like a poem, poetry that has a form as opposed to free or blank verse. The form sometimes gives you ideas."

The ability to relish a technical or formal challenge is probably a crucial factor in John Sayles's success, but it's hardly the whole story. If one contemplates his prodigious output, for instance, it is easy to imagine an enormously disciplined, career-oriented writer. But according to Sayles's friend Bruce MacDonald, the red-haired Boston actor who has a pivotal role in *Secaucus 7*, "John is the opposite of a grinder. The stuff just seems to flow out of his typewriter. I just think that, most of the time, he'd rather be writing than doing anything else."

Sayles views his specific gifts (like the ability to remember up to two pages of dialogue, verbatim, for several hours) as tricks akin to "being able to bend your fingers back. You either do or you don't. I don't even think about the memory thing that much, about having an 'ear.' It's just that when I start writing what a person is saying, that's the way it comes out. I write fast, for sure, and I don't turn things in late, but I don't think I'm very disciplined. What I do is, I tend to get myself into situations where I have to write myself out of a corner. If I have three days to write a movie, I can write it in three days. I really can write anywhere. Once I get into the story I can write in bus stations or in airplanes. I can watch TV or listen to music or talk to people while I write. I write faster—not better—if there aren't as many distractions, but I can write with distractions. I don't write better any time. I write as good as I write, and I write until it's OK, and then I hand it in. None of this is really discipline, though. It's just that I can do it."

A natural athlete might, I think, talk this way about his inborn skills, with a modest confidence and a hint of jock-macho nonchalance that others could mistake for arrogance. Sayles, in fact, is to the manner born, since he really was a star athlete in his teens. Tall and muscular still, but with signs of the sedentary writer's life beginning to accumulate around his middle, he looks every inch the high-school jock grown up. Born in Schenectady, N.Y., in 1950, Sayles was the son of two school teachers, part of a German-Irish family whose men-folk, most of them, went into police work. He says he got good grades in school without working very hard, took physically taxing factory jobs in the summer, and set out on ambitious hitchhiking expeditions that eventually took him back and forth across the country four times. It was these experiences, together with several stories told by friends, that formed the basis of the linked group of stories (actually the remnants of an abandoned novel) about the teenaged wanderer Brian McNeil in *The Anarchists' Convention.*

Sayles entered Williams College with the class of '72, because, he says, "I didn't know what else to do, and I didn't want to go into the Army." There, while continuing to play intramural basketball and baseball, he began, for the first time, to read novels, to act in college plays, and to write. Bruce MacDonald was also at Williams then, as were several other *Secaucus 7* collaborators, Maggie Renzi among them. MacDonald recalls that Sayles wrote a review of every play he saw there, and then filed the pieces away in a drawer. He never sent them anywhere, and wrote them, he says now, "just for the fun of writing stuff, and for the practice."

Even allowing a sizable margin of error for modesty, and a little more for bluster, Sayles does explain a surprising number of the major turning points of his life in the most direct, throwaway manner imaginable, ascribing them less to any conscious game plan than to what he felt like doing, to what came most easily to him or suited his tastes. His inclinations, along with his talent (and his confidence in it), simply guided his steps in a very straightforward fashion.

Sayles claims, for example, that he began taking creative writing courses at Williams "because it was always the easiest course. They graded you on poundage, and I wrote long stories, so I got A's in that, which brought my average up to C for my other courses, which I mostly didn't go to."

He continued to write after graduation, blindly mailing his stories to a gradually diminishing circuit of magazines, and amassing the requisite number of rejection slips. Finally, in 1975, *The Atlantic* accepted his O. Henry Prize-winning tale "I-80 Nebraska, m. 490-m. 205," one of the earliest fictional treatments of the CB radio craze, and of truck drivers as concrete cowpokes. Soon afterward, *The Atlantic*'s editors returned a fifty-page story Sayles had submitted with the suggestion that it might be the beginning of a novel. By this time, after sojourns in Atlanta (where he did day labor, digging in red clay) and Albany (where he was a nursing home orderly), Sayles had taken up residence in the semi-slums of East Boston. Here, subsisting on the unemployment benefits he earned when layed off by a Cambridge sausage factory (the place eventually became a principal setting of *Union Dues*), Sayles wrote *Pride of the Bimbos,* in twenty-seven weeks, while warming himself at the kitchen stove.

The aborted novel from which the picaresque Brian McNeil stories were torn, "like hunks from a rotting carcass," quickly followed, and there was *Union Dues* after that. Sayles was spending his summers in North Conway, where *Secaucus 7* would later be shot, "playing large retarded people, like Lennie in *Of Mice and Men,* the Indian in *One Flew Over the Cuckoo's Nest,*" at a summer theater. It was the near-impossibility of selling *Union Dues* from New Hampshire that prompted Sayles to finally acquire an agent—an agent, it turned out, who had business connections with an agency in Hollywood.

"I had known I wanted to work on screenplays," Sayles said, "and I was interested in directing, but I didn't want to go out there and knock on doors. I knew it wouldn't impress 'em that I had written a novel. So I wrote to the agency out there and said, 'You're representing two of my novels as screen properties. I'm interested in screenwriting. Here's a sample screenplay.' And I wrote a screenplay as a sort of audition. It was about the Chicago Black Sox bribery scandal of 1919. They said, 'Sure, we'll represent you.' So Maggie and I moved out to Santa Barbara. And the first decent offer I got was the rewrite on *Piranha*."

All of his work on genre projects, Sayles says, has been undertaken "both for the fun of it and for the money. I didn't get offered that much at first, and these things *were* fun to work on. Once you agreed on a premise—like, this is about piranhas eating people in North American waters—you could pretty much do anything you wanted. Even in the genre films, as limited as we were in time and opportunity, you could do something. Even hack work is about something. Like, *Battle Beyond the Stars,* which began with just Corman's idea of doing *The Seven Samurai* in space, is about death, different life forms' attitudes toward death. It's no big heavy thing, it's just something to base the characters around.

"All I ever really try to do in these genre pictures is to bring some kind of awareness to them. In *Piranha* the horror is caused by the military, and I hope that there's some kind of awareness, from the characters themselves, that we've been down this river before. In *Alligator* or *The Howling* I try to bring them into the twentieth century, to make them a little more consistent. The tension that is interesting to me is taking something totally fantastic and sticking it in a very realistic setting. I try to say, 'OK, what would *really* happen if you walked outside, and there's this giant alligator there? Who would try to catch it, who would react with fear, who would just say, "Great, let's go see the giant alligator!"?' "

Sayles's work in his horror and action scripts is, as a rule, mild, deft, and craftsmanly. He contributes verbal textures, narrative grace notes, and succinct character touches that help to tidy up or to decorate a movie's surface. An exception is the impressive *The Lady in Red,* the story of the woman who accompanied John Dillinger to the Biograph that night. It's an exception because, after extensive research, Sayles wrote a script, rich in social observation, that he says he might have enjoyed directing himself.

And *that,* in his terms, means that his commitment to the material went beyond what he deems essential on a piece of "hack work" like *The Howling.* Again and again in Joe Dante's pop-gothic romp about werewolves, one finds oneself being pleasantly startled by, say, two nervous people, stumbling through a dark and foggy forest, muttering exactly the sort of oaths that real people in the same situation might be expected to mutter. Sayles's "ear" certainly comes in handy. And in *Alligator,* he says, "my original idea was that the alligator eats its way through the whole socio-economic system. It comes out of the sewer in the ghetto, then goes to a middle-class neighborhood, then out to the suburbs, and then to a real kind of high-rent area. That's still sort of there on screen, but they couldn't shoot so many scenes—which makes the alligator move so fast, that you don't get the progression."

I submit that embellishments like these, while pleasing in themselves, are scarcely comparable to rethinking or reimagining genre legends. *The Howling,* in particular, is practically wall-to-wall with undeveloped implications. The pious new-shrink monologues of chic psychotherapist Patrick McNee are miniature essays on the hazards of "repressing the beast in ourselves." And then, in the film's best sequence, the libido of a pair of copulating lycanthropes appears to be the generative cause of all matted hair, the rippling flesh, and the distended fingernails; "the howling" is an orgasmic shriek. Unfortunately, each of these moments is presented as a discreet, limited joke, and the film as a whole fails to derive its tone from them. Joe Dante himself contends that werewolf movies are "a dead genre," and, with Sayles, he settled upon a fun-and-games approach to *The Howling,* piling on de-mystifying naturalistic flourishes, and movie in-jokes that set up a winking complicity in disbelief between filmmaker and viewer. Taken purely on its own terms, the picture evinces a failure of imagination.

Because John Sayles enjoys solving formal problems as a writer, and can do so without affronting his creative dignity—and because he's a writer with enormous reserves of wit and intelligence to draw upon—it's possible to believe that he's achieved his success as a screenwriter-for-hire (the success that made *Secaucus 7* possible) without exerting himself to the limit. He can hunker down and turn out a script as if he were carving a chair leg instead of a statue. In the words of Joe Dante, who has worked with Sayles on *Piranha* as well as *The Howling,* "John is one of the most unspoiled of all the people I know who have gone to Hollywood and 'made it.' He's a real person, and as a writer he has a sense of character that guys who have written fifty-five *Starsky and Hutches,* and then want to do your movie, just don't have. That's what comes through so strongly in *Return of the Secaucus 7,* and it makes me think that John could become a really major writer of screenplays. What I think happens on the genre scripts is that John streamlines his ability to do that, because he doesn't think the producers will appreciate it. I think your first experience in movies is indelible and stays with you on everything else you do. Well, John's first three scripts were for Corman, and Roger's not interested in character."

John Sayles, I suspect, owes not only the pace of his career, but also some of the liveliest (and some of the flattest) qualities of his writing to the stability and practicality of his temperament. Sayles's best fiction brings a wide variety of closely observed persons fully to life, imagined from the inside out. His lesser work tends toward toneless surface duplication; it reads like journalism thinly recast as fiction. (Sayles admits that he owes at least one of the *Anarchists' Convention* stories directly to his tape-recorder memory: "Golden State," about a pair of loquacious winos, is he says, "all verbatim dialogue.") In *The Anarchists' Convention,* stories full of life stand side-by-side with others that are almost dead, and one envisions every one of them flowing from Sayles's typewriter at an uninterrupted steady pace, smooth and clean and even.

Sayles's flexibility poses a peculiar problem. As I watched *Return of the Secaucus 7,* with its lovingly sketched characters and light-fingered plotting, I said to myself, "This is a screenplay written by a novelist." As I read *Union Dues,* a somewhat shapeless book that employs an almost symphonic interweaving of several sharply individualized voices, I thought, "This is a novel written by a scenarist."

"Writing fiction and writing screenplays have complemented rather than interfered with each other," Sayles says. "No, there's just storytelling. With novels you have more control, but I'm trying to get as much control as I can in movies. Who knows if I'll get it? If I can't, I'll stop doing it. As far as I'm concerned they're just different ways of storytelling, and it's nice to get paid for something you want to do.

"Most critics figure that the dialogue is the screenplay, but I write shooting scripts, I write images. I always try to do things with as little dialogue as possible. Especially on an action thing, like *Piranha* or *Battle Beyond the Stars,* I think about how I would tell the story if it was a silent movie, so that Japanese people could understand it without subtitles. I have a lot of pictures in my head, and I reinforce them with dialogue."

Sayles continues to write screenplays and novels concurrently, as if to furnish himself with an essential safety net. When I spoke with him in March, he had just completed a "marathon, three-day re-write" on John Frankenheimer's *The Equals,* a martial arts adventure, to be shot in Japan, with *Urban Cowboy*'s spooky bad guy Scott Glenn in the lead. So he's still getting "hack work" assignments, and better ones all the time. On the other hand, he had recently lost a promised $800,000 investment, earmarked for a pet independent project called *Lianna.* And Brooke Adams, penciled in for the title role, had dropped out "because she got cold feet about the material." Sayles had planned to begin shooting *Lianna*—a feminist coming-to-consciousness story with an academic setting and an intense lesbian love story at its center—in Hoboken later in March. "It's fairly complex," he admits, "and it isn't something that a lot of people are eager to invest in."

Meanwhile, Sayles was doing rewrite after rewrite, polish after polish, on studio development deals, to write and direct, that had been dragging on for over a year. For the Ladd Company, he was preparing *The Blood of the Lamb,* a loose variation on *The Man Who Would Be King*: two drifters infiltrate a fundamentalist religious sect, intending both to expose and to rob it, only to find themselves rising in the group's hierarchy—and getting off on the power. For Fox, Sayles was preparing a script based on an idea of co-producer Amy Robinson's: a high school romance, across lines of class, set in Trenton, N.J., in the mid-Sixties—"It goes in depth into things they only scratched the surface of in *Breaking Away.*"

Laughing, Sayles says that, "All my movie projects are in limbo. My whole *life* is in limbo. I don't have many drafts or polishes left on any of them, so I should find out soon whether they'll give me a go-ahead to make them. Basically, you know, for the next year and a half I have an open calendar! Everything may happen or nothing may happen.

"I want to do the stuff I want to do, and if the studios want to do them too, then I'll end up doing them with the studios, and if they don't, I'll probably end up scrambling around for money again and either doing them or not doing them, depending on whether I get the money. The problem with independent films is that you almost never make enough money to make your next film. Very few people get to make more than a couple of independent films without either starting to work for the studios, or giving up, turning into an underground filmmaker. Very few people get to make that many narrative films independently. It would be great if I could pull it off, but I have no idea.

"It would be good for me to get one studio movie made and have it make some money, so at least I'm on their list, whether or not I want to capitalize on it and make a whole bunch right away. It would help me to raise independent financing 'cause I could say, 'Look: 20th Century-Fox made $10 million on this movie. All I'm asking for is a lousy $400 thousand. You could make $10 million too.' But who knows? It's been over two years since I shot *Return of the Secaucus 7*, so I'm getting a little tired of this. It's nice to have the control you have writing a novel. If these things don't pan out I may just say fuck it and just sit down and write for a while.

"I could start from scratch. I'm not afraid of starting from scratch. It's hard, but I've done it before. I went through the slush pile as a writer, and I did OK. I pretty much went through the slush pile as a screenwriter, too, and I did OK. And I started from scratch as a director. So if I want to do that again badly enough, I can figure out a way. At least I don't have to wait for someone else to tell me I can work.

"It's like when I was a kid I wanted to be a center fielder and get paid for playing baseball. Then I started getting bored playing baseball 'cause I didn't get to hit enough. If I could be a DH—a designated hitter—that would be pretty good. Except you have to stay in all those damn hotel rooms."

# Putting People Together: An Interview with John Sayles

TOM SCHLESINGER/1981

JOHN SAYLES WROTE, DIRECTED, produced, acted in, and edited *Return of the Secaucus Seven,* a movie that is receiving high acclaim nationwide. Only 30, Sayles is also an award-winning short-story writer and novelist: his novel *Union Dues* was nominated for a National Book Award. He broke into film through the Roger Corman training ground, New World Pictures. After writing screenplays for *Piranha, Battle Beyond the Stars,* and *The Lady in Red,* Sayles gathered his profits and financed *Secaucus Seven* for a mere $60,000.

But there are no man-eating fish, intergalactic battles, or machine-gun volleys in *Secaucus Seven.* Eight sixties-generation cohorts converge on a New England cottage for a ten-year reunion—a weekend of reminiscing, comparing notes on turning 30, and planning for the future.

Sayles, who also scripted *The Howling,* has several writer-director contracts with major studios in the works. He made a surprise visit to the Cinema/Chicago screening of *Return of the Secaucus Seven,* at which time this interview was recorded.

*How did you get involved in the film industry? Did you go to film school or have any formal training?*

No, actually I got an agent by writing two novels and a short story collection, and then selling the first novel myself. I was acting and directing in

---

the summer theater and I couldn't sell my second one, so I called up this guy—I had never met him—and he became my literary agent. Immediately, his agency had a deal with a film agency on the west coast. I wrote them and said, you're already representing my book as a film property, so here's a screenplay as an audition piece.

*What did your first screenplay concern?*
There is sort of an ironic story there. I wrote about the Black Sox scandal of 1919. When I went out to Los Angeles they said, we love the screenplay, we want to represent you, but forget about the Black Sox scandal because the rights have been in litigation for twenty years. Then about a month ago, a friend of mine who directed the TV movie that I wrote (*Perfect Match*), told me he knew a woman just starting out as a producer who bought the rights to Eliot Asinof's book, *Eight Men Out,* which is really the definitive work; if you have that, you have the rights to the story. So we're going to get together on that. It's six years later and I had just written it off.

*Did you have any kind of formal training in screenwriting?*
I hadn't gone to film school. I had an agent, I moved out to Santa Barbara, and I was just writing when I got a job doing a rewrite of *Piranha*. New World Pictures used my script and *Piranha* made millions of dollars, so I wrote two other scripts for them. Basically, I was just self-taught. I had seen a lot of movies—that was my film school.

*Do you structure or outline your stories before you begin the actual writing?*
I had written a couple of books, so I knew how to write dialogue with my eyes closed. As far as structure was concerned, basically the way I write a movie is I just sort of close my eyes and think it out, sort of see it in my head, and then I write out an outline if I have the time to do that.

*Do you ever use scene cards?*
No, I end up just going from an outline and just going from the beginning until it is filled out.

*When you are doing this outline, do you break it up into a beginning, middle, and end? Are you conscious of setting up the problem, putting up obstacles, and moving toward the resolution?*

Yeah. For instance, in *Piranha.* I was sort of on my own. One nice thing about working at New World is that they're very clear about what they want. They say, I see this as an action picture with some humor and there should be a certain amount of either attacks by fish or threats of attacks by fish. So I decided that given a 90 to 100 minute movie, there should be a piranha attack every ten minutes. You open the picture with one and then every ten minutes you have another attack or some kind of action sequence. The basic problem with the story was, how do we get the piranha into the river? The first part of the story was about this but then I asked, why doesn't everyone just stay out of the river? They wanted the piranhas descending on the summer camp at the end so I had the end point. I drew a picture of a river and a lake and I said, okay, here's a schematic, visual thing of what happens but there's no point where the people are going to have a rest. So I drew a dam in the middle of it: the first half of the movie is getting to this dam; the second half of this movie is the piranhas getting around this dam, and then it started taking shape and incidents started taking shape before I had any characters.

*The piranhas were, then, your protagonists?*
Oh yeah. Somebody from one of the more "intellectual" film journals was talking to me about *Piranha* and how horror movies are always an allegory for something and I was trying to convince him that *Piranha* was actually an allegory to the cultural revolution in China and the piranhas were the Red Guard, and the four bad guys were the Gang of Four, and the heroes were actually Mao having let these things out accidentally and trying to get them back in. It works, but almost anything works when you think about it that way.

*Are you partial to any duration in your stories? In other words,* Return of the Secaucus Seven *took place over a weekend; do you prefer working in shorter time periods where you can condense the action and take a slice-of-life type approach?*
Actually, *Secaucus Seven* was that way mostly because of the budget. *The Lady in Red,* which I wrote, happens over three years. A lot of filmmaking is handling time. You're just given (in the case of rewrites) or you just make up the time period of the thing, so that the movies have a certain pace to them. *Lady in Red* didn't turn out the way I wanted because they just didn't

have the budget to make the movie right. I wanted that to be a real breathless, '30s, Jimmy Cagney everybody-talking-fast type movie. It turned out a little more like Louis Malle. Different movies have different speeds.

*Within the scenes as well as the juxtaposition of the scenes throughout?*
Yeah, and like in a horror movie, you try to give people a break after a big action scene. I wrote a picture that didn't get made called *The Terror of the Loch Ness*. MGM didn't feel that there was enough action in the picture. They didn't feel that the beast itself was that fascinating—which I did—and they wanted oil rigs exploding and submarine battles under seas, so I just had this list of about 25 action sequences in a one-hour movie. It was like *Voyage to the Bottom of the Sea* where every two seconds the whole ship would shake; and that was too bad. Then the minute they budgeted it, and they saw what all that action was going to cost, they said, okay, let's cut some of the action. But, basically, it doesn't matter what the time period of the story is. It's more important how you handle the time period as far as the audience's relief and tension is concerned. I think people like Hitchcock are the best at that because they'll have some stupid little scene and if you looked at it on paper you'd ask, what is this scene for? But he put it there because he's sort of lulling people so that he can shock them or give them a break after a big suspense sequence.

*Are you conscious of putting in this kind of relief in your outline? Setting up the whole structure so that there is a rhythm of rising and falling action?*
Yeah.

*What type of screenplay form do you use when you write?*
I got used to writing shooting scripts. I found that the most useful way to write, so I'd just write a shooting script with shot numbers. I don't get into a big discussion of angles, things like that, but I'll say "dissolve" or "cut" depending on how I want the time to go into transition. I'll say a "close up" or a "long shot" and it's up to the director whether or not he wants to follow it.

*Does this approach ever offend the director?*
Not really. Especially not at New World where the directors were getting handed the project with a month to do pre-production. They better have

a good idea what's going on. It hasn't worked as well at the major studios where there are people and agents and this and that and the other thing and they keep talking about "fleshing it out" and I think what they mean is that even if you have characters who are obviously likeable because of the things they say and do, they want somewhere there to be: "We see RALPH, a handsome, likeable young man . . ." Unless you tell them everything that's going on in stage directions, they don't get it. So you end up having to write three or four different kinds of scripts: a selling script, which I can write, and then one for the producer and one for the director. With *Secaucus Seven,* it looks like there are no stage directions at all because I knew I was going to direct it.

*What type of script do you write when you have a writing-directing deal with a major studio?*

I am now in writing and directing deals with studios and that's part of the problem. I'm supposed to direct these if they get made so I'm writing them for myself. Then I hand them in and they say, well, we don't see anything here. Then I have to go back and spell it out in the rewrite without being too condescending.

*No matter how good a story is, if the characters are flat, undeveloped, or inconsistent, it seems to fall apart. Furthermore, the characters will then be reacting to the plot elements rather than generating them. Do you ever do character biographies before you begin to write?*

With *Secaucus Seven,* I didn't. With the things I've done for hire, I haven't because basically, I'm given the plot—we want a guy and a girl and that kind of thing—and then I just have to invent that as I go along. Rather than having a scene where the shark has just almost eaten them both and they're resting and they're talking about their lives very exposition-like, I try to have their action, their jobs, bring their character out. I'm very concerned with what people do for a living. So in *Piranha,* I had one guy who used to work in the mill that had been flooded in order to make a resort. He had a grudge against this lake. He almost hated the river and hated the lake because it had taken his job away from him. The girl was a skip tracer, and it was her job to find people as it was his job to hate this lake and sort of drink. So immediately, when they were on this river, there was something about it—she was always looking for someone and he was always grumbling. With *The Lady in Red,* it was the story of a woman who went through several jobs. She started out as this farm kid who worked for her father, who was an asshole. She ends up working in a sweat shop, becoming a dime-a-dance girl, being in prison and doing work there, then becoming a prostitute and then becoming a bank robber. So it's a progression of jobs for her.

*Did you use a similar approach in your TV movie* Perfect Match*?*
That was a true story I was given. Once again, I had the characters of the people. It was about a woman who had given up her child for adoption when she was 16. She developed a blood disease and had to find her daughter. They found her daughter and she had not been told she was adopted by her older adoptive parents, who were very protective. I tried to give them active things that they did that would help their character. I wanted this woman who had given her child up to have really straightened out her life and also to be somewhat glamorous, so that when she met her daughter, the daughter would be weaned away from her adoptive parents, and there would be a real conflict there. So I made the real mother a fashion designer in San Francisco. I made her adoptive father a guy who ran an icecream store because that's a very childlike thing. The story is about the girl trying to get away from this very childlike life and become something more glamorous. So I think what people do can help you with who they are.

*And this is what generates the story?*
It, finally, has to come out in the action. For screenplays, at least, that thing that Fitzgerald said—that action is character—works. And I'm much more interested in character than action so it's been nice sometimes for me to do these hired-gun jobs where they give me a plot or at least a situation because I don't have to think it up. I never would have woken up in the morning and said I had to write a movie about piranhas eating people, but once I was given one, if they agree on what they hand you to begin with, you can make the people whoever you want and they'll never give you a problem.

*When you're given a plot or you create one yourself, do you forge any kind of emotional network between the characters involved in the plot? And how do you go about doing that?*

This is actually one thing I learned from a book about screenwriting. There was an interview that Peter Bogdanovich did with Allan Dwan (*Sands of Iwo Jima*), who started screenwriting years after he had been directing in silent movies. He had this rule, which I also use in my fiction writing, that if you drew lines of emotional connection between the characters, you had to have at least two coming from every person. I saw *Roller Coaster* the other night and George Segal had a business-type relationship with his wife. He had emotional connections to other people, mostly antagonistic, but he only had one line to his wife. So basically, the wife was not needed. Unless you've got her into the story, and had a line going from her to another character, you really didn't need her.

*Did you use this approach in* Secaucus Seven*?*
In *Secaucus Seven* I ended up with all these people, a bunch of people that have lived with each other for a long time. If anybody has only one line drawn then it better be for a good reason, so I ended up with this sort of molecular structure where everyone had two or more lines to other characters and I could write on those lines what the relationship was. Only Chip had one line and that was the point of his character, that he was just hanging on by his fingernails. I've done that with most of my scripts and usually it means I cut a character or so. Now with something like *The Lady in Red,* there were a lot of characters that only had one line but they weren't emotional, they were for plot reasons. You try to make their dialogue as realistic as possible but you don't really have to know who that person is, as much as what their function is. There was a cop named Hennessey who at first we saw as a bag man for the mob, and then he had another line, sleeping with the madam, and then he also had a connection with the FBI. He was more or less the composite, corrupt Chicago cop, sort of the spider in the middle of the web. But he was a very minor character, he was just well-connected.

*Sometimes if you isolate this emotional network from the story, it almost sounds like a soap opera. For instance, in* Secaucus Seven, *the main action concerns a couple splitting up and the best friend sleeping with the wife. Did this network arise as a result of the characters or for the sake of something happening during the weekend?*

I think the emotional network arose from people I had known, and just knowing groups like that, and how over the years those lines do start to connect and tangle. Again, *Secaucus Seven* was a special case.

*But isn't budget always a consideration when writing a screenplay?*
At New World and other places I ask, how much do you want this to cost? I can write it big and I can write it small. And they always say, oh, just write it the way you want to. And then they don't put up enough money to film it the way I wrote it so I have to cut all this stuff. I don't know if they realize it or not but you just can't, at the last minute, take a scene out without the whole thing collapsing, if you write with any kind of subtlety and you don't have one scene where all the exposition happens. If you pace your exposition through a lot of scenes and they take one out, you've got to find another place to put that exposition or the whole plot makes no sense. So with most of the movies I've written, the whole plot makes no sense, if you really think about it. They move fast enough so you don't worry about it too much.

*They'll always put in a chase scene instead of an expository scene and that may take out one of the missing links in the story.*
In *The Lady in Red,* all the scenes where the people machine-gun other people are left in the movie and the ones that explain why the people are machine-gunning other people are gone—they didn't use them. Half the time, you don't even know why these people are shooting each other.

*Which is enough to want to make your own movie. How did that come about?*
I worked as an actor a couple summers in a summer stock company called the Eastern Slope Playhouse in New Hampshire, which is where we shot the film. I knew some of the actors there and the producer, and he knew everybody in town. Because I was only writing horror movies and it was going to be three or four years before I was writing more legitimate movies, not legitimate but bigger budget movies, I wanted to speed up the process. I knew I was going to have about $40,000 together and I wrote a screenplay that we could shoot for that much money. We were able to put the whole cast and crew up for $800—which, on location, is what you usually put one person up for, like one of the grips.

*And the living quarters were large enough to shoot in?*
We kicked people out of their rooms and we dressed it to look like a living room. We'd shoot at high ceilings that we could bounce light off of. We'd move our equipment from one room to the other rather than taking it out, putting it in a truck, driving to another location. Hardly any of our locations were more than a mile away from where we were staying. The scenes of the stream were right across the street so we just dragged some cable across the street, that kind of thing. And I wrote it that way.

*How, specifically, did having the budget first shape the screenplay?*
I knew I was going to have non-Screen Actors Guild actors, and all the people I knew that were good, and not in the Guild, were around 30. So it became a movie about turning 30, among other things. I knew I wouldn't have enough time for camera movement or a whole lot of action, so there was going to be a lot of people talking, which is what these people I know do on a weekend. How do I keep the audience's eyes moving? Well, I had a whole bunch of people and made it like *Nashville* where you can always cut away to another little subplot, and it seems to be moving even though the shots are static. The movement then is in the editing and there will be a good reason for editing, as it is so annoying when something cuts and it doesn't need to. We couldn't afford to be moving around to a lot of locations and I was filming in New Hampshire so it became a reunion in New Hampshire with a bunch of people turning 30. Next I say, okay, who are these people? I started to think of people I knew who were that age and what they were getting into. I had several composites of people I knew and stories or sort of emotional poles that could happen to them in a weekend.

*Then you started to draw lines between the characters?*
Once I made the characters different enough from one another without making them melodramatic or contrived, then I started saying, who are these people to each other? A couple of them were living together and a couple of them used to live together, and then it just sort of came from that. Specific scenes were originally there for audition purposes. I made this film as an audition piece, so I knew it was going to be a lot of talk and I'd just get offers from soap operas if I don't have some action, so I included the basketball scene and the diving. I tried to think of any location or thing

people could do where you could still tell something about the characters, but it should be action. So then I had the action scenes and I had to figure out how to integrate them.

*Without upsetting the overall structure.*
Exactly. During *Piranha,* they called from Texas where they were shooting and said they can't get a raft. Disney won't give us their Huck Finn raft. Why can't they be going down the river in a houseboat, there's a great houseboat here. Well, if they're in a houseboat, unless the piranha can fly, there's really no danger. So you get used to that. The whole plot of *Piranha* is contrived so you have to keep it moving fast enough with as little of the contrivance showing as possible. The same thing is true for a movie that wants to do more than just entertain, like a lot of the originals I have written. The nature of film or any kind of writing is that you're contriving to put people together in a certain way. You just try to do it subtly enough so that people don't notice or don't care, one or the other.

*In* Secaucus Seven*, there doesn't seem to be any one main character. There is a romantic conflict but you seem to be taking an overview of everyone.*
That's a screenplay that I never would have brought to the studios. The only way this movie is going to work is if you believe these people, spend some time with them and feel like you've met them. Some of them are having a more dramatic time than others, but for the others, it's still their lives and important to them, and will become important to the audience if you do it right.

*Can* Secaucus Seven *be placed into a particular genre of film?*
I think the American equivalent of that is the movies they made during World War II about a bunch of guys going through basic training and then into the army. It really wasn't about one individual. Occasionally, like in *The Big Red One,* there would be a narrator, but he wasn't necessarily the hero; it was about a group of people. That's the only American equivalent I can think of. As I said, I would not have given this script to the studios for that very reason; they would not have been able to accept that point of view. I couldn't have talked anyone into making this movie, which is a good reason to make it.

*How much did you vary from the shooting script?*
You have to realize that a script is only an outline. Even though there is almost no ad-libbing in the picture, it still is not a living thing until actors come there and make something out of these characters. Each actor is the star of their own movie. In *A Streetcar Named Desire,* there is a little part where the doctor comes at the end and Blanche says, "I've always relied on the kindness of strangers." There's a story that William Redfield tells about meeting the doctor from the original production of *Streetcar,* and he says to him, I hear this play is very good. What's it about? And the doctor says, well, it's about a doctor that comes all the way from Baltimore to help this poor lady. And as far as that actor was concerned, that's what the play was about. He's got a minute on stage, and that is his play.

*How has your acting affected your writing?*
Because I have acted, I try to look at all the characters that way. How do I play this person? Is the person consistent? Is there some action, something that this character wants, or is it because we just need another body there? If he's just there because they need another body, then you have to give them something that they want, or try to do, or react to.

*Once the characters are defined and the interrelationships established, do you ever send them through a traumatic event to show their development and growth?*
One way to do that is to set people up beforehand by showing something of their character. Then I think people get satisfaction out of guessing right as to how people are going to react in a certain traumatic event. All the spinoffs of the *Seven Samurai* set up these characters with fairly broad personalities, so when they get into a fight, they say, oh, this is the guy that is good with the knife, and this is the coward, and this is the guy that is this so that basically they do their acting through their fighting. In the samurai movie that I've written, most of the character comes out of descriptions of swordfights. Whether they can do that or not will be interesting to see, but very little of it is actual talking.

*Did you use subtitles?*
I try to keep it down to a minimum because audiences don't like subtitles. Mostly it's an action, the way the samurai treats this American guy. Sort of

like they tried to do in *Shogun,* having the audience be as out as the character was and using the subtitles only when he starts understanding Japanese. These old swordfighters and karate masters don't talk very much. They throw you around and you learn lessons by how hard you get beat up when you do the wrong thing. They lose a lot of their students that way, but that's how they do it.

*It sounds like how you learn to be a screenwriter. One last question, do you have any idiosyncracies concerning your writing habits, like when you write, where you write, or whether you have a magic pen?*
I write under pressure and everywhere, mostly on airplanes.

# John Sayles: From Hoboken to Hollywood—And Back

DAVID OSBORNE/1982

THE GANGLY YOUNG KID from the East, walking the California foothills, paused in Ventura to admire the Pacific. Three days in the Coast Range had left him looking more like a tramp than the next Orson Welles, so when two elderly rummies strolled up to his bench and asked if they could join him, he didn't see how he could refuse.

The tall one with the white mane introduced himself as Daniel Boone; his short friend was known as Cervantes. It wasn't long before Sneaky Pete and Mister Miles arrived, Daniel Boone again making the formal introductions. The conversation wasn't bad for seven in the morning, and when the bottle of Thunderbird began making the rounds, the kid figured, hell, when an alky offers instead of asking, now there's an occasion.

"Somehow I'd picked the most popular bench in all of Ventura," John Sayles remembers with a shake of his head. "They just sort of flocked around. I looked like I'd been sleeping under a car for about three days, so they weren't exactly self-conscious around me. Besides, I had thirty-three cents to go in on the second bottle with." In a few hours, his visitors were dozing on the sand, and Sayles was at the local A&P buying pen and paper to jot down the scene. He is not one to let good material slip away.

In the decade since, the thirty-two-year-old Sayles has written two novels, a number of short stories, a good twenty screenplays, and a play. The first story he sold, "I-80 Nebraska," won an O. Henry Award; his second novel,

---

*Union Dues,* was nominated for a National Book Award. But it was the unexpected success of his homemade, $60,000 movie, *The Return of the Secaucus Seven,* that thrust Sayles into the limelight. A bittersweet look at sixties people turning thirty, *Secaucus Seven* tapped a warm vein of nostalgia among Sayles's contemporaries, longing for some public confirmation of their strange journey through the seventies. The film walked away with the Los Angeles Film Critics' Award for Best Screenplay; won "top ten" honors for 1980 from *Time,* the *Los Angeles Times,* and the *Boston Globe*; and opened doors for Sayles both in Hollywood and in independent filmmaking.

Sayles has completed two new independent films, writing and directing both: *Lianna,* the story of a woman who leaves her husband and children for another woman, and *Baby, It's You,* a film about a high school romance that crosses class lines. And if negotiations with Warner Bros. pan out, next year he will direct his first studio film, tentatively titled "Blood of the Lamb," about ex-radicals and fundamentalists.

You'd never know all this by looking at him. Large, rumpled, habitually clad in worn running shoes, baggy pants, and an old T-shirt, Sayles looks more like someone you might meet in a New York subway than in Hollywood's glare. A slouchy six-four and 210 pounds, he brings to mind a high school athlete gone to seed, one of those big, dumb school heroes whose beer bellies tell you all you need to know about life after the glory days. He arrives for an interview half an hour late, yawning, one hand to the tender back he regularly abuses in a neighborhood basketball game. Though the mercury has taken a dive, he has no jacket. ("I've never seen him in a coat," says one friend.)

"He comes on like the village idiot," says Upton Brady, his editor at the Atlantic Monthly Press, "but behind that is one of the great storytellers—and a very, very sensible character." In college and summer stock, Sayles admits, he was apt to play "large, retarded people." But when he decided, in 1978, after years of writing movie scripts, that he wanted to direct his own, his plan was anything but harebrained. He saw two options for getting his way: write a blockbuster script or make an audition piece to prove his directing talents (though, in fact, he had never looked through a movie camera). The second option was quicker. He had $40,000, scraped together from book royalties and the sale of three scripts to Roger Corman, and *Secaucus Seven* was born.

Born poor, of course. With so little money, Sayles knew he would have to do without costumes, makeup, travel, much camera movement (otherwise, there would be too many takes of each shot), and guild actors. Lacking action sequences, the plot would need to move from character to character to keep its momentum. And the roles would have to be accessible to inexperienced actors willing to work for almost nothing—meaning friends and acquaintances, most of them about his age.

Not only did he write, direct, and act in the film, but he edited it himself. "I learned how to work the editing machine by reading a manual they gave me when I rented it," he says. "They never would have rented it to me if they'd known, but I acted like I knew what I was doing." The film, made as a calling card for studio executives—with almost no thought to national distribution—has grossed $2 million.

*Secaucus Seven* was written after *Lianna*. Sayles shopped that script around Hollywood just long enough to know he'd never make it there, and then began looking for independent backing soon after *Secaucus Seven* was released. After a long search, his producers, Jeffrey Nelson (who coproduced *Secaucus Seven*) and Maggie Renzi (Sayles's nine-year companion, who played Kate in *Secaucus*), raised almost $1 million by selling shares in the film to about thirty investors. Sayles shot it in Newark, New Jersey. The cast, mostly stage actors, includes Linda Griffiths and Jon DeVries.

Unlike a spate of other recent films involving homosexuality, *Lianna* brings the issue of children to the fore: Lianna forfeits any chance to keep her son and daughter when her husband finds out about the affair. "Originally I got interested through various couples I knew that were splitting up," says Sayles, "and how different it was between those who had children and those who didn't. I also knew a bunch of women who were hitting the streets for the first time, who had gotten married right out of school, and really hadn't done anything for themselves—hadn't ever gotten their own apartment, hadn't ever gotten a job. There're a lot of women who get divorced at forty-five and don't know what to do, but I was interested in what that did to a younger woman.

"I wanted to combine the two, and I tried to think up a situation where the woman was the one who got kicked out of the house, and wasn't around the kids—so I asked myself what she could have done to have that happen. And knowing some women in the past who had come out, knowing some of the problems they went through with families and friends, not to mention their own heads and the people they were in relationships with, I sort of combined the three ideas. It all made for a good, complex story that could have two or three things going on."

Sayles acknowledges that in making a film about lesbian life he may be criticized by some as being presumptuous. "All writing is presumptuous," he says. "You're presuming you know something that other people should hear. There's more pressure, more public eye on it, because it's a film, and so few films get made about anything vaguely controversial. But, you know, I've been writing short stories and books for years where the main character is a woman, or an old man, or a turtle, and the women haven't said how dare you, and the old people haven't said how dare you, and the turtles haven't called me up and said how dare I write about them. *Union Dues* is written from about seventeen points of view, and I'm not any of them, really. So that doesn't bother me. There are people who will react to the film politically. But no matter who you are, they would react that way, rather than just watching it and seeing what it says and does."

Before making *Lianna,* Sayles talked with gay women in the industry, some of whom had read the script. "I got some very good advice," he says. "But the main thing I got was that no matter what film you make, somebody is going to feel like it's not their story. The same thing happened with *Secaucus Seven.* Any movie you make that's about a specific time and place, people tend to say, 'No, that's not right; this is what happened to me.' So talking to half a dozen gay women, I got half a dozen different stories. And that finally was my answer: 'Well, you say it happens this way; I just talked to five other women who say it happens that way. Remember, this isn't about you, it's about one woman.'" But might audiences draw a negative image of an entire group from that one woman? "That's a risk you just have to take," Sayles replies. "You have to have the nerve to take that risk in writing, if you're going to communicate at all."

Sayles and Maggie Renzi share a slightly ramshackle brownstone in "an Italian-Puerto Rican family neighborhood" in much maligned Hoboken, New Jersey. Why Hoboken? Because "Manhattan is so expensive it's ridiculous" and "Hoboken is less assaultive." Sayles can leave his old Rambler on the street for weeks at a time, unmolested. Besides, he can head down to the local gym, where he dwarfs the Puerto Rican players, whenever he gets the urge for basketball.

There is a pattern: from largely Italian Goose Hill in Schenectady, New York (his parents were teachers), to grim East Boston, where he wrote his novels, to Hoboken. And study at Williams College, Sayles likes to suggest, was something of an accident: Guidance counselors kept trying to get him into college, and the application to Williams was at the top of the pile, so the kid from working-class Schenectady ended up at a tony school in the Berkshires.

If that's where he acquired a patina of easy confidence, he doesn't say. Anyway, confidence, he says, is "just picking your shots." Perhaps it shows in his writing, he allows, since "part of not having self-doubt is who you're working for, and I always write something I like first. I always wanted to write, not to be a writer. I think people who start out saying, 'Gee, I want to be a writer, can I cut it?' and want to be known as a writer and get things published, tend to worry that their writing is not going to measure up. Whereas I always just liked to write, and I would do it whether I showed it to somebody or not."

It started back in grade school, with "rip-offs of 'The Untouchables.'" After high school came dreary writing courses at Williams, then a period of several years as a nursing home orderly, construction worker, and meat packer, when writing was done after work. "I used to get rejection slips from magazines that said, '*Ar Arrad* is the Armenian national quarterly. There are no Armenians in your story. Why are you sending us this crap!'"

In 1974 he sent a fifty-page story called "Men" to the *Atlantic Monthly*. Recognizing talent but unable to handle the length, the editors turned it over to the Atlantic Monthly Press, where editor Peggy Yntema was intrigued. "I wrote John and said, 'Who are you?'" she recalls. "And he wrote back and said he worked in a sausage factory." She recommended he turn "Men" into a novel. He got laid off, and in six months on unemployment he knocked out his first book. "It was a real jeu d'esprit," says editor Upton Brady. "There aren't many books you read about a dwarf private detective in drag playing baseball." Since the novel was about baseball and masculinity, Sayles wanted to call it "Balls." The book was published as *Pride of the Bimbos*.

Sayles's talents have since ranged over subjects as diverse as labor history and sixties radicals (the novel *Union Dues*), man-eating fish (*Piranha*, the Corman *Jaws* knockoff that was his first Hollywood job), science fiction (*Battle Beyond the Stars*), aging leftists ("The Anarchists' Convention," the title piece of his short story collection), professional wrestling (his play *Turnbuckle*), werewolves (*The Howling*), and Cuban refugees in Miami (a novel in progress, "Los Gusanos").

Sayles writes at breakneck speed (he turned one script out in three days), and he does it wherever he finds himself—in a car, in front of the television. At home he writes standing up at a typewriter, thanks to the vertebrae he's been missing since birth. Why does he write? "I do it because I like it," he replies, shrugging. "And I'm making a living as a writer 'cause I'm lucky."

So far, he has not been nearly as lucky in Hollywood, though the doors opened wide after *Secaucus Seven.* Within days of the film's first showing, at Filmex, Sayles had signed two deals, one to write an extraterrestrial script, "Night Skies," for Steven Spielberg and Ron Cobb at Columbia, the other to write and direct "Blood of the Lamb" for the Ladd Company. Soon there was a second writing-directing deal, this one with Twentieth Century-Fox for *Baby, It's You.*

Today "Night Skies" sits on a shelf, judged too expensive by Columbia. And the two writing-directing deals, Sayles discovered, were "sort of like getting drafted by the Red Sox and sent to Pittsfield. If you all of a sudden turn into a great ballplayer, they'll bring you up. But they have the money to just look at drafts. If anything exciting comes along, great, they'll make it. If they don't think it's commercial enough, or it doesn't turn them on, they won't."

"That's the most discouraging thing about being a writer," he complains. "I was hired by both Fox and the Ladd Company based on *Secaucus Seven.* But I can't go to them and say, 'OK, *Secaucus Seven* was something where I had total control. I wrote a script that wasn't a regular commercial script and it was very successful, so that's what I want to do again.' No, they're hiring me because I did one thing, and they're hoping I'll come up with another thing. And that hasn't happened yet."

Sayles and Fox parted ways after several drafts of *Baby, It's You.* "We had enough disagreements that it was clear they had some movie in their head that they couldn't express to me," Sayles states. "But it wasn't the one I wanted to make." Amy Robinson, of Double Play Productions, who originally brought the story to Sayles and engineered the deal with the studio, then turned around and raised $2.9 million from independent investors. Sayles finally shot the film last spring, after *Lianna.*

*Baby, It's You* is the second film produced by Robinson and her partner Griffin Dunne. It's part high school nostalgia, part love story about people from different sides of the tracks, combining three common Sayles themes: class, coming of age, and the sixties. It's about a Jewish princess bound for Sarah Lawrence and an Italian tough who doesn't even finish high school.

"It follows these characters over two big hills," explains Sayles. "One is from 1966 in Trenton, New Jersey, to 1967 at Sarah Lawrence, which was a huge jump in what was expected of somebody who was young. Jill, the female character, goes from a high school in which getting good grades and being straight makes her popular to a time and place where you need to be just the opposite to be accepted. And people actually did that in those days—they totally restructured their personalities, at least on the outside, in the space of a year.

"The other big jump is from high school, which is the last bastion of true democracy in our society, where you have classes and eat lunch with the guy who's going to be picking up your garbage later in life, to the year after, when she goes to college and he runs into the fact that he's going nowhere. It's about class in America, and where the divisions are. It's about how certain things are possible in high school, but when people enter the real world, they become impossible."

Jill is played by Rosanna Arquette, who also stars in the upcoming television miniseries *Executioner's Song*. Opposite her is Vincent Spano, who at twenty has already had major parts in *Over the Edge* and the yet-to-be-released *Black Stallion Returns*. The film was shot almost entirely in New Jersey, using schools in Cliffside Park, Hoboken, and Newark. The $2.9 million gave Sayles four times the budget of *Lianna*. For the first time he was able to buy the rights to recordings, including several Sinatra tunes, a Springsteen classic or two, and the obligatory pile of sixties rock.

Paramount expressed interest in distributing the film, but potential problems developed recently. After viewing a rough cut, Paramount reportedly asked for changes in the second half of the film. Sayles balked. "It gets interesting and complex in the second half," he said after the screening, adding with a sting, "which is why Paramount doesn't like it." Then he went off to complete the editing, planning to hand the finished film over to Double Play Productions. (Double Play has the right of final cut, but the director has the right to remove his name from the film if any changes displease him.) Sayles, however, described the state of affairs not as "resistance" but as "a disagreement"—and quipped, "I suppose I could always go back to cutting meat. I've still got my union card." Paramount, for its part, called the whole affair "a tempest in a teapot."

If studio distribution has proved elusive, so has directing a film for Hollywood. As with *Baby, It's You,* his deal at the Ladd Company for "Blood of the Lamb" was put into turnaround after several drafts. It has since been picked up by Warner Bros., but Sayles must rewrite it before any decisions are made. The story sounds like a natural: Two bored ex-radicals infiltrate a fundamentalist religious group.

"One thing you're almost always dealing with is that most of the people can't read," Sayles says. "They can't tell a good script from a bad script. Some of them have decent story sense, and they can look for certain elements—and that's the art of writing a selling script, to make those elements come out, so they see right away what is commercial about it. You might extend the lead part, so it seems like a star part—knowing full well that what you've extended it with is very expendable stuff and will probably go out in the cutting. Or you might put something in that you know they won't be able to afford, but that makes it more exciting. The rest of the stuff, you try to put there, too. You're fooling them a touch, but at least you're bringing out the parts they're going to respond to."

At the moment, however, Sayles is weary of the whole game. "Development deals just take up too much energy, without a real promise of ever turning into something," he says. "I'm less enthusiastic, having gone through this whole two-year period of getting jerked around with scripts. I don't want to go through it again with casting and directing and everything else. There's a lot of movies I'd like to make that probably could only be made through a studio system, with the kind of financing they have. But I don't know if my taste and sense of what's commercial is close enough to theirs that I'll ever get together with them on anything."

What's the difference? "I've written genre pictures, and basically I think anything can be a good picture in any genre—it just has to be honest to what you start out doing, and not throw a lot of things in there because somebody's decided they need those elements to sell a certain audience. I guess one difference is that I'm interested in looking at characters in some kind of depth. I don't think it hurts an audience to know who a person is; I don't think you have to have in every picture some kind of cataclysmic event. I think there's room for those pictures, and I like some of them.

I think there's enough of an audience for any picture that attempts to do something or say something in an entertaining way, if it's well enough made."

Surprisingly, though, Sayles does not dispute the studios' reluctance to seek the audience for small, character films. "If you're sitting there working for Fox or Warners, and you have four movies that have the potential to make millions, and five that might break even or make a small profit if you work hard on them, which ones are you going to work on and which ones are you just going to dump and take as a loss? None of the major distributors are set up to do special handling, to go city by city, over a year period. They're set up to do a two-week test in a major market, and if it flops there, forget it. I'm not saying their taste is great in general, but I don't see why they should be interested in making something like *Secaucus Seven.*"

On the other hand, Sayles acknowledges, it's almost impossible to keep making movies independently. Independent filmmakers cannot deduct their expenses on a film until it is released, a fact he was blissfully ignorant of when he did *Secaucus* and filed his tax returns. As a result, he had to pay $12,500 in back taxes for 1978, and he expects the IRS will keep a close watch for the rest of the eighties.

"What it means is that even if I wrote three movies a year and got paid a lot for them," Sayles observes, "there's no way I'm going to get far enough ahead to finance a film myself again. This time around it would be tax fraud. Even if you're lucky and every picture you make makes money, unless you have a lot of things coming out at the same time and can always write the cost of one against the success of another one, basically, the way the IRS is set up, it's just totally against small pictures being made. Without some kind of flow of big money behind you, any gain you make is eaten up by taxes."

The only option is to raise money from others, and that is never easy. "It's not the greatest investment in the world. You can't take the money you're spending on a picture as a deduction until it opens. That may be a year later, and even then you can't take it off unless it's a flop immediately. If it's successful, it's going to take another year or two to make its money back. Meanwhile, you could be making twenty percent with municipal bonds or something, with no risk. So why invest in a film that will probably lose money?"

Still, there are people who, for one reason or another, have decided to invest in a John Sayles film. So far his strategy has been to concentrate on writing and directing, let others raise the money, and keep a level head. After all, this is a man who broke into the business writing "actorproof" low-budget horror films; who wrote three endings for *Piranha,* and four for *Alligator,* his best one unused because the thirty-two-foot reptilian model was too good a publicity gimmick to destroy; who wrote a love scene for werewolves in *The Howling*; who has grown used to watching his scripts filmed with a random third of the scenes missing; who was called on last spring to dash off twenty pages of dialogue for a draft he'd never seen of a movie being filmed halfway around the globe.

"Nobody stuck a gun to my head and said, 'You have to work in an expensive medium that relies on other people,' " he says with a shrug. "So if I thought my Godgiven rights to direct something were being threatened, it'd be one thing. As it is, it's a pain in the ass, but nobody guaranteed me anything. It's up to other people and their money, and I *am* asking people for their money. I wouldn't invest *my* money in somebody *else's* movies."

# John Sayles: An Interview

KENNETH M. CHANKO/1983

ALTHOUGH WRITER-DIRECTOR JOHN Sayles is finishing post-production work on *Baby, It's You,* his first movie to be distributed by a major studio, and is working out a deal at another studio to direct another film later this year, he has hardly "gone Hollywood." *Baby, It's You* was made for $3 million—a lot for Sayles, a drop in the bucket for a major studio—principally through bank financing. It was a situation, Sayles said, in which the bank knew that as soon as the movie was finished, one of the majors would pick it up. And sure enough, it was—Paramount is scheduled to release *Baby, It's You,* a teenage love story following the couple beyond their high school years, next month.

It was Sayles's insistence on having the story explore the characters' lives *after* high school—a daring concept for a teen movie in Hollywood these days—that got the project into a bit of trouble.

"It's a cross-class high school romance between a Jewish girl who is definitely going to a four-year college—and a pretty classy one—and an Italian guy who's definitely not going anywhere after high school; in fact, he doesn't even finish high school," said Sayles. The interview was conducted in a small editing room on the West Side of Manhattan where Sayles and several others were working on the movie. He mentioned that the office space was built for the year-long editing of Warren Beatty's *Reds.*

The first half of *Baby, It's You,* which stars two screen newcomers, Rosanna Arquette and Vincent Spano, deals with their high school years

---

From *Films in Review,* February 1983. Reprinted by permission.

when the relationship is possible. The second half has the girl in college and the guy down in Miami trying to meet Frank Sinatra, washing dishes to make ends meet.

"Fox liked the high school part of the picture, but they didn't want it to go on to college. As far as Amy (Robinson, the producer) and I were concerned, the only thing that made it interesting was that it did go on to college, that it wasn't just another nostalgia piece (the movie spans the late 1960s to early '70s). None of the studios felt confident enough to do it.

"It would have cost $5 million at a studio," Sayles explained, "with all the unions and everything. Whereas with a bank loan, Doubleplay (the production company) was able to make it for $3 million without any of those union contracts to honor. We worked with a pick-up crew that had worked on a lot of independent features, as well as with European filmmakers. Our cinematographer was Michael Ballhaus, who shot 11 of Fassbinder's movies, and a lot of his assistants came over from Germany. A woman who worked on *Gallipoli* and other Australian films did the hair; our key grip was from Canada. We had very good people, a really great crew—and very efficient."

Sayles knows from efficient. The first movie he directed and wrote, *The Return of the Secaucus Seven* (he also edited it and acted in it), was made for $60,000. The story of college friends reuniting ten years later, *Secaucus Seven* was released in the fall of 1980 and had an unexpectedly successful run for a small, independent film. It has grossed about $2 million to date, according to Sayles. The movie also appeared on several top ten lists that year, including *Time* magazine's.

The 32-year-old Sayles, who was born in Schenectady, NY and who now lives in Hoboken, NJ, where almost all of his second directorial effort, *Lianna,* was shot, was able to raise the bulk of the $60,000 to make *Secaucus Seven* from book royalties (he's also a critically acclaimed novelist and short-story writer) and from sales of screenplays to Roger Corman.

"They're fun to do, and they're a technical challenge, but I also do them so I can use the money to make my movies," said Sayles, referring to such scripts as *Piranha, The Lady in Red* and *Battle Beyond the Stars*. More recently, he wrote the screenplays for Joe Dante's *The Howling,* a kind of poorman's *Jaws* called *Alligator* and John Frankenheimer's *The Challenge.* "I like the people who are doing them, and I've gotten to work in all kinds of different genres.

"I don't necessarily want to direct all my screenplays. It takes so long to write and direct and to do the editing that just writing the screenplay goes fairly fast and painlessly. I wouldn't want to spend a year of my life doing *Alligator,* but it's been about that amount of time for *Lianna,* and it's close to that for *Baby, It's You,* although they overlapped a bit. When I'm writing for somebody else, I'm helping them do *their* story.

*Lianna,* which has just been released in New York and several other cities, is a case in point. It's a serious story of a lesbian relationship that explores its effect on the younger woman, who has a husband and two children. "It's not like *An Unmarried Woman* where she happens to have money. She has to go out and find a job and deal with her friends, her kids, and the community." Sayles wrote the story five years ago, before he started writing *Secaucus Seven,* and finally got to shoot it last year. Like his first movie, he also edited *Lianna* and has a supporting role in front of the camera. However, *Lianna* cost $300,000 to make.

"It took us a year-and-a-half to raise the money," Sayles recalls. "They (the producers, Jeffrey Nelson and Maggie Renzi) went looking for $800,000 originally. We wanted to shoot it in 35m and to take more time with it, but we just weren't getting it, the money just wasn't coming. It goes to show that if you're willing to lower your standards enough, you can do anything," Sayles said with a rueful laugh.

Sayles approached several studios early on with his *Lianna* screenplay, but the response was not encouraging. "They'd say 'There's a kernel of an idea here, but we're afraid of this, and we're afraid of that.' It would have never survived the writing phase at the studios."

Sayles considers the writing and reworking of the screenplay the most critical stage in the movie-making process. "To have it go through a studio committee is usually damaging. I mean, it's a legitimate process—they have to consider whether this story is worth spending $5 million on; what elements can they sell, who can play which parts. But it's like getting a bill through Congress. It gets watered down. So I figure if it gets watered down at all, it's not worth doing at a studio."

Sayles said he doesn't feel he has an identifiable style per se—"It's more a sensibility. I'll always go for the better performance, the better acting take, which sometimes will leave you with a more ragged cut. When you hear about this guy's style or that guy's style, I think it comes out of the conditions they had to work under. I'm not really interested in style.

Like in my fiction writing, I'm willing to change styles if it fits the story better."

Knowing he had just $60,000 to make *Secaucus Seven,* Sayles wrote it so the amount of camera work wouldn't matter that much. "There was shot after shot that would have looked nicer, and I knew exactly how it would have looked nicer, if I could have moved the camera," Sayles admits. "With *Lianna,* setting is a little more important. Camera movement is still not quite that important, although once again if I had had more time or money or the skill to get it done on time there are certain things that could have looked better. In *Lianna* we spent much more money on set design than in *Secaucus Seven,* where all we did was move furniture around. In *Lianna,* when she moves from the faculty housing, where she was living with her professor-husband, to a bare apartment, the contrast is important. Also, we had to make a local bar look like a women's bar rather than one where ethnic types come to watch boxing.

"In *Baby, It's You,* since we had more money and time, and because it is a much more 'active story,' there's a lot of camera movement. These kids just never stay still. I got a lot of good ideas from Michael Ballhaus, and eight out of ten of them I was able to use. I also got to shoot it in 35m and, in addition to better resolution, you get a better depth of field than in 16m. That was important because this is a high school movie and the characters are in a hallway or in a class, and how these characters are perceived is a key element to the story. There are always a lot of students around, so it was good that everything didn't go out of focus once you got five feet away from the camera."

There are many different movies Sayles said he would like to make, but the complexity of characters is something that will always be explored in his films. "And I think that sort of goes against traditional movie language, the white-hat/black-hat thing. That sort of thing works in a certain kind of movie—like *The Road Warrior.* There's very little you have to know about that guy; in fact, the less you know about him the better.

"But even in the genre stuff I've done, like *The Lady in Red,* there was always a reason why these people were shooting at each other. It might get cut out, but I always write it in. I don't like to do things in movie shorthand. I'll take the time to consider why these people are falling in love, instead of just having them walk along a beach."

Sayles is an admirer of Akira Kurosawa's films (*Battle Beyond the Stars* borrowed its basic plot from *The Seven Samurai*), and he also likes Sidney Lumet's work because "he's another person interested in that complexity. If you look at *Serpico* and *Prince of the City* you can see that. *Serpico* was complex enough, but it's simplistic compared to *Prince of the City.* He presents so many more sides to the issue in *Prince.*"

Would Sayles like to continue to write novels and direct films? "I'm finishing some touch-up research on a novel about the Cuban exile community in Miami. I've got some chapters written. I just have to make some time to do it.

"Because directing is very political and social, it takes up more of your time than writing does. It's more demanding because you have to make the movie when the money is there. A book can just sit there, it doesn't depend on anyone else. That's what's nice about it. You don't have to rely on anybody else—you either do it or you don't. Fiction writing is a break from movie-making for me."

As far as Sayles's next movie is concerned, he displayed a marked ambiguity about whether he'd rather do it independently or at a studio. "It's not easy either way—you give up something at both ends. You give up the ease of not having to search for money when you make an independent film, having to scrimp on the mixing time and everything. If you go with a studio, having people drive you around and bring you Coke—that's Coca-Cola, I mean, or Tab in my case—then you pay for it in other ways, which is that they can always say—and rightfully—'look, we're risking three million or five million or whatever, be a little responsive to our needs.'

"It's great to not have to go around and raise your money—a thousand here, ten thousand there. But if I can't get the same kind of control doing it through a studio—artistic control, which is always important to a project as far as I'm concerned—then I'd just as soon go back to looking for the money myself and do it independently."

# A Male Director's Look at a Lesbian Relationship

JUDY STONE/1983

WEREWOLVES AND MAN-EATING piranhas. Lost activists from the '60s. Lesbians of the '80s. The White Sox baseball scandal of 1919. Striking coal miners in the embattled '20s. This uncommon variety of subjects may not be equally the *spice* of life for John Sayles, but it's been the bread and butter that has kept him hopping from Hollywood, Calif., to rundown Hoboken, N.J., the home base that's as unfashionable as this gangling, down-to-earth screenwriter/director/novelist/actor.

Next month, the Dream Factory where he once churned out such horror movie scripts as *Alligator* and *The Howling* will finally release his first big $3 million budget movie, *Baby, It's You,* after it premieres at Los Angeles' Filmex and the San Francisco Film Festival. His second low-budget independent production, *Lianna,* the story of a lesbian love affair, opened Friday at the Lumiere.

Sayles achieved fame, if not fortune, with *The Return of the Secaucus 7,* a perky, often witty look at some bewildered survivors of the anti-Vietnam war movement. He plunged every cent of his hard-earned Hollywood money into that one, a $60,000 risk that had a theatrical gross of $2 million, leaving him with a profit of about $200,000.

Even though Sayles recently became the lucky beneficiary of a five-year, $30,000 per annum grant from the John D. MacArthur Foundation, he doesn't look any more prosperous than the last time he dropped into

---

From *San Francisco Chronicle,* 20 March 1983. 

*The Chronicle*. In fact, he appears a shade embarrassed by the unanticipated windfall.

Although he's only 32, the 6-foot-4 "ex-jock" seems to have sprung out of the '30s Depression era in both his manner and concerns. Both grandfathers were cops; his parents teachers. He grew up in a working-class neighborhood in Schenectady, N.Y., and has been a construction worker, nursing home orderly and meatpacker during and after earning a BA in psychology at Williams College. Unkempt and relaxed in a rumpled blue shirt and well-worn cords, he was in town the other day with Maggie Renzi to talk about *Lianna*.

His pert, blue-eyed companion for the last nine years, Renzi is used to doing double-duty. She acted as the untidy housewife in *Secaucus* and was assistant film editor. She co-produced *Lianna* and played Lianna's understanding neighbor.

Sayles had written *Lianna* years ago but couldn't find a producer. Without experience in directing or editing, he made *Secaucus* to show what he could do. The response exceeded their expectations. The script won the L.A. Film Critics' award for best screenplay of 1980 and made several Top Ten lists. As a result, Sayles decided to proceed with the independent production of *Lianna*. He had already chalked up enviable writing credits: his first short story, "I-80 Nebraska," made the 1976 O'Henry collection. His first novel, *Pride of the Bimbos*, about a five-man softball team barnstorming the South, was followed by the novel *Union Dues* which was nominated for both the National Book Award and the National Critics' Circle Award.

*Lianna* began to develop when John and Maggie were living in Santa Barbara and Sayles was commuting to Hollywood. "I knew a lot of people who were breaking up and had children," said the writer, who does not have children. "I was witness to some really bad custody battles. It was a time when judges started giving joint custody. I knew women whose husbands had died or were divorced. They were going from being a woman in a family to starting out from scratch economically. I wanted a situation where the woman would have to leave the house and who might not get custody. I thought of some gay women I had known who were coming out and all of this combined to make an interesting story about someone who at 33 begins to grow up."

Lianna, the mother of an eight-year-old girl and 13-year-old son, falls in love with her child psychology professor and leaves her husband who teaches at the same small-town college. "Lianna makes this leap," Sayles said, "and naively blurts out the news to people very close to her. Because of the reaction, she has to re-examine her own life. She's as much an outsider to the gay world and a lot of those feelings as the audience."

Sayles said he was not making a film just for gay audiences. "I concentrated on things that I think are common to all relationships, like loneliness and those power things that happen between people no matter what their sex is."

He reported that *Lianna*—which broke all house records in its first days in New York—has had a "mostly positive" response from lesbians despite minor criticism. Some viewers felt the bar scene was not typical of a women's bar. At a sneak preview in Boston, half the audience was composed of gay women. "There was a kind of immediate knee jerk reaction to seeing something about women written by a man and for the first ten minutes you could feel the hostility," Sayles noted. "By the middle, people were with the film and by the end, they showed they liked it."

How did he feel about that knee-jerk reaction? "I can understand it," Sayles responded. "Some of it is just left over from hard political times. In any huge political movement, there's almost always a moment when, say, the black people kick out the white. Whether it's necessary or not, it almost always happens. There was that moment in the women's movement when they felt they had to kick out all the men because they had to think on their own. That fear of being co-opted is a real one."

Lesbians weren't interested in helping finance a film written by a man, Renzi noted uncritically. "That didn't seem like a hip idea to them. Also, the two women in *Lianna* don't end up happily ever after. I think it was hard for women to put money into something that wasn't a completely positive story."

It took 18 months for her and co-producer Jeffrey Nelson to raise $300,000 to finance the film, which had to be rebudgeted from its original $800,000. The money was raised in a limited partnership with 24 people who had never invested in a film.

Renzi admitted she felt some initial discomfort with the sexual aspects. She and the women who worked on the film did some re-thinking about their preconceptions. "When I was growing up, my mother told me all my closest friends would be women. With two sisters, I'm used to intimacy with women. There's a fine line between that and a sexual relationship. Even though I had the part of an onlooker, as an actress I had to ask myself if I would have been comfortable enough to do one of the scenes involving physical intimacy."

Linda Griffiths who plays Lianna and Jane Hallaren who is the psychology professor were uncomfortable at first with the love scenes. Sayles tried to put them at ease by stressing the emotional connection they felt. Renzi said he helped the actresses by being completely clear about what they had to do. "He didn't say, 'All right, girls, go to it.' He'd tell them, 'move your hand here,' 'stroke her back.' He made it as calm and quiet and matter-of-fact as possible. Jane and Linda were very supportive because they knew John wouldn't pull anything."

"I don't believe in tricking people," Sayles continued. "Sometimes a director gets good results that way. I'd just as soon not. There are two things in film: the results you get and the experience of making it. I have one of those end-justifies-the-means problems. I don't want to do anything in the experience of filming that makes you feel hypocritical when you see it. I don't think you can make a movie with principles about the way people should treat each other and treat actors terribly."

Right now he's wary of Hollywood. After *Secaucus* premiered at Filmex, Sayles signed two deals which are now in limbo. Up until press time, it looked as if *Baby, It's You* would also end up nowhere. Sayles directed-wrote the mid-'60s romance between a Jewish girl heading for Sarah Lawrence College and an Italian tough who doesn't finish high school.

Sayles shot it in Newark, N.J. and at Sarah Lawrence. "It's about class in America," Sayles said. "It's about how certain things are possible in high school but when people enter the real world, they become impossible. High school is the last bastion of true democracy in our society." Meanwhile, Sara Pillsbury, who owns the rights to Eliot Asinof's book, *Eight Men Out,* about the White Sox scandal of 1919, is peddling Sayles' film version in Hollywood and plans to produce it.

Sayles is confident he will shoot his next independent production, *Matewan,* in September if Renzi is able to raise $1.2 million. The film is set in West Virginia and is based on a famous 1920 massacre. The bloodletting was the culmination of a struggle between the United Mine Workers which was trying to organize the highly individualistic coal miners and the operators who had brought in private detectives to break the union.

"John is more committed to this union thing than I am," Renzi interjected. "For me the film talks about violence. The mountaineers live with an incredible amount of violence. It's where they have been shooting an eye for an eye forever. This is *not* going to be a vigilante movie. Vigilante movies like *Death Wish* scare me. I want this film to say it's never right to murder."

"I don't have the answer to non-violence in situations like the West Virginia one," Sayles commented in his mild way. "I liked *Gandhi* but if you take that principle and try to spread it everywhere, it doesn't necessarily work. The West Virginians historically were always in a situation where their money was taken right out from under their own feet and, in fact, they were kicked off their own land if they said anything about it. If a dispute got to court, the miners lost. One of the reasons I want to make the movie is to figure out that kind of thing. Where would you stand? Where would the audience stand? It's a very tough question."

# Sayles Talk

RICK LYMAN/1983

THE AIR IS VERY rarefied here. You need collateral to take a breath.

The sound of fine china meeting silverware tinkles delicately in the lightly scented air while tuxedoed waiters move in watchful glide patterns around the cloth-draped tables. The rich smell of coffee fills the dining room while tall windows framed by scrupulously tended plants offer a sumptuous view of a private waterfall.

In stalks the genius.

He's over 6 feet tall, thin and he lopes slightly. He eyes the room. Three-piece pinstripe suits peer authoritatively from behind crisp copies of the *Washington Post* and the *Wall Street Journal.* A few poke their heads from behind the papers and watch the strange creature approach, secure in the knowledge that a member of the hotel staff will eject him if he proves as unsuitable as he appears.

The genius' companion and business partner, Maggie Renzi, sighs and says in a subdued tone, "Oh God, we look like a couple of old hippies."

John Sayles, 33, award-winning novelist, short-story writer, screenwriter, actor, film editor and director, does not respond. His brown corduroys, well-worn, stop just above a pair of ragged tennis shoes. His shirt, also light brown, says "The Gap" on the breast pocket. It is most definitely not a button-down. In fact, there are no buttons at all, just shiny snaps, in the urban-cowboy motif. His hair, pulled back behind his ears, sprays out at

---

From *Philadelphia Inquirer,* 6 March 1983. Reprinted with permission.

the nape of his neck like the bristles of a broom that has seen too many seasons.

He points one worn Nike in front of the other, lopes to the center of the room and asks the emotionless maitre d' for a table for breakfast. He is admitted graciously—everyone has to eat, after all—and the pinstripes disappear behind their papers.

Would they see the irony if they knew that Sayles' career exemplifies everything this plush room is not? His stories are personal and bawdy, pro-labor, anti-conservative. And his movies are strictly independent, filmed away from the Hollywood power structure on a relative shoestring. He lives, for heaven's sake, in a small house on an unpretentious street in Hoboken ("It's near New York without *being* New York").

And he chokes on all this genius talk.

Sayles, who is at the plush Four Seasons Hotel in Georgetown as part of a nationwide tour to promote his new movie, *Lianna,* was named last month as one of eight recipients of the annual awards issued by the Chicago-based MacArthur Foundation.

The awards, which have become known as "genius grants," are given to individuals the foundation chooses who have distinguished themselves in their fields. The grants, which vary but run to tens of thousands of dollars a year for five years, are meant to give the recipients a stretch of time to pursue their interests without wondering how next month's rent will be paid.

Sayles doesn't take to being called a genius, shrinks away from any affectations that smell of pomposity. He orders a simple breakfast of gooey rolls and hot chocolate.

"I can't believe they booked us in here. This is the fanciest hotel I've ever stayed in," Renzi says. "How about you?"

Sayles squints, swallows his latest bite and says, "Yeah, well, except for the Plaza in Paris."

He smiles, extinguishing all traces of self-seriousness. "Steven Spielberg was filming in Tunisia or someplace, and we'd been talking about doing a movie called *Night Skies,* a kind of *Drums Along the Mohawk* with aliens instead of Indians. He wanted to get together and talk about it, so he flew me over to Paris for a day and a half," Sayles says. "I'd never been there. It was great, but I didn't have much time."

"He got to see one small museum," Renzi adds.

"Anyway, Spielberg decided he didn't want to make a movie with hostile aliens, so he did *E.T.* instead," Sayles says. "Besides that, though, this is the fanciest hotel I've ever stayed in."

Sayles, a Schenectady, N.Y. native, graduated from Williams College in Massachusetts in 1972. He lists among his previous occupations those of orderly, meat packer and construction worker.

His first short story, published in 1975, was about "a five-man drag baseball team that barnstorms the South." It won an O. Henry Award. His first novel, *The Pride of the Bimbos,* was published the same year. He calls it "Fellini-esque." He started making just about everybody's list of Big-New-Talents-We-Should-Keep-an-Eye-On.

His second novel, *Union Dues,* published three years later, was nominated for both a National Book Award and a National Critic's Circle Award. His collection of short stories, *The Anarchists' Convention,* was published in 1979.

In 1977, Sayles got hooked up with B-movie czar Roger Corman and sold the producer his first screenplay. He's now done six of them: a witty *Jaws* spoof called *Piranha*; a rugged, Dillinger gangster thing called *The Lady in Red*; a sort of *Magnificent Seven in Outer Space* adventure called *Battle Beyond the Stars*; a successful werewolf flick called *The Howling*; a cult favorite about a giant reptile loose in the sewers of New York called *Alligator,* and a samuraiish chop-socky called *The Challenge.*

He's often asked why he did such B movies. What's an award-winning novelist *author* doing making a movie like *Alligator*?

"People think I chose to do those movies or something, that there's some kind of pattern, that I'm making some kind of statement," he says. "It was just a job. I was *hired* to write those movies."

It was in 1977 that he, Renzi and others raised $60,000 to finance *The Return of the Secaucus Seven,* the first movie Sayles wrote and directed. He also played a small role (he was the night clerk at a motel in the small town where a group of '60s liberals has its reunion). And he edited the movie himself.

*Secaucus Seven* won the best screenplay award from the L.A. Film Critics Circle in 1980, when it was finally released, and quickly became an arthouse staple. *Time* magazine, among other publications, picked it as one of the best 10 movies of that year.

In the fall of 1981, using the same production team, Sayles began filming another of his screenplays, something he'd had kicking around for several years, called *Lianna*. It opened in New York last month to some glowing, and some not-so-glowing reviews, and is making the national circuit now. It opened here on Friday.

Like *Secaucus Seven,* it was low-budget, costing only $300,000 to film. That wouldn't pay the taxi-cab bill for most Hollywood productions.

*Lianna* is filled with Sayles' brand of charming, fully rounded characterizations. It's about a naive young New Jersey housewife who has a passionate lesbian affair with her night-school college professor. Some of the criticism of the movie has held that Sayles was stretching when he wrote it, straining to be daring and controversial.

"I can't believe anybody would feel that way. The movie just isn't like that," he says. "*Lianna* is not the story of a love that dared not speak its name."

It was written five years ago, he says, well before the filming of *Personal Best* and *Making Love,* two movies that also dealt with gay subjects. Where did the story come from?

"I made it up," he says, then pauses, smiling. "No, I was witness at the time to a couple of really hard custody fights, and I knew a couple of women who were coming out [as lesbians] at that time, people who were growing up at the age of 35 or 40."

Lianna, the housewife, is "not quite a heroine," Sayles says. Like those people he knew in Hoboken, she finds herself growing up in her mid-30s. "She doesn't do anything wrong on purpose, but she's naive," he says.

His third movie, which opened two days ago in Seattle ("a great movie town. I don't know why"), is called *Baby, It's You.* It's a coming-of-age movie set in North Jersey in the '60s. "It's not a comedy, more a *Rebel Without a Cause* kind of thing," Sayles says. It's more serious than *American Graffiti,* for instance. It's all about New Jersey and high school and cars."

Like his other movies, it was made independently. He, Renzi and others made the rounds raising the money, one chunk at a time. ("Raising money is exactly as terrible as you'd think it is," she says.) Only after it's shot, cut and ready to go does he sell a film to a distributor.

"We're happy being independent," Sayles says. "I feel much more like I have one foot in the movie industry and one out. I suppose it would be nice to have a big budget, but really it doesn't matter to me as long as I get the final cut and casting control."

Renzi is hitting the fund-raising trail, in between *Lianna*-promotional interviews, to raise money for Sayles' fourth movie. Called *Matewan,* it's based on a true story involving union attempts to organize West Virginia coal miners. Company thugs were sent to the small town to bust the union. They pushed people around and beat them up, until finally, having had enough, the townspeople "banded together and murdered the thugs" in the middle of Main Street.

It will be Sayles' most ambitious project with an estimated budget of $1.2 million—not much by Hollywood standards, but a staggering sum for him. "It has 48 speaking parts," he says, as if astounded by the fact.

He's also sold Warner Bros. a screenplay called *Blood of the Lamb,* but the studio hasn't given him the go-ahead on it. They just keep asking for more rewrites. "You keep doing drafts as long as they keep paying you," he says. "That's how the movie business works."

In addition, he's finished the outline and "about five chapters" of a novel, which he hopes to finish writing this year. It's called *Los Gusanos,* Spanish for "the worms," and it's set in Miami's Little Havana community of Cuban refugees. "I've been down there a half-dozen times, researching," he says. "It's definitely not a comedy."

He polishes off the last of his sticky buns and rises. The tuxedoed waiter wafts forward to see if there will be anything else. No, he says, and begins loping out.

Does he consider any of his new projects to be a departure for him?

He laughs. The question smells too much of Hollywood pomposity.

"Everybody wants to call things a departure. What's a departure? It's *all* a departure," he says. "I mean, when your first story is about a five-man drag baseball team, it's hard not to have a departure."

And with that, he turns and departs.

# Interview with John Sayles

ANONYMOUS/1983

*Editor's Note: John Sayles recently chatted with us about the production of* Lianna. *What follows are edited excerpts from that conversation. It may be of interest to know that* Lianna, *which deals with a woman who realizes that she is a lesbian at the same time as her marriage is breaking up, was written by Sayles four years before he wrote* The Return of the Secaucus Seven. *At the time he realized that he could not raise enough money to do* Lianna *so he concocted the story for* Secaucus Seven *in order to have a script which he could do for the amount of money he had available.*

ON *LIANNA*, WE SHOT thirty-six days—six consecutive six-day weeks. We shot in Hoboken, and the crew, except for three or four people from Boston, were coming from nearby Manhattan or New Jersey or Brooklyn. They would come across the river every morning, and then go home at night. It's nice, for people to get to go home and forget about the movie.

I shot in Hoboken because we live there and that's where we could ask for the most favors. Hoboken is where *On the Waterfront* was shot, but we never, until the very last shot, pointed the camera toward the river and the city skyline and even then we didn't make a big deal of it. So it's just supposed to be an Eastern liberal arts college, vaguely urban but not New York City.

---

From *American Cinematographer,* April 1983. Reprinted by permission.

There were probably 20 different locations. One of the problems with the way that I write and the budgets I work with is that I write with a lot of characters and a lot of small scenes and they tend to happen in a lot of different locations. With Lianna, I did some re-writing to accommodate the budget. Originally, I had written it for the West Coast when I was living there so the scene in the pool was at the beach.

We live in a house in Hoboken and during the shooting our ground floor was Ruth's bedroom. Another bedroom in the house was Frieda's. The second floor was the production office with all the phones and the mimeo machine and then the editing room was the third floor.

*Lianna* doesn't have the home movie feeling that *Secaucus Seven* did. With *Secaucus* we weren't going to make it look great with the kind of money we had so we went for a rougher edge, whereas with *Lianna,* we wanted to take some of that edge off. The movie's depressing enough in some places that we didn't want to go with the real hard-edge film noir look, so we kept it a little softer. It's not a heavy melodramatic film and I don't think that look would have been right for it.

There is very little camera movement in *Lianna.* There's some in the dance scene but generally the dancer moves and the camera doesn't. There's one scene that we tried to do hand-held, but some of it works and some of it doesn't. The big argument scene between Lianna and Dick moves around but it moves with the characters. When it works, you're not aware of the camera and this was my intention—to give the feeling of a little space around them and them moving around each other. Now and then there are simple tracking shots if people are walking and there's a little movement in the love-making scenes. Generally, it was not a priority to do a whole lot with the depth. These are very articulate people, both in *Secaucus Seven* and *Lianna,* so they can do a lot of expressing of their own. Sometimes they're not saying what they mean, and sometimes they're trying to get off the hook by being articulate when really they're emotional; but still they're very articulate. With *Baby, It's You,* the picture I directed after *Lianna,* the characters are high school kids who are not that articulate and the film depends a great deal more on the visuals. Fortunately for that one I had more money.

My first priority is always with the acting and the believability of the characters. The second priority is visuals and sound. I'm always telling the actors if you feel like you've got another one, tell me about it and we'll do it again or if you want to try something different, try it. We'll make time for that. Then in the editing, I'll always take the actor's best take, even if it makes a choppy cut, because unless it's totally distracting, the choppy cut will go by faster than a not-so-good performance.

Once you know how much camera movement you can or can't have, once you know what your subject-matter is and whether it needs size or not, you can really concentrate on making a kind of movie you can afford. If you only have $10,000 what kind of movie can you make for $10,000? You don't try to make *Lawrence of Arabia,* but you may try to make a small story in the desert if you have a desert nearby.

*Lianna* cost $300,000. There were $40,000 worth of deferments and the day that we signed our contract with UA Classics we were able to pay those off. The deferments were to crew members and not to actors. So $340,000 was the total budget for the film, and that eventually included the blow-up, although we didn't plan it that way. We only budgeted to an answer print in 16mm. Then, when we were looking for distribution, it didn't make sense to sit around waiting for a distributor to come along and blow it up, so we blew it up ourselves and ended up paying for that, too.

Of the $300,000, I ripped up my check for writer/director, editor and actor although, I had to be paid for certain things on paper because I was, at that time, in the writers' guild, and we had to pay the guild benefits. Basically I'm taking points instead of getting paid as a writer/director and editor.

I own a bigger piece of the film than I would have if I had just gotten paid up front, which I think is fair. The producers got very little money up front so the above-the-line was very, very small. The actors were getting scale; even the lead actors were getting only slightly above scale plus a few points. I think the top four actors in the billing have a couple of points in it and I think they'll actually see some money on that, which is good.

I leave the specifics of deal-making to the co-producers. I will say my piece as far as "I really want this person" or "we can get somebody else" or whatever. We have never had much trouble with deal-making. One of the nice things and I think one of the totally necessary things about that kind of filmmaking is that everybody has to be pulling in the same direction and so far, I've been very lucky. Even in a big-budget production that I did, *Baby, It's You,* which is like a three million dollar picture, the crew and cast and everybody was pulling in the same direction.

It took a year and-a-half for Maggie Renzie and Jeffrey Nelson to raise the money for *Lianna,* even after *Secaucus Seven* had done well, mostly because we weren't offering any creative control. We hadn't cast it yet and we weren't guaranteeing any known box office people. Although the fact that *Secaucus Seven* did well got us meetings with people, it didn't necessarily get us the money. And so it ended up being financed totally by a public offering and what are considered unsophisticated investors—people who had never invested in a play or a film before. There were 30 some investors from $50,000 to $1,500. Anyway, as we were raising money I got to talk to various gay women in the film industry who had just heard about the script. They very nicely sort of said, "Here, if there is going to be a movie about this we would like it to be a good one. We feel like this character isn't developed enough in this way and this isn't really true anymore," that kind of thing. I opened Ruth up a little bit more even though she is the character I'm likely to know the least about because it is very much a movie from an outsider's point of view. Lianna is an outsider. It is the only way I felt comfortable coming at it. I added a little to Ruth. I softened the husband a little bit. He was even a bigger rat in the beginning. And, I decided to play Jerry myself because on paper he is a total jerk, and I played him as a partial jerk. Also I changed *Lianna* from being set in Santa Cruz to the East Coast which I think helped it because in Santa Cruz there's a feeling that you can get away from people and the faculty life isn't quite incestuous. I think it did help setting it in the East where you're always going to run into these people at the A&P and there is not this huge beach to go walk on where you can get away from people. You feel like there is a little less acceptance of anything goes in a campus on the East Coast in New Jersey than there is in Santa Cruz where some of the biggest radicals in both lifestyle and politics have taught in the past.

We shot in 16mm. We sniffed around Super-16 for a while. We looked over the new Aaton Camera and I liked the idea of shooting in Super-16, as did Austin DeBesche, who was the DP. But the equipment beyond the camera is so hard to get. To show in interlock, you have to do all kinds of monkey-business. To get an editing machine modified so that you can cut in Super-16 is trouble. This is the kind of film where very often you want to show it in interlock in another city to a potential distributor or exhibitor while you're still working on it. So it just made more sense to shoot in straight 16mm. With *Secaucus Seven,* I thought it was just going to play on

PBS and that its life would be in 16mm, so we framed it for 1.33 Academy format. But this time, we did plan for 35mm distribution and we framed for 1.66:1 by using markings on the viewfinder. We went for 1.66 instead of 1.85 because a lot of the film's life is going to be overseas and with 1.66 you're safe.

We shot about a 10:1 ratio and I'd say I only cut about seven minutes of the scenes that were completed and went into the first assembly. After we had a little preview screening in Boston I cut about four more minutes out of the thirty-five print.

We wrapped in November and we did our sound mix in February—which is pretty fast. I didn't give myself enough time for the sound work on it so I ended up doing a lot of last-minute work, but we really couldn't afford that many assistants. We had a woman who had done some editing before, supervising the syncing of the dailies. We didn't get to screen the dailies, which is a real disadvantage to the cinematographer. We saw them on the flat bed. Because we didn't put them up on the screen there are one or two shots in the final prints that are soft and one of them got even softer because there's an optical on it for the opening credits. Those are things you're not going to catch on a moviola screen until it's way, way too late. But at least on *Lianna* I got to view dailies. On *Secaucus Seven* we got weeklies—And even then, they usually didn't have the sound with them. I just got to see what it looked like. I had to have the way the film was progressing in my head. On *Lianna,* we changed a few things because of what I saw. We re-shot one scene because I just didn't like the way it came out. I needed different coverage and I re-wrote it slightly.

# John Sayles: From Hoboken to Harlem, Via Outer Space

GERALD PEARY/1984

BY THE TIME YOU have finished reading this sentence, John Sayles, author of *The Anarchists' Convention, The Last of the Bimbos,* and *Union Dues,* will probably be finished writing several sentences of his own. "I work fast," Sayles says—so fast that he penned a prizewinning short story riding in a car from L.A. to San Francisco; so fast that, as he reveals in the interview below, he composed the whole first draft of a screenplay, *Alligator,* on a cross-country plane ride.

Sayles isn't just speedy. He's skillful, stylish, and quite incredibly successful. Since 1978, when *Union Dues* was nominated for a National Book Award in fiction, Sayles has had nearly a dozen screenplays—he's not sure of the number—put into production. These go from *Lady in Red,* a low-budget saga of the last days of John Dillinger, to his coauthorship (with Richard Maxwell) of a new multi-million-dollar martial arts extravaganza, *The Challenge,* directed by John Frankenheimer and starring Toshiro Mifune.

Along the way, Sayles has become Hollywood's most employed horror and science-fiction writer, the scenarist behind a trilogy of semitacky, totally cheapo, thoroughly enjoyable Roger Corman flicks—*Piranha, Alligator,* and *Battle Beyond the Stars.* When he has the time and a decent budget ahead of him, John Sayles can produce a first-rate, classy genre script, such as the one he wrote for *The Howling,* among the cleverest and most literate horror movies in years.

---

From Rod Serling's *The Twilight Zone Magazine,* June 1984. Reprinted by permission.

There is also John Sayles, independent filmmaker, whose latest productions are *Baby, It's You,* a teenage tale set in Trenton, New Jersey, in 1966, and *The Brother From Another Planet,* about a black extraterrestrial on the loose in Harlem. And of course there's *Return of the Secaucus Seven.* That Chekhovian romp in the New England countryside, about a reunion of friends from the anti-Vietnam War movement, was made on a miracle $60,000 budget. Sayles wrote, edited, directed, and even acted in *Secaucus*—which has brought in $2 million dollars, making it the most popular and financially lucrative independent feature since *Hester Street.*

Then there's *Lianna,* made for "under a million" and without Hollywood stars. It's a kind of lesbian *Doll's House,* the story of an immature, repressed young woman who walks out on her bourgeois life, husband and children for an affair with her female psychology professor. Again, Sayles wrote, directed, and edited, and he appears on screen, behind a repulsive moustache, as an open-shirted filmmaking teacher on the make. *Lianna,* says Sayles, was "one hundred percent shot in Hoboken, New Jersey," where he lives. As he proudly points out, *On the Waterfront* was also a Hoboken product. In fact, Sayles walks every day past the playground swing where Marlon Brando's crude Terry Malloy once courted Eva Marie Saint.

Thirty-three-year-old John Sayles is tall, muscular, and certainly athletic-looking for a guy who spends too many hours a day hunched over a typewriter. There is a slightly rustic look, too. He could star in a Roger Corman remake of John Ford's *Young Mr. Lincoln.* More likely, he'd play "Shoeless Joe" Jackson in his own movie about the Chicago "Black Sox" scandal, a project he's been dreaming about for years.

TZ: *Did you read science fiction or fantasy as you grew up?*
SAYLES: No, but I think that's been an advantage. I have all these great fresh science fiction ideas that probably have been done already, but I don't know it. People who read science fiction come up and say, "You got that scene from Zelazny," or somebody like that. I answer, "Who is Zelazny? A screenwriter?"

TZ: *Surely you've read H.G. Wells and Ray Bradbury?*
SAYLES: I never read either of them. I never read the *Dune* books. Who's the guy who wrote 2001? Clarke? I never read anything by him. I read one book by Philip K. Dick called *Martian Time Slip*. It just happened to be

where there were no other books around. I liked it. I like science fiction, but mostly in the movies I saw, not the fiction.

TZ: *Which horror and science fiction movies do you like?*
SAYLES: I like the original *Thing*. I like *Them*. If you ever see *Alligator* and *Them* together, you realize that the Los Angeles River is the common setting. I like the original *Invasion of the Body Snatchers*. I like the film where the ship crashes into a cow pasture and everybody has those little inserts at the back of their heads. I forgot the name of it. I like *The Day the Earth Stood Still* and *War of the Worlds*.

I saw most of them originally on the Early Show when they had a "Horror Week" or something. When I visited Florida as a kid, they had a guy on tv named P. T. Grave, a guy down in a dungeon who was tortured by a giant hand. There was another horror film host who howled. I also liked the really trashy pictures, the Japanese ones like *Mothra* and *Rodan*. They were on tv late at night. I think if you were tired and a kid, seeing them was sort of like being stoned.

TZ: *Was there any horror movie you didn't appreciate?*
SAYLES: I didn't like *The Mummy*. That one freaked me out. There is something depressing about ancient Egyptians. Their whole culture was based on death.

TZ: *Didn't you write a play about a mummy?*
SAYLES: Yes, it was called "New Hope for the Dead." The title supposedly comes from a *Reader's Digest* article about cryogenics. The main character's an Egyptian mummy, but the action takes place in modern-day America.

TZ: *Do you consider any of your short stories to be in the realm of the fantastic?*
SAYLES: A little bit of "Fission," maybe, where the young guy, Brian, is tripping. He takes acid and doesn't quite know it, and the story gets "out there" a bit. "Schiffman's Ape" is a little bit of a fantasy because I invented a new species of monkey for it.

TZ: *What about "I-80 Nebraska, M.490–M.205"? Your hallucinating truck driver, Ryder P. Moses, is a character out of a wild tall tale, and his existence is never verified in the story.*

SAYLES: "I-80 Nebraska" has an element of the fantastic in that the whole story's told over CB radio. There's something eerie about a whole life on the radio waves. Ryder P. Moses is the Flying Dutchman character. You are never sure he's real until his truck smashes up at the very end. Even then, you never see him.

TZ: *Have you thought of filming "I-80 Nebraska"?*
SAYLES: Actually, that was the first thing I ever had optioned. Some guy who was a plastic squeeze bottle magnate optioned it for a thousand dollars back in the days when they had tax shelters. He wanted to shoot a movie in Boca Raton, Florida. The tax shelter fell through three months later, and the movie didn't happen. But he still had the option, and he kept being contacted by people from Texas who wanted to do it if Don Meredith would star in it. I even wrote a treatment. If the trucker genre hadn't been trashed by so many bad movies, Roger Corman might have made it. Those other trucker movies had nothing to do with trucks at all. They were *Walking Tall* in a truck, *High Noon* in a truck. Only *Truck-Stop Mama* was good, made by Mark Lester, a good B director.

TZ: *When did you first encounter Roger Corman?*
SAYLES: I met him at a story conference for *Piranha*. Because the piranhas were going to get boring after a while, we planned a spread of attack and threats of attack instead of steady action. Roger also asked me to get a couple of piranhas into the ocean at the end so they could breed and we could have a sequel. He thought New World owned the rights, but it was the property's original Japanese owners who had rights to *Piranha 2*.

They never got around to doing it, though I saw some of their script. They had flying piranhas, so that even if you stayed out of the water, they could fly through the air and grab you. Guys on oil rigs were being eaten.

TZ: *Did you ever write* Piranha *in fiction form?*
SAYLES: They said I could write the novelization if I wanted. I said I didn't. But afterward a novelization was published in England as "a novel by John Sayles." They actually put my name on the book jacket! The Writers Guild won a small settlement for that.

TZ: *How did you get involved with* Alligator?

SAYLES: I had already worked with its director, Lewis Teague, on *Lady in Red,* a movie that's very popular in Europe. That was one of the best scripts I've written, though Lewis had only twenty-one days to shoot it, a budget of under a million, and no voice in casting the first four leads. Robert Conrad was Dillinger, a small part. Pamela Sue Martin, recently on *Dynasty,* was the lead. She's okay, but she hadn't done a big part before.

Anyway, they had this script for *Alligator,* but it wasn't a good script. So Lewis talked the producer, Brandon Chase, into hiring me. They gave me this script that was set in Madison, Wisconsin. The alligator lived in a sewer for the whole movie. It never got above ground.

TZ: *What turned the alligator into a fantasy monster in the original script?*

SAYLES: A brewery had a leak and the alligator was drinking the malt, or something like that. It never made sense why it was a *giant* alligator. They killed this alligator at an old abandoned sawmill. Someone had left the power on at the old abandoned sawmill. And someone had left a chainsaw lying around the old abandoned sawmill. They plugged the chainsaw in and threw it into the alligator's mouth. All the alligator's thrashing around didn't even pull the plug out, even as the chainsaw cut him to bits.

So I rewrote *Alligator.* All I kept was a giant alligator, and I started from scratch. I wrote the whole first draft on the cross-country flight from L.A. to New York.

TZ: *Were you following concrete instructions?*

SAYLES: No, Lewis just said, "This script needs plot, character, mood."

TZ: *What was the alligator like?*

SAYLES: They had built an alligator years earlier, and it was sitting on a shelf. When they took it off the shelf, it fell apart. They had to build another alligator. Well, there was a lot of good stuff I wrote that never got shot, whole subplots, because this alligator couldn't cut it. This alligator couldn't do the things they said it could. It couldn't go in the water, for instance. Since there was only one foot of water in the sewer, I decided the alligator should end in the Mississippi River and drown. But that wasn't filmed. Earlier I'd wanted to burn the alligator, have a guy pour gasoline on it. I liked the idea of the alligator walking around on fire. They said no, because the alligator was booked for a personal appearance in a flatbed truck for publicity. We couldn't destroy it. We had to cut away from it.

TZ: *So what did you do?*
SAYLES: Finally we blew it up. I wrote the scene over the telephone. Lewis called and said, "Well, it's time to shoot the end." I said, "Oh well... let's have the alligator take dynamite off somebody. We should do some crosscutting at the end. Also, someone should drive a car on top of the manhole cover..."

TZ: *And underneath the alligator and the hero are trapped...*
SAYLES: Lewis said, "That sounds fine." He story-boarded the conclusion and did a great job. I said, "Don't put any dialogue in except, 'Move your car! My boyfriend is down there with the alligator!' "

TZ: *Do you think the horror movies you have written are frightening?*
SAYLES: Nothing in *Piranha* is really scary. The piranha is nasty but not scary. *Alligator* isn't particularly scary either. That alligator wasn't a very mobile creature. It was kind of like being afraid of a Sherman tank. Some of the stuff in the sewer is pretty well done and suspenseful, but only when the alligator eats the cop at the beginning is *Alligator* scary. That's because of the dangling feet.

There are some things that director Joe Dante stuck into *The Howling* that are creepy, including one pure "pounce." They are going around this guy's room and this dog jumps out. I didn't write the scene, so I didn't expect it. It scared the shit out of me when it happened. That's like the guy leaping out in *Wait Until Dark*. It isn't real suspense or anything. *Alien* is another pounce movie with little suspense. In a bad pounce movie, there's a conceit that if the pouncer is off-screen, the character on-screen can't see it. If it's off-frame, it's like being hidden behind a wall.

TZ: *How did* The Howling *originate?*
SAYLES: There were *Howling* and *Howling II* books by Gary Brandner. I wasn't crazy about them. They had a "What kind of man reads *Playboy*" sensibility. In the original novel there was a rape scene, and then the woman went away to one of those small towns that doesn't exist anymore.

There people say, "Howdy, ma'am. Howling? What howling? We don't hear any howling." So you knew they were werewolves.

I didn't use anything from the books except that there were werewolves around. But Avco Embassy Pictures had to purchase both books. Otherwise somebody else could buy *Howling II* and scoop them.

TZ: *When did you get involved with* The Howling*?*
SAYLES: Joe Dante got a script for *The Howling* and said, "It's terrible. Can I bring in someone?" I had worked with him already on *Piranha*. I wrote *The Howling* and *Alligator* at exactly the same time, and also I was directing a play in a New York theater across from the Port Authority Bus Terminal. The theater's heat broke down, so I wrote a lot of both scripts in the Port Authority with bag ladies talking to me.

TZ: *Was Joe Dante responsible for all the scenes in* The Howling *from classic horror movies? And for having Roger Corman in a telephone booth [in homage to director William Castle in a telephone booth in* Rosemary's Baby*]?*
SAYLES: Yes, almost all the marginalia is Joe's, including having Roger and fanzine editor Forrest Ackerman in it. On *Piranha*, Joe had people reading *Moby Dick*. He's into that kind of stuff.

TZ: *Does Corman like movie references in his films?*
SAYLES: Roger doesn't want people laughing at silly things. He likes humor, but he wants the right kind of humor. Usually the joke references that end up in the films are the ones he didn't get.

TZ: *For* Battle Beyond the Stars*, were you instructed to look at* Star Wars *for your script?*
SAYLES: Actually, Roger wanted *The Seven Samurai* in outer space, though some of his art design things were ripped off from *Star Wars*.

TZ: *Was that a satisfactory film?*
SAYLES: It's about two-thirds as good as it could have been. We didn't have the budget to do certain things. For instance, there is a character in the film who is a giant lizard. Originally he was supposed to be a big black guy with a yakuza tattoo on his back and be much more of a humanoid than this guy in a lizard suit and a Captain Hook routine. The character

lost lots of depth. It's tough to act in a lizard suit. Originally my script was more about death and how these beings, Nestor—five guys who look exactly the same and have only one consciousness—dealt with death. If one of them died, it was only like losing a bit of skin. Nestor complete each other's sentences. When one learns something, the whole race of Nestor learns it, even those back on the planet. What it is, they are bored shitless back on the planet. Everyone knows what everyone else is thinking and all that stuff. So they send some beings out to have adventures because it's sort of like tv. The others get to have adventures in their heads back home. The Nestor part was cut down, which happens when you're on a tight schedule. At the end of the day, they say, "We didn't get to this page, so there it goes!"

TZ: *And the ending?*
SAYLES: They wanted to end *Battle* five minutes early because one of their process shots of spaceships taking off didn't work. They said, "Can you write a scene that has Richard Thomas and the woman who is the lead in a space capsule? We don't have many sets left. And do it without a close-up. Richard Thomas has grown a mustache since we last shot." I wrote the scene on the phone.

There are some good things in *Battle Beyond the Stars*. George Peppard did nicely with his character, who was a sort of space trucker. He didn't like to act without a highball in his hand, so we incorporated that by making him a belt that dispensed ice. The women characters are less than they could have been. They tend to get cut down on Corman pictures and have bigger breasts and smaller brains than I originally envisioned.

TZ: *What was your work on* The Challenge*?*
SAYLES: John Frankenheimer brought me to Japan to change all the Chinese people into Japanese people in five days. I went to Kyoto one day and saw the locations for a big battle scene at the end. I was given a floor plan so I could confer with Frankenheimer. It was fun, kind of like playing Gettysburg. The other four days I was locked up in the Imperial Hotel in Tokyo while Toshiro Mifune, the star, took everyone else out to dinner. The typewriters kept breaking down, and there are not a whole lot of English typewriters there. I was tired. I'd been up for three nights. Finally they went downstairs to an office and saw an IBM Selectric sitting there. They said, "Toshiro Mifune!" and took it for me.

TZ: *How is the movie?*
SAYLES: Mifune is great. Scott Glenn is good. I'd say it's about one-third to one-half stuff I wrote. It's uneven. There's some weird stuff in there.

TZ: *Would you ever take your name off the credits of a film?*
SAYLES: At this point, my agent always says, "If you didn't take your name off *Lady in Red*, you might as well keep it on this one." Yes, I could, if they turned things around totally, but I don't think they have. *Lady in Red* still has some feeling and substance. *Battle* turned out pretty good. *The Howling* turned out very good. It's the closest to what I wrote.

TZ: *What made you, a heterosexual male, want to do a movie like* Lianna?
SAYLES: I never saw anything odd about a hetero male wanting to write about a lesbian relationship. I've written about old people, black people, Hispanic people, men, women, children, werewolves, alligators, Neanderthals—most which I have never been and never will be.

TZ: *How did gay women react to it?*
SAYLES: In general, they've been very enthusiastic and supportive of the film, if only because there is some recognizable human behavior coming from gay women on a movie screen—something fairly rare. I wish straight audiences had been as enthusiastic in some cities.

TZ: *How much does the high school world of* Baby, It's You *resemble your own background?*
SAYLES: The milieu is very similar to the one I grew up in. I wasn't a Sheik type [the movie's "greaser" hero], but I knew a lot of guys like him. One of the reasons Amy Robinson and I were able to work on the story together was that our high schools had been very similar and we're only two years apart in age. She had a better hit on the girlfriends, and I was more familiar with how the guys were thinking and acting.

TZ: *Many people have compared* The Big Chill *to* Secaucus Seven, *and the plots are obviously somewhat similar. How did you feel about it?*
SAYLES: I had a pretty good time at *The Big Chill*. The characters were so different in their values and politics that it felt like a totally different movie than *Secaucus*, even if the plot things were similar. Whether it's "derivative" or not is no skin off my ass one way or the other.

TZ: *Last year, you won a so-called "genius grant" from the MacArthur Foundation which pays you $30,000 a year, tax-free, for five years. Are you using it to make* The Brother From Another Planet*?*

SAYLES: No, the MacArthur Award pays the rent, and what's left over pays my taxes. I'm making *The Brother* with every cent I've earned screen-writing in the last three years.

TZ: *You've described* The Brother, *filmed in Harlem, as "a very noneffects, low-budget science fiction movie about persons and cultures rather than a lot of hardware." Will the film be as wild and satiric as it sounds? Or will it be more somber, like* The Man Who Fell to Earth*?*

SAYLES: It'll be wild and satiric and somber all at the same time. Wish me luck.

# John Sayles

ROBERT SEIDENBERG/1985

IN THE MOVIE WORLD, John Sayles is a maverick.

He writes dozens of horror and sci-fi genre flicks, finances and makes his own deeply personal films, and writes prize-winning fiction. Rather than coasting down the Hollywood mainstream, he chooses to duck in and out of less-traveled roads, leaving a distinct imprint on all that he touches.

And Sayles has not only forged new territory—and helped pave the potholed sidestreets of American independent filmmaking for those who follow. He also has, by most standards, attained success.

Applause for John Sayles has come from both the critical establishment and the moviegoing public. His directorial debut, *The Return of the Secaucus Seven,* cost only $60,000 to make but brought in more than $2 million. Dubbed the "original *Big Chill*" by many, this story of '60s radicals reaching their 30th birthdays, arguably is this decade's most popular American independent feature.

And last January the MacArthur Foundation bestowed upon Sayles one of its awards for "exceptionally talented individuals." The so-called "genius prize" of $34,000 a year for five years was prompted by Sayles' film work, novels *Pride of the Bimbos* and *Union Dues,* and a short story collection, *The Anarchists' Convention.*

A first diagnosis of Sayles' cinematic oeuvre likely would read "schizophrenic." How could the same man write movies about man-eating fish

---

From *Buffalo News,* 24 February 1985. Reprinted by permission.

(*Piranha*) and giant urban alligators (*Alligator*) and then turn around and create such intelligent dramas as *Secaucus Seven*?

But Sayles perceives no paradox or conflict. Writing the genre scripts is not only fun, he insists, but it brings in enough cash to finance his own films.

In this way, Sayles bypasses the studio system and retains creative control over his work. And that's something upon which he has always insisted.

He suffered drawn-out battles with Paramount over the final cut of his third feature, *Baby, It's You,* a bittersweet tale of an ill-fated adolescent love.

He was forced to finance *Lianna,* his second feature, because the story of a woman falling in love with her female psychology professor was of no interest to studio execs and "would never have survived through the studio story system."

And in the midst of raising funds for his next project, *Matewan,* Sayles financed, wrote, directed, edited and acted in his most recent feature, *The Brother From Another Planet.*

*The Brother,* which has just started playing in the North Park Theater, is a story of a mute, black escaped slave from outer space who spends much of the low-budget, low-tech film wandering through Harlem trying to track down a heroin ring while avoiding the pursuit of two bounty hunters (one of whom is played by Sayles). In many ways, *The Brother* combines the two strands of Sayles' filmmaking: low-budget humanistic and sci-fi genres.

A 34-year-old resident of Hoboken, N.J., Sayles is a mild-mannered man who resembles an outdoorsman more than a library-locked author. He is humble yet confident, incredibly easy-going, and appears well-rested from his brief hiatus from directing and script writing.

On the eve of *The Brother*'s New York opening, we met at a SoHo restaurant to talk about his new film and the events leading up to his recent recognition. It came as no surprise that when asked to step outside for a photo session, Sayles replied, "If we can do it where a lot of people won't stare at us—like a sidestreet or something."

Q: The Brother From Another Planet *seems to be a merger of the sort of films you directed previously and the kind of work you do for other directors. Did you do this consciously?*

A: Well, I'm aware of that and I was aware of that while I was writing it. But to me, traditionally, science fiction has always been a way into other films, just like the Western can be. I think it was E.L. Doctorow's first book, *Welcome to Hard Times*, which is a Marxist Western, but he used the Western format to get into things about primitive economics and psychology. He basically wrote a Western, but not just to be another Western.

Q: *Does* The Brother *then signal any sort of change of direction for your filmmaking, away from more personal stories like* Secaucus Seven *and* Lianna?

A: Not at all. It's just that I thought up this idea and I wanted to make a movie of it and I did. I really tend not to, sometimes unfortunately for me, think a whole lot about the commercial possibilities of something until I finish the script and I've decided to make it. Then the commercial thinking goes into how much can this afford without us wasting either all of my money so that I'm in big trouble or the investors' money. And that's when you set the budget.

The economic thinking goes not into what the characters do or say or what the story's about but into how many extras are in the background. Or whether to have a wide shot of the Port Authority bus terminal or just show two guys from the very top of the escalator so you can shoot it in a bank instead of paying all the insurance you would have to to really go to Port Authority.

The way you cover something and the way you write it can save you a lot of dough. And I've written enough low-budget films and made a couple of them so now I have a good idea of what costs money and what doesn't.

Q: *So it's not as if while writing you would decide to do something to make the film more commercial?*

A: You try to make it more understandable, you try to make it better. I think you can guess this is going to make it more commercial, but you're just as likely to be wrong about that as if you're just trying to make it good. You know, people who try to make total exploitation movies strike out just as much as people who try to make more serious movies that challenge the audience a little bit.

I'm always aware of that stuff. I've written lines in movies for other directors and thought, "Uh-oh. We're going to have a talk about this. There just went $2 million. People aren't going to like that. Or the studio's going to think that people aren't going to like that."

"You can't kill the dog," they say or whatever it is. Or the girl. You just showed that she has brains or something like that and there's no room for that in this kind of movie usually. So you hope you can sneak it by.

Q: *Do you feel any conflict writing for such unabashedly commercial movies and, at the time, doing your own films?*
A: Not really. Basically, when I'm working for other people, it's like working as a carpenter. And when I'm writing and directing stuff it's more like I'm the author of a book, because I'm also either going to edit it or work with the editor on it. So I'm going to have that kind of control over it. Whereas when you're writing for other people, you don't have that much control. You try to make it as good as it could be.

What I always aim for is, "Okay, this is a genre movie. If I was going to go see a movie about werewolves, what kind of movie would I want to see?" That way you're careful not to condescend to what you're writing or to the viewer.

I think that's one of the reasons why, say Steven Spielberg and George Lucas have been as successful as they've been. They really like those movies. They write stuff that they would love to go see, so they aren't condescending to their audience. And they can sense that. Now and then you'll get away with something condescending, but rarely are you slick enough to get away with it when you're really just saying, "Here. Take that, idiots."

Q: *You're not overcome with cynicism when you're writing scripts for these movies?*
A: No. They're actually fun. I try to think, "Okay, what would be a neat scene here?" And I've never taken a movie in a genre that I don't like, like a slasher movie. And some of the things I've been writing lately have been more about people—and those are even more difficult.

I actually have bigger arguments over those because they're not fantasy. I say to the directors and producers, "People just don't talk or act that way. It's going to be awful hard for me to find a way to do what you want me to do and have the characters act in a somewhat recognizable human manner."

Whereas if they're from outer space, "Sure, they were born without tact or born without brains or whatever they were born without. Their species just doesn't have it."

Q: *Where and how does your fiction writing fit in with all of this?*
A: Time-wise it doesn't. Mentally, I do a lot of thinking about this novel that I'm trying to get done. But I have two screenplays, maybe three, to finish before I can sit down and work on that. It's only time. To make these movies, especially to finance something yourself, takes so much. If you write as many screenplays as I do, even if you get minimum, you get yourself into the 50 percent tax bracket. So that in order to raise $300,000 to make a movie you have to go out and write $600,000 worth of screenplays, which is a lot.

And I'm lucky I can do that. Most independent filmmakers I know don't have any source of income like that. They're still waiting tables or whatever, and they're just making living expenses.

But the fiction will always be there; I don't have to raise money to write it. Whereas with movies you sort of have to strike while you've got some momentum—to either raise money or get a job.

Q: *How many screenplays have you written?*
A: Including the ones that I've directed, probably 25. Maybe about 18 of those have gotten made or will get made into something—a TV movie or a feature.

Q: *Is there anything that hasn't been produced that you would love to see made?*
A: Sure. I wrote a movie called *Matewan,* which we've been trying to raise money for. And the first script I ever wrote—that I keep rewriting every two years—is a thing called *Eight Men Out,* which is about the Black Sox scandal of 1919 when the Chicago White Sox threw the World Series.

And there's a film I wrote at a studio—the only thing I ever sold to a studio from my own idea—called *Blood of the Lamb,* which has gotten stalled at Warner Bros. I'd like to buy it back from them and direct it.

But I really can't direct it for them anymore, even if they wanted me to—which they don't—because I had to quit the Directors Guild of America in order to make *The Brother.* The studios have a signatory agreement with the guild, so unless they wanted to go a very roundabout way to have me do it—either in Mexico or for some separate little company they would set up—I really can't work as a director at the studios.

Q: *Why did you have to quit the Directors Guild?*

A: I couldn't afford to stay in and make movies for under half a million dollars. First of all, it's unusual for directors to finance their own movies, so that's not something the guild is really set up to do. They're really set up to deal with management.

But when you're in the guild not only are you supposed to pay yourself if you're financing it—which is no problem because I can always rip up the check—but you also have to hire a Directors Guild first assistant director, second assistant director and production manager, and they all get paid very well, minimum. So even for a four-week shoot, which is what *The Brother* was, it would have been about a third of our entire budget.

Not only could I not afford that, but there were two other problems.

Number one: you can always ask somebody, "Well, we're going to say on paper you're getting this much and then pay you less." But I don't want to be in a guild where I have to always break the rules to stay in.

And number two, I can't justify to the crew members why these three people, just because they're in this club, this guild, are being paid six to 10 times more than they are for the same four weeks of work. And since this was not going to be the last movie I make for under half a million dollars, it just didn't make sense for me to stay in the guild.

Q: *You quit right before starting production of the* The Brother*?*

A: I had to resign. But they were nice about it. I have no problem with the guild. It's just that I couldn't afford to stay in and operate the way I'm operating.

I had already sort of cut myself off from the studios in that I let it be known that I didn't want to direct anything that I didn't have final cut or casting control on. And that sort of automatically limits the number of phone calls you're going to get from the studios. I think being in the guild or not is a lesser problem than that.

Q: *How did you initially become involved with film?*

A: I always wanted to, but I knew that you didn't just go out and start throwing screenplays at people. Students ask me this in screenwriting classes, and I always say the way I got into the business was that I wrote two novels and a short story collection.

The agent I got to sell my second novel had a deal with a film agency which was actually representing my books as film properties. And that was somebody I could send a letter to and say "You are representing these books as film properties. I want to do screenwriting. If I write a screenplay will you look at it? And if you like it will you represent me?"

So I adapted this book, *Eight Men Out,* and it turned out that the head of the agency had at one time been the agent for that book. So he knew the material, and he thought I did a good job and told me "Sure. If you come out to California we'll represent you."

So I went out and lived in Santa Barbara for a couple years. And I would go down to meetings—but I've never really gotten a job from a meeting. And one day my agent just called and said "There's a rewrite. It's $10,000. It's called *Piranha*. It's for Roger Corman. You want it, you got it."

And I said "Okay." And I had a good time working on that one, and the movie was successful enough that Roger hired me to do two others for him. And then I started getting jobs because a couple of directors that I worked with there got jobs outside of Corman's factory, and they asked me to come and rewrite things for them. And it all sort of spread from there.

Q: *Why did you decide to leave California and come back East?*

A: I had always been interested in writing and directing, and I saw that the most likely way open to me—since I wasn't independently wealthy—was to get screenwriting work and try to parlay that into a directing job. A lot of people have done that recently—Walter Hill, Larry Kasdan, Paul Schrader.

And it just wasn't happening that fast. I was writing a lot of movies, but it was all the kind of stuff that would take about five years until the genre fans would get a hold of it and realize the same guy wrote all five of these movies. Most of them were movies that didn't even get reviewed in most papers and that the industry doesn't pay much attention to.

So it was happening very slowly and I decided to go the other route, which very few filmmakers take. A few have—Stanley Kubrick started this way—using money that I made from one thing to finance an independent film of my own and then show it to a studio and say "Okay, now will you give me a job? I'll write and direct. Here's some film that I've done."

Q: *The reason for making* Secaucus Seven *was to come up with something to show the studios that you could direct?*
A: I wanted to make *Secaucus Seven* as a sort of audition piece. I wanted to get something on film that was a feature, that did a few things. I thought "I'm not going to have any time or money to shoot action, but I know basketball really well. I could cover a ball game in half a day. I'll put some of that in so they can see I can move the camera around a little bit. But then how do I work that into a story?"

The second consideration was "Okay, I've got this much money, and I want to make a film. *But,* this might be the last chance I get to do this. Why make something that everyone is making? Why not make something that I really want to make? That I won't get to make any other way except if I do it myself?"

So then I started trying to do the two things at once and having just enough production value so that it could qualify as an official movie. But I didn't really expect it to get shown theatrically. I thought it would maybe get a PBS sale and show on TV and then be useful to show to the studios.

I always knew that people, if they saw *Secaucus Seven,* would like it. But there weren't too many precedents for movies that small with no known actors getting theatrical distribution. That's what I felt was lucky about it. We were sort of in the right place at the right time.

It's happened a couple times before. *David & Lisa* sort of did that, but that was about 15 years earlier. And now and then something like *Marty* will break through and get some attention and get seen by people. But usually those films are just tax writeoffs.

Q: *Did you even try to get studio funding for* Secaucus Seven*?*
A: Naaw. It also was a story that wouldn't have survived through the studio machine. I knew that much from my meetings. If you start talking about something like that, about an ensemble group, they say "Well who are the main characters?" And I say, "There are eight or nine." And they say, "Wait a minute. This isn't a war movie. And we don't have Robert Redford in a two-minute little cameo."

And they would have wanted something more to happen. Probably the guy who is weird and burned-out would have had to commit suicide at the end or something like that.

Q: *Did the "audition piece" work? Did* Secaucus Seven *lead to* Baby, It's You *and a studio deal?*

A: What it did lead to—in a slow kind of way—was a few studio writer/director deals. One was *Blood of the Lamb*, which never panned out. And *Baby, It's You* came a little after that. But it actually made me more saleable as a writer than as a director.

And then *Baby, It's You* moved around from Fox to nowhere to, finally, Paramount, before it actually got made. And in the meantime I made *Lianna* myself.

While I was editing *Lianna,* we were doing all the location work and casting for *Baby, It's You.* I remember one night coming out of a mixing session on *Lianna.* I had been up all night writing the sound charts and working, literally, for about a week, on two hours of sleep per night.

So I fell asleep during the last 30 minutes of the mix, and then somebody woke me up and I had to go down and see actors for *Baby, It's You.* And they overlapped when they played, too. *Lianna* came out about a month and a half before *Baby, It's You.*

Q: *You didn't try to get studio funding for* Lianna *either?*

A: The minute I mentioned the subject matter they said, "What else are you working on?" Nobody ever was that interested. And once again, it wouldn't have survived through the studio story system. I mean, somebody said "And you mean she has children, too? Maybe we could take something about a single woman or somebody who's married. But she's got children, ah, too sticky. What else are you doing?"

Q: Baby, It's You, *in your opinion, survived the studio system? Are you happy with the film?*

A: "I'm very happy with it. I nearly didn't survive, but the movie did. I had a huge fight with the studio over the final cut. And eventually, they went with the cut I wanted. But that was after a lot of battling, after me promising to take my name off the film as writer and director. After being off the film for a month while people did another cut of it.

They test marketed that and it didn't market any better than my cut had. So I think they just figured "Let's keep away from the bad publicity of having the writer/director take his name off the thing."

I kept saying "I'm not bluffing," and they didn't believe me. And I said "Look, I'm not going to put my name on it unless I do the final cut." And we weren't talking about little minor things, we were talking about major differences.

I had the usual contracts that "so-and-so films will hereinafter be known as the author." I was their employee, so I was out of line in certain ways. But in others, I just wanted it to be a good movie and it wasn't going to be. And I didn't shoot a different movie than I wrote. They got to read the script. They should have known what we were making.

Q: *Was the story for* The Brother *really inspired by a dream of yours?*

A: A couple of dreams. While I was editing *Baby, It's You* and having a lot of work-related dreams. My first dream was that I was writing a movie for Joe Dante, a quick rewrite due the next day. And it was really dumb. It was called "(Bleeps) from Outer Space." I sort of saw the title come out in 3D.

And I saw at Cannes this year that there's a movie coming out called *Morons from Outer Space*—somebody's tapping into my dreams.

Next I had another dream where I was directing a nice atmospheric film noir movie with a guy roaming around an urban environment; and the guy was a bigfoot. It was called "Bigfoot in the City" and there was a lot of saxophone music and hiding in alleys.

And then I had this short dream about a black guy in Harlem who wasn't talking, actually couldn't talk and get help. He was wandering around and nobody paid much attention to him. It was really, "How alienated can you get?" Not only are you out of a job and out of a home in New York City, and black, but you're not even from the damn planet and you can't tell anybody about it—or you don't want to tell anybody about it.

*The Brother* has elements of all three dreams. The guys that David Strathairn and I play are sort of the (bleeps) from outer space. And there is some film noir type stuff at the beginning and the end, with steel drum music instead of saxophone music; but it has that quality to it. And then there's a lot of stuff that's just about this alienated guy and his perception of what's going on around him.

Q: *You planned from the start to make the Brother mute?*

A: Yes. And that also had a lot of technical and economic advantages to it. When your lead character doesn't talk you don't have to shoot a lot of synchronous sound; you can have him walk down the street, and even if people yak at him he doesn't have to answer. You can do a lot of cutaways without sync sound, which saves you time and money.

Also, if he doesn't talk he never has to explain himself. And whenever you do something that's fantastic—as long as it doesn't seem like a trick that you're not explaining—the less you explain the better. Now and then the Brother will answer a question, but it's usually by just pointing his thumb up or down. And that's all he really needs to say about himself. People just figure he's another weird guy wandering the streets.

Q: *We've seen a lot of movies lately about aliens. Did that make you at all hesitant about releasing* The Brother *at this time?*
A: That didn't really affect it much. But once again, it was like when I made *Lianna.* I didn't know what *Personal Best* was about, and I didn't know that they were making *Making Love.*

As a matter of fact, I talked to Scott Glenn, who had a big part in *Personal Best.* I ran into him in Tokyo and I told him "When I go home I'm going to go back to editing this movie called *Lianna.* It's about two women who fall in love. What have you been doing?"

He said "Well, I've been working on Bob Towne's first movie, which is called *Personal Best.* "What's it about?"

"Track and field."

That's all he gave me, the sucker. I don't know if he didn't want to disappoint me or if they told him to try to keep it down about the lesbian angle. Track and field! Okay. I guess it was, from his point of view. For him, the coach, it's track and field, and whatever they want to do on their own time...

Q: *How do you feel about a situation when your film predates something similar? How did you feel when you saw* The Big Chill*? Lots of people called it a* Secaucus Seven *ripoff.*
A: I had already been warned that people thought it was a knockoff of *Secaucus Seven.* I just thought it was a more-thoughtful-than-usual Hollywood movie. There were certain things about it that I thought were good, and there were certain things about it that I didn't buy, that I didn't think were realistic about those people. I thought the people were very different than the people in *Secaucus Seven.*

But to a certain extent, once you decide to do a movie about a reunion of a bunch of people who went to college together, certain things are going to happen: they're going to talk, they're going to make the beds, people are going to pair off in certain ways.

It's sort of like complaining because you made a Western and somebody else came along and made one and you said "He used an Indian and a horse. What a ripoff."

But I loved *The Big Chill* soundtrack. And I liked seeing some of those actors, and there was good dialogue written for them. So it didn't bother me that much.

The only real effect it had on what I do is that *Secaucus Seven* got re-released in some places on a double bill or just to take another look at it. So we probably made $500 more than we would have.

Q: *Why didn't you use all the recognition you were getting around the time* The Big Chill *came out to your advantage and at that point attempt to get studio funding for* The Brother*?*

A: We were having such a hard time raising money for *Matewan*, and having all these discouraging meetings with people, that I just didn't want to deal with them again. And I didn't need to.

It would have been nice to have another $100,000 and another week of shooting. People would have gotten more sleep. I would have gotten more sleep. But we didn't need that much more money. And more money would have brought along things that would have gotten in the way.

For instance, we were able to shoot up in Harlem without a big crew, with a crew that was half black—which would have been hard to find in the union. And we didn't deal with the Teamsters at all.

Our presence there was a very small, integrated presence instead of a huge white film company of studio union guys coming and pushing everybody out of the way and saying "Now we're going to recreate Harlem in this four-block area that we've roped off."

Q: *Did you use the money from the MacArthur grant to fund* The Brother*?*

A: Whenever I could. I get $2800 every month, which is pretty good. And I either threw it right into the film or paid the rent and my other bills with it. So I could go right down to zero in my bank account, knowing that next month some money was going to show up.

I also used money from scriptwriting and the cable sales of *Secaucus Seven*. That money had to go through four or five hands before it finally got to us.

I had also saved a lot of my salary from writing and directing *Baby, It's You*. That's the only movie that I've ever been paid as a director on because I was in the guild during that one, and if you're in the guild you get paid a lot. I probably made about $50,000 directing that one.

Whereas with something like *Lianna* or *The Brother* I don't take a salary as writer, director or editor; I only take money as an investor. I just sort of pieced all the money together to pay for *The Brother.* And while we were editing the movie I was writing two scripts for the Jean Auel books, *Clan of the Cave Bear* and *Valley of the Horses*.

# Dialogue on Film: John Sayles

## ANONYMOUS/1986

JOHN SAYLES'S FIRST ASSIGNMENT in the film business was to revise a screenplay for Roger Corman, *Piranha,* in 1978. Coming from short story and novel writing (his *Union Dues* was nominated for both a National Book Award and the National Book Critics Circle Award in 1977), he was surprised to discover that the major challenge lay in explaining why the characters "... once they had figured out there are piranhas in the river, don't just stay out [of it]."

Several more screenplays for Corman's New World company followed, but Sayles, unhappy that most of what he wrote never ended up on the screen, turned to independent production, financing his first film with monies from his writing. *The Return of the Secaucus Seven* (1980) was almost unanimously praised, but did not, as Sayles had hoped, lead to a studio-backed project. However, a pattern had been established: Sayles wrote more screenplays, and came out with his next independent feature, *Lianna,* in 1983. *Baby, It's You,* released later the same year, was his first venture for a major studio, and also earned critical acclaim.

*The Brother From Another Planet,* Sayles's most recent directorial effort, is another low-budget, independent production. Although classifiable as, possibly, a science-fiction comedy, the film demonstrates again the director's concern with portraying a community and presenting characters with lives and interests different from his own.

---

From *American Film,* May 1986. Reprinted by permission.

In 1983 Sayles was awarded a MacArthur Foundation "genius grant," and with its assistance continues to work on his fiction writing and future film projects.

QUESTION: *You're said to be an extremely fast writer. Can you describe how you work?*
JOHN SAYLES: My writing speed is like a gas—it fills the amount of time available. I wrote *The Brother From Another Planet* in six days because that's the time I had. But I did carry it round in my head for a long time before writing. I don't think speed is important unless you have a deadline. I think you just write till it's good. If I have more time it doesn't necessarily get any better. The main thing I've found is that once you have the structure, you're really filling things in. I've often worked by writing the structure first—a very tight outline.

When you're dealing with assignments, you're essentially dealing with traditional movies that are going to last between ninety and one hundred and twenty minutes. I usually target for one hundred. And I say: In the first twenty minutes, we should know what this movie is about and who the main characters are. And I know that by page sixty, we have to have had the first big confrontation or whatever. Genre movies are easier to plot that way than personality movies. But with those, too, like *Secaucus Seven,* each character has a progression. They start with something they need or want at the beginning of the movie, and by the end they've either gotten it or not, or learned something that they didn't know before. So even there, there's some kind of structure.

So I'd say speed really has more to do with your working habits, and also with knowing where you're going. I've never just sat down and said: I'm going to write a screenplay and let's see where it takes me.

QUESTION: *Where do you find the actors you use in your films?*
SAYLES: In most of the movies I've directed I've known some of the people beforehand, either from having seen their work or, as I was an actor for a while, having worked with them. We always have so little time to shoot that I usually work with people who have worked in theater because they can retain two pages of dialogue with no problem. Then you rarely have to do another take because an actor has lost a line.

In *The Brother From Another Planet* there are five or six parts where I already knew the actors. In fact, the woman who plays Randy Sue, a Southern woman who lives in Harlem, was somebody who came in second for a part in a play I wrote and directed. When I did *Baby, It's You* I got her a part playing a waitress. Then when *Brother* came up, I wanted someone who was very strong and tough and from the South—and I thought of her. So I actually wrote a part for an actress who was willing to work for scale. Also important. And it helps to have a casting director who gets used to what you really want—we've worked with Barbara Shapiro in New York a couple of times. And on *Baby, It's You* with Margie Simkin.

QUESTION: *Do you spend much time rehearsing, and when it comes to shooting, do you improvise a lot?*

SAYLES: I really have never had much time for rehearsing. On *Secaucus Seven*, we read through the screenplay with the actors the day before we started shooting, and any kind of rehearsal took place while the lights were being set up. It was pretty much the same with *Lianna*. With *Baby, It's You*, we actually had three days budgeted with the principals for rehearsal. I told Vincent [Spano] we didn't need him and to just go watch a lot of Frank Sinatra movies. And I got Rosanna [Arquette], who played Jill, together with the three girls who played her high school friends, and we just drove around and they talked about boys and records and we went and had hamburgers—so they got used to each other. We didn't talk about the script at all.

And I really haven't had the money to improvise. The deal I make with actors is: I'll always use your best acting takes. You're always going to have priority. If it's in focus, if you're recognizable, if it's the best acting take—I'll use it. The technicians don't always want to hear that, but the priorities in the movies I make are the acting and believing in the characters and caring about them. Often I'll say to an actor: If you really feel you have a different way to do it, or you can do it much better than you just did, we'll do one more take. In that way there's some improvisation. But in general I've done very little. You try to write it so that it seems people are making it up. It's in the writing.

QUESTION: *You mentioned not having much money. How do you make your movies on such low budgets?*

SAYLES: For *Secaucus Seven*, for instance, I had the budget, a small one, first, and the idea that I wanted to make a movie. So I asked myself what kind of film could I make well for this kind of money? And what actors could I use?—things like that. I was up in New Hampshire doing summer theater with a group of actors and they were all around thirty. So . . . I'm going to make a movie where almost everyone in it is around thirty. Where can I set it? Well, we had this summer theater that would be easy to rent for another month—so I had the location. Then, I'm not going to be able to move the camera much because that takes experienced people and time and money. How can the picture have any movement if I can't move the camera? But look at *Nashville*, where you had a whole bunch of characters, and so there was always an excuse to cut away from one conversation to another. So even if the camera work is rather static, the cutting can add movement.

Then there was the other aspect, the social consciousness part. Most people who are trying to break into movies make a small horror picture. But I may only get to do this one time, and if that's the case, if I'm only going to get one shot, why not make something that I would want to see, that I wouldn't get to see unless I made it myself, or somebody not working in the studio system made it? I had met a bunch of people who had been very politically active in the sixties, Vista and all that, and who were still trying to be, but at the same time they were trying to decide whether to get married or not, to have kids or not, trying to make a living. And so the idea evolved from that—a group of people having a hard time turning thirty.

With *The Brother From Another Planet,* I realized: Here's a movie we can shoot in Harlem so that all the crew people I know in New York can go home at night. You don't have to pay for board, you don't have to pay for dinner; they just have to show up on the set, and then they go home. And there are a zillion really good black actors in this area who are totally underemployed. There's a lead character who doesn't talk, and if he doesn't talk you can shoot a lot of MOS [silent] footage, which is much cheaper, especially on New York streets, with the horns and the brakes and the airplanes overhead.

This was after I had had two years in a row doing scripts for studios. So I said I can finance myself, and I won't have to deal with those fuckers. I won't have to hear about whatever changes they want. I could just hear their comments: "Wow, maybe Eddie Murphy would be interested! Why can't we have him say something?" So I just decided I wasn't even going to call them up. I financed it myself, and shot it in four weeks, and all of the very hard things you have to do when you have a very low budget. I actually had a pretty good time shooting, but the producers, Maggie Renzi and Peggy Rajski, said never again will they shoot a movie that fast in an urban area.

QUESTION: *You seem to be able to write and direct your own work. Do you have any desire to direct stuff you haven't written? And would you change anything you have done?*

SAYLES: I wouldn't want to direct someone else's stuff right now because I have so many things I've written myself that I haven't yet gotten to direct. For the past four years, we've been trying to raise money to make a film that I wrote maybe six or seven years ago—about a 1920 coal mine massacre in West Virginia. And I've been trying with some other producers to get money to do a film about the 1919 "Black Sox" World Series scandal. And I've got four or five other ideas in the formative stages. It takes so much out of your life to direct something and actually get it made that, maybe if I end up ten years from now, and I've gone through my things and I don't have any ideas—maybe then I'd want to direct somebody else's script.

I'm still interested in writing for other people. I don't always think I'd be the best director for some things I write or some ideas I have. Basically, I make a living by writing screenplays for other people, and sometimes that's fun. As far as changing things, you can take any minute in anything I've made and find that there's a better way to do it. I can't afford to be a perfectionist. Given more time, more money, sometimes given better thinking on my part—there would be a better way to do it. Perhaps a more interesting way.

There are things in *Baby, It's You* that I regret having cut, but I was trying to run some kind of middle ground between making a commercially viable movie and making the movie I had written. I had been sucked into writing more than I really needed, so there was a richness in the peripheral characters that just didn't make it to the screen. About forty minutes of really good stuff. When we saw the longer version, we realized this is an epic-length movie, but it's not an epic-length subject. With a different system or different moviegoing habits, we could have stuck with a two-hour-and-ten-minute movie.

So of all the movies I've made, that's the one that's the least about a group of people. Most of my movies are about communities. Even *The Brother From Another Planet* is about a community and how they react to an outsider. *Lianna* is about a group reacting to one woman's change in her life.

QUESTION: *You've spoken about your actors—how do you put your crew together?*

SAYLES: You try to get the best possible people for the money you've got. And the best possible people in a low-budget movie are those who can work fast. There are plenty of DPs [directors of photography] who can do beautiful stuff, but they do it by waiting for the light, by knowing what time of day it's going to be beautiful. They take a couple of hours and they move this light here and this one there. And you can't work with them. If they have to work with your schedule they're going to be unhappy—and not turn out good work.

I try to avoid people who feel like "We're the technicians, and there are those idiots doing this acting, 'creative' stuff up there." I try to find crew members who are interested in what the people on the other side of the camera are doing. And vice versa, of course.

Basically, what you want is everyone working in the same direction. They're not trying to make it a tug-of-war. They're all interested in it being the best thing possible. All of them, right down to the grips and the PAs [production assistants]. They're interested in *seeing* the movie that they're working on.

# Director's Humanism Keeps Him Away From Mainstream Movies

ELEANOR O'SULLIVAN/1987

YOU CAN COUNT ON the fingers of one hand the number of highly respected American directors who work, indeed thrive, outside the Hollywood mainstream. They include Woody Allen, Jonathan Demme, Jim Jarmusch, David Lynch and John Sayles.

Sayles, who was raised in Schenectady, N.Y. and has lived in Hoboken for six years, is along with Jarmusch, the most actively non-mainstream of the group, both in terms of his films' subject matter and his lifestyle. The common thread in Sayles' films is an abiding generosity of spirit and eagerness to explore the human experience. His films are without stars and generally shot on modest budgets. But what they lack in glamour they possess in revelations and insights about the human condition.

Sayles' description of his movie-in-progress, *Eight Men Out,* could easily apply to his other films, *Return of the Secaucus Seven, Lianna, Baby, It's You, The Brother From Another Planet* and *Matewan,* to be released Friday.

"It's definitely an ensemble piece, about a group of people and a time, of how people thought at a certain time," Sayles said. "The slant of the movie will be to try to make people understand that time."

The time of *Eight Men Out* is 1919, during the Black Sox World Series scandal. The time of *Matewan* is 1920, the place the mining towns of West Virginia. In the depressed town of Matewan, coal companies are importing scab labor, blacks from the south and immigrants to keep pay rates down. The miners strike and the town is torn by strife. A union

---

From *Asbury Park Press,* 23 August 1987. Reprinted by permission.

representative named Joe Kenehan tries to unite the miners and sell them on the union. In the microcosm of Matewan, Sayles provides a history of unions in this country, as well as a portrait of poor struggling families.

"I could have saved a lot of money in the budget doing a contemporary story, but I felt like going back to the origins of the union, and its early crisis moments," Sayles said. "That way you can get a simpler and purer look at things without as many complications, although it's a fairly complex movie.

"When you look at its origins, you see all the elements of what it (the union) becomes or doesn't become. Although in *Matewan* you're very sympathetic to the strikers, there are the seeds of dissent within the movement already, especially within the United Mine Workers. The minute Joe says, 'Sometimes we're going to have to give something up for the union as a whole,' he gets a lot of resistance from local miners."

Although it has a gripping, edgy quality, *Matewan* also is a grim look at the life of the miners. This is hardly the stuff of most contemporary movies, a fact Sayles acknowledged. *Matewan* is far removed from what he called "the cinema of affluence," which would include the majority of contemporary films. They contain little or no acknowledgment of struggle, adversity and poverty; their purpose is to entertain.

"But people forget that entertainment for entertainment's sake has a political message in it, too," Sayles said. "It may not be an overt one but it's certainly there and it's an easy one to accept: 'This is kind of a nice world, a nice way to think about ourselves.'

"Other realities are for other people and they deserve those realities, is the message. If those other people are having a hard time then there's probably something wrong with them, the message says. But there's nothing wrong with you or the system that makes your good life possible, so you don't have to worry about it too much."

Sayles' humanism precludes that breezily unrealistic approach. Even his most mainstream movie, *Baby, It's You,* with Rosanna Arquette and Vincent Spano, has a decidedly dark side.

"The idea in most contemporary movies is to basically pay attention to yourself and that basically you can run your life without having anything upsetting come into your path if you work things right," Sayles said. "That's a very political statement."

Fifty years ago, Americans made *The Grapes of Wrath,* which has much in common with *Matewan,* a hit movie. But that was at a time, Sayles said, when moviegoing was a three-time-a-week diversion. It was also possible for audiences of the 1930s to identify with the plight of the migrant family Joads, as many Americans had endured similar struggles. Would Sayles agree then that *Matewan* is an anachronism?

"Anything that is geared for people over the age of 20 is an anachronism," he said. "*Out of Africa* was an anachronism because it was about adults. Anything that doesn't have that kid appeal is an anachronism and you're taking a big chance—'Who's going to see this movie?' 'Are we going to get enough money back?' "

"But why I make something is because there are things and people happening out there that I see in life that I don't see on screen. I'm interested in them. The movies that I write, and write and direct, I want to go beyond the two-dimensional feel of most contemporary movies."

Cinecom is distributing *Matewan* in New York on Friday, followed by about 12 major cities two weeks later, then half a dozen more cities a week after that. Sayles said Cinecom's executives, who took a chance on (and were handsomely rewarded for doing so) *A Room With a View,* are hoping that word-of-mouth will turn *Matewan* into a crossover movie, one that moves from the essentially art house circuit to mainstream theaters.

Sayles said the word from early screenings of *Matewan* is good, but he is also aware it's not going to be an easy sell.

"Reviewers and interviewers tell me they really like it and then, they wonder, 'How are you going to get people in to see it?' It's not a star vehicle, strike one. And it's not a pure genre movie, although it has a lot of elements of the western action story. But it's not like *Silverado* so you can't advertise it that way.

"The kind of strike three is that it is going to have to start small, because of the economics of distribution and economics of how we make movies. You can't buy the first two weeks; you have to rely on people hearing about it. In some places you hope your track record will help. And if a fraction of a fraction of a fraction of people in New York City remember your movie and go in those first two weeks, then you have good business."

Sayles has had pre-production work on *Eight Men Out* to keep him busy while waiting for the film's premiere. Whether he will travel from Hoboken to Manhattan to see his film is another matter.

"Life in Hoboken is easier than being in Manhattan. I like to go in there and see a movie that isn't in New Jersey, but the pace of New York City and the expense and the center of the world attitude is not my favorite thing to be around.

"It's more relaxing for me and easier to work in New Jersey. And not being in Hollywood, I can know a lot of people who are not in the movie business, so movies are not always the focus of the conversation."

# Miners' Bloody Battle for Union Relived

EDWARD GUTHMANN/1987

NO ONE CAN EVER accuse director John Sayles of sticking to the safe and predictable road. In five feature films made over the past eight years, Sayles has portrayed: a gang of '60s activists (*Return of the Secaucus Seven*), a naive college professor's wife who turns gay (*Lianna*), a middle-class coed who falls for a working-class hood (*Baby, It's You*) and a speechless black extraterrestrial who visits Harlem (*Brother From Another Planet*).

Now, in his biggest, most ambitious film yet, Sayles has turned his lens to West Virginia coal miners and their efforts to unionize. Set in 1920, *Matewan* recalls an actual confrontation between coal miners and the hired thugs who acted as the law in company-owned towns. That incident, known as the Matewan Massacre, left 11 men dead and triggered the 1920–21 Coal War of West Virginia. It also serves as the final, bloody set piece in Sayles's film.

Unlike Sayles's earlier films, all of which were produced on low budgets, and all of which concentrated on quirky characters and personal relationships, *Matewan* (pronounced "MATE-wan") is a historical epic about a community of people. Neither didactic nor simplistic, and more than two hours long, it's one of the least conventional films to open this year. One critic called it "a descendant of the populist cinema of John Ford (*The Grapes of Wrath*) and King Vidor (*Our Daily Bread*)."

"The size of it is the main difference," Sayles says. "It's the first big period piece I've done." A prolific writer, occasional actor (*Hard Choices*),

---

recipient of a MacArthur Foundation "genius grant" and gentle path blazer in the growing field of American independent film making, Sayles, 37, visited San Francisco recently to promote his new effort. Looking like your neighborhood grease monkey in jeans, running shoes and cotton shirt unbuttoned halfway to the waist, the 6-foot-4 Sayles couldn't have looked more incongruous in the subdued elegance of San Francisco's Majestic Cafe.

Made for slightly less than $4 million, *Matewan* actually was conceived a decade ago—way before Sayles made his 1980 directing debut with *Return of the Secaucus Seven*. An offshoot of Sayles's 1977 novel *Union Dues* (a National Book Award nominee), *Matewan* sat on the shelf for years while Sayles made other films, wrote screenplays for other film makers (*Clan of the Cave Bear*, TV's *Unnatural Causes*) and directed a trio of memorable music videos ("Born in the U.S.A.," "I'm on Fire," "Glory Days") for Bruce Springsteen.

Predictably, *Matewan* was a tough project to get off the ground. "Over a three-year period, we kept thinking we had the money to make this thing and then it would fall apart," Sayles says. "When we made *Brother From Another Planet* (in 1984) it was basically something to do because the money had fallen through for *Matewan*."

Tracing the film's origins, one goes back to the summer of 1970, when Sayles, a Williams College undergrad with no film-making aspirations, was hitchhiking across the United States. After several detours down the back roads of West Virginia, he remembers, "I had gotten a real feel for the people: That's sort of how I got interested in the history, from coal miners who gave me rides."

At the time, West Virginia was still reeling from the January 1970 assassination of Joseph A. "Jock" Yablonski, a reform candidate for the United Mine Workers presidency. Yablonski, his wife and daughter were murdered in their home, a special prosecutor proved, by partisans of UMW leader W.A. "Tony" Boyle. Boyle was convicted on three counts of first-degree murder.

As bitter as that episode was, Sayles says, it didn't compare to the events of 1920–21. When he spoke to the young miners, he remembers, "inevitably they'd say, 'You think it's bad now, you oughta hear what my daddy and granddaddy went through.' "

At the time of the Matewan Massacre, Sayles says, West Virginia miners were little more than slaves. "They were paid by the ton, but they worked without pay just to get to the coal. They had to lay the track, bring in the timber, support the roof. They might work a whole day and not make any money."

Instead of cash, workers were paid in company scrip and were forced, under threat of dismissal, to shop at the company store. "One of the extras on the film had been a miner as a young man," Sayles says. "In order to save money to buy a farm, he lived with a married couple instead of in company housing. The company came to him and said, 'Hey, buddy, you're not spending enough money at the company store. There's a tailor coming through the company store next week, and we want you to buy two suits. Otherwise you're going to lose your job.' "

In *Matewan,* when the miners threaten to strike, the Stone Mountain Coal Co. reacts first by planting spies in coal camps, and later by bringing in Italian and black scabs—also known as "transportations"—to divide and weaken the ranks.

"There was a lot of unemployment among black coal miners in Alabama, so the companies would go down and say, 'We've got jobs in West Virginia,' not telling them it was a strike situation. They'd lock them in a boxcar, open it once a day to put in bread and water. This went on for three days. When they arrived at the coal camp, the company told the workers they had to pay $200 for train fare."

To enforce that kind of tyranny, and to bust any unionizing attempts, the coal companies hired brutal "gun thugs" from the infamous Baldwin-Felts detective agency. "They would blackball guys and send a description of the (union) organizers and troublemakers to all the other mines. A lot of guys would disappear on their way home because they were trouble-makers. That was the covert part. The overt part was that most sheriffs and police chiefs in the state, if not all of them, had their salaries paid by the mine companies."

From his first visit to West Virginia hill country, Sayles felt an affinity with the people. "They're real bedrock Americans: very individualistic, and very patriotic at the same time. There's a strength and self-reliance to them because the life was so hard. They were the people who hacked a living out of mountains that didn't have especially good farmland."

It's the kind of individualism, Sayles believes, "that also gets you in trouble. It tends to isolate you from other people, so you get these eye-for-eye, tooth-for-tooth situations like the Hatfields and McCoys feud (which took place in the same county a half-century before). You get a situation where an outside force comes and takes your land away, and because you fight as individuals and not as a unit, you can't really oppose them. That's why the Matewan incident was so remarkable."

After years of pitching his *Matewan* script to the studios—all of which objected to its political content and lack of a "star" part—Sayles finally got a go-ahead from Cinecom (*Swimming to Cambodia*), a small company based in New York that fronted the film's $4 million budget. Working with Oscar-winning cinematographer Haskell Wexler (*One Flew Over the Cuckoo's Nest*) and his longtime producer and girlfriend Maggie Renzi, Sayles assembled a cast of professional actors and West Virginia locals—some of them descended from Matewan Massacre survivors.

Sayles also wrote a part for himself—that of a semicomical, fire-and-brimstone preacher who thinks labor unions are the devil's work—but scored his greatest casting coup with Broadway star James Earl Jones (*Fences*) in the minor role of Few Clothes, a black miner. The film was shot last summer and fall in seven weeks.

Instead of shooting in Matewan, which looks too modern today for the purposes of the film, Sayles went to nearby Thurmond, a tiny hamlet that still retains the look of the early '20s. "The main street is still railroad tracks. The buildings, most of which predate World War I, are all brick. The green copper telephone wires are still standing from the '20s. Now and then we had to throw a net over a satellite dish, but otherwise it was perfect."

Sayles's next film, *Eight Men Out,* based on the book by Eliot Asinof, is the true story of the 1920 Chicago Black Sox scandal, in which several ballplayers agreed to throw the World Series to the Cincinnati Reds in exchange for gamblers' kickbacks. Charlie Sheen and Christopher Lloyd head the cast.

"One of the things that's interesting to me about the story is that in 1919–20, the same time as the Matewan Massacre, there was a huge change in America. Things were moving with a vengeance from that kind of 19th century world to being a 20th century world. The Jazz Age was starting. People had come back from World War I. Immigrants were coming in. Prohibition was coming in. Cars were invented. It was the kickoff for the modern world."

# On the Road With John Sayles

GEORGE VECSEY/1987

SOUNDING A BIT LIKE one of the old-timers in his most recent film, *Matewan,* about a coal-field union war in the 1920s, John Sayles reminisced recently about the old days when a young man could hitchhike all over America without too much fear of violence, all the way back in 1970.

"My hair was kind of medium length and I carried a duffel bag my father brought back from World War II, so I got a lot of rides from hippies and a lot of rides from servicemen," he recalled from ancient memory.

Sayles was a student, taking time off from his summer factory job, avoiding the interstates as much as possible, passing through the back country of West Virginia. Some of the people who gave him rides told him stories about the grim day in 1920 when security guards and striking miners massacred each other in a narrow coal town named Matewan.

"Jock Yablonski was just dead, there was a lot of turmoil," he said, referring to the murder, in January of 1970, of the reform candidate for the United Mine Workers presidency.

"Almost everybody would say, 'If you think this is wild and woolly, you should talk to my old man about the coal wars.' I started to pick up a little oral history, even if I couldn't put it together."

Midway through his college education, a late bloomer more familiar with factories than foreign films, John Sayles was already storing up impres-

---

sions for his future as actor, novelist, screenwriter and director of quirky films with a social context.

Sayles, at 36, has made films about lesbians, artsy private colleges, black street life, sort of daring the mainstream of moviegoers to come on in. In making a film about a union war in the gritty coal fields, he is doing it all over again, totally by choice.

"You know, at the end of *Death of a Salesman,* somebody says, 'Attention must be paid.' I want people to pay attention to miners. There was a little bit of it in *The Molly Maguires,* that this is the hardest job in the world. You crawl down there and die."

*Matewan,* (which is currently screening at the UA cinemas in Costa Mesa), was produced by his friends Peggy Rajski and Maggie Renzi, and made on location in those same West Virginia hills, including three days in an exhibition mine with a four-foot seam that played havoc with Sayles' bad back and his terror quotient.

"When the lights go out, you are like in a coffin," he said.

His fascination with the coal wars and the people of Appalachia led him to write a screenplay that sat around for nearly a decade while he was becoming known for *The Return of the Secaucus Seven, Lianna, Baby, It's You* and *The Brother From Another Planet,* the 1984 cult classic about an innocent black alien plopped down in the middle of Harlem. "I've lived on the fringe, in and around black neighborhoods, and I played ball with black people, and been around minorities, so I wanted to show what that was like to other people," Sayles said about the *Brother* film.

"I want people to like the stuff I do, but not enough to lie to them," he added. "*Girls Just Wanna Have Fun* movies are also making major statements about the way people get along, or don't get along, politics, violence, men and women."

Large and athletic, Sayles lives on the left bank—of the Hudson River, that is—in Hoboken, N.J., Springsteen country. (He has directed three videos for Bruce Springsteen.) He keeps up with movies at the nearby Secaucus Mall and makes films whenever he and his pals can scrape together the money. In 1983, Sayles was awarded a MacArthur Foundation "genius grant," which provided him with $34,000 a year for five years.

Sort of the Woody Allen of Hoboken, Sayles uses many of his regulars—Maggie Renzi, David Strathairn, Josh Mostel, Nancy Mette—in *Matewan,* but he also makes maximum advantage of a deep-voiced newcomer (to

Sayles' films) named James Earl Jones, who does his best not to dominate the screen as the natural leader of the black miners.

"He will be great for the ancillary sales," Sayles said. "We'll be able to say, 'With James Earl Jones.'"

*Matewan* opens with the narrow beam of a miner's lamp and the labored efforts of a miner's lungs. It soon becomes apparent that this is a film about people trying to organize a union and other people trying to stop them.

Union-war films are probably not the hottest topic at Hollywood power breakfasts these days, probably not trendy vehicles for trendy young stars who are being rushed into yet more movies about trendy young subjects for trendy young audiences.

"I always want people to leave the theater thinking about their own lives, not about other movies," said Sayles, referring to the movies he both writes and directs.

Talking about his other life, as a hired screenwriter, he said, "When I write a genre movie like *The Howling,* that's fine, it reminds people of other werewolf movies.

"But in my movies, I want them to say, 'This is something I see in my life, not in the movies.'"

Sayles does not expect too many people to come to his movie just because of its strong union theme, although, he said, "It's really about 'union' with a small 'u,' not just trade unions. How do people get together? People rarely get together unless they have a common enemy. It's a lot about America and what it was supposed to be, and the labor movement and what it didn't turn out to be."

Along with his new movie, Sayles has written a book, *Thinking in Pictures: The Making of the Movie* Matewan, soon to be published by Houghton Mifflin. He describes how he created a pacifist union organizer, Joe Kenehan, who tries to unite rival black, Italian and mountaineer miners into one union, while the coal company hires a sadistic World War I veteran and his agents to keep the miners from joining forces.

"It has the elements of a western," Sayles said. "Who's gonna get killed and who's not? In the westerns, Joe Kenehan would say, 'I used to be in the Army,' and he would pick up his gun and take care of the guy—the classic Gary Cooper, a-man's-got-to-do-what-a-man's-got-to-do.

"I use that genre, but Joe is a pacifist and Joe loses, so that causes people to question pacifism. Maybe psychologically it was more important for the

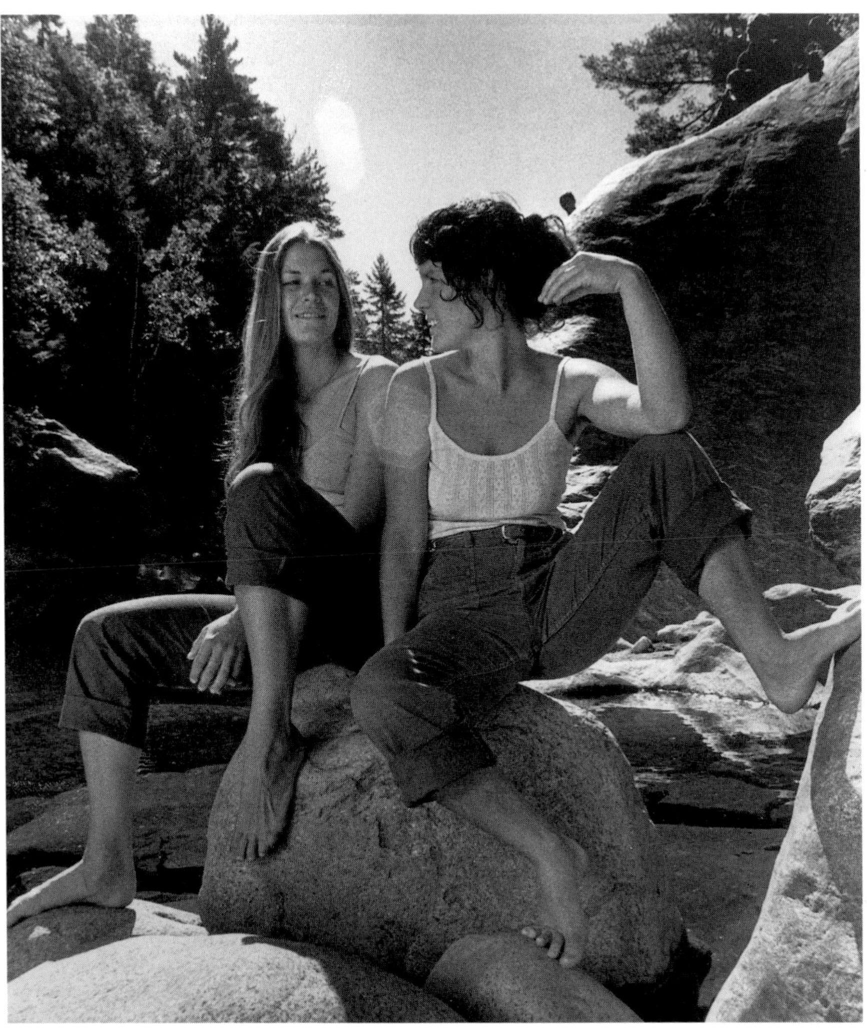

Karen Trott and Maggie Renzi in *Return of the Secaucus Seven,* 1980

Linda Griffiths and Jane Hallaren in *Lianna,* 1983

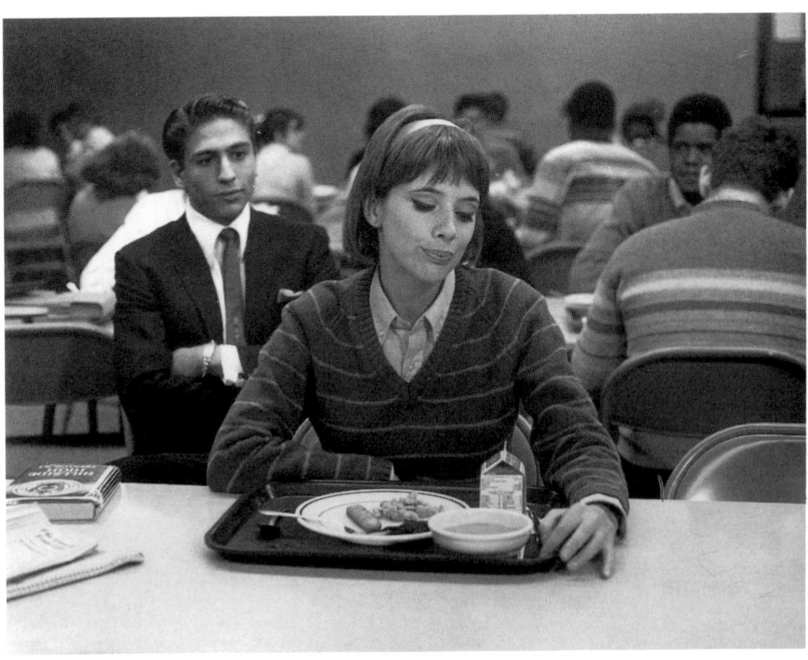

Vincent Spano and Susanna Arquette in *Baby, It's You,* 1983

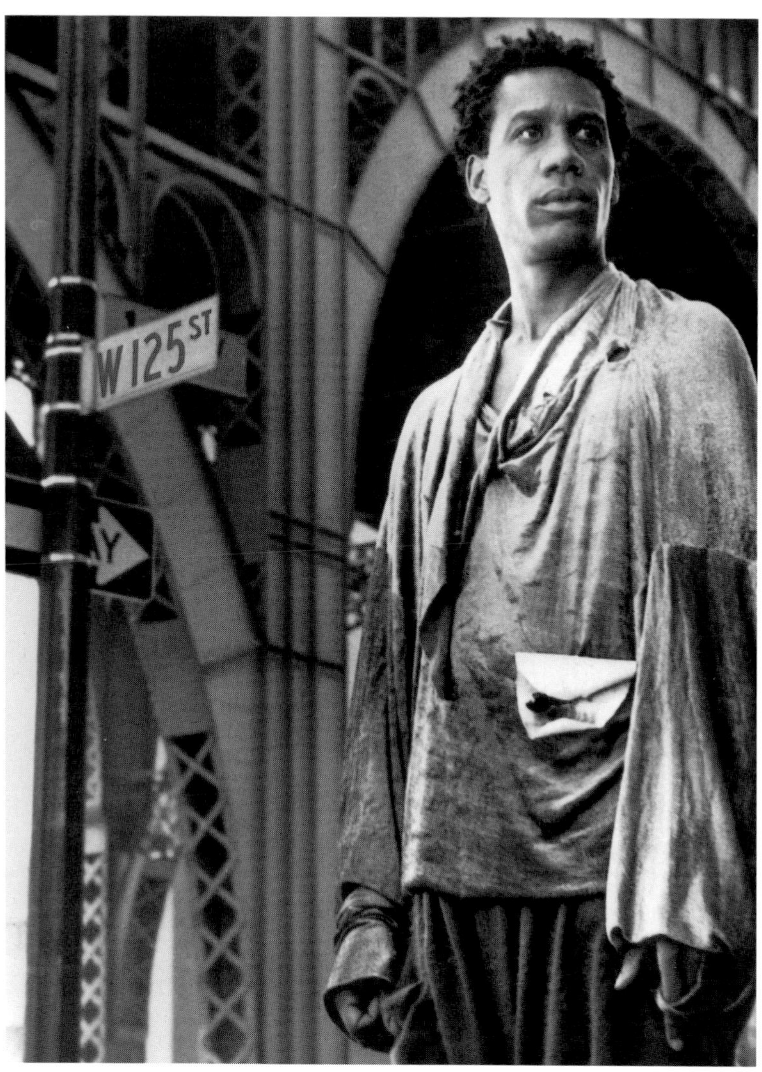


Joe Morton in *The Brother From Another Planet,* 1984

James Earl Jones in *Matewan*, 1987

David Strathairn in *Eight Men Out,* 1988

D. B. Sweeney in *Eight Men Out,* 1988

Jace Alexander, Todd Graff, and Vincent Spano in *City of Hope*, 1991

Tony Lo Bianco and Joe Morton in *City of Hope*, 1991

John Sayles on the set of *Lone Star*, 1996

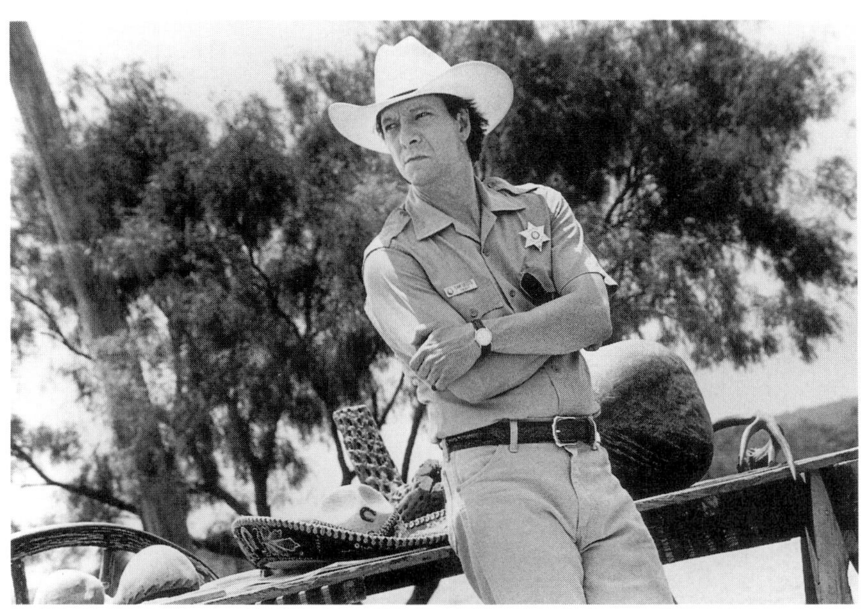

Chris Cooper in *Lone Star,* 1996

miners to shoot back, or for blacks to burn down their cities during the '60s. I don't know. I'm just raising the questions."

He said he was encouraged by the response to *Matewan* at Cannes, where it was shown as part of the Directors' Fortnight, a sidebar to the main film festival.

"The French being the French, all they were interested in was, 'How is it that one American independent film maker is doing classic American cinema of Ford and Hawks?' They were into the form, like *High Noon*.

"The Italians wanted to talk politics. Each of them was from a sliver of the political structure. They asked me, 'How do you make this movie in Reagan America?' I said, 'I don't think he's worried about me.' "

Sayles has worked his way to this independent stance from a traditional childhood in Schenectady, N.Y.—high school football and basketball, summer jobs, parents who were active in the teachers' association and, he noted, a number of law officers in the family.

He had never met a prep-school student until he went to Williams, where he cut a lot of classes, played intramural sports, and majored in psychology because "I was more fascinated with case histories than with classical English courses."

Starting college in 1968, he said, "I went to peace marches as a civilian. I was so out of it, I did not care about campus politics. I came late to a lot of stuff."

He figured he would wind up "not as a doctor, maybe working in a psychiatric hospital." Instead, he impulsively began acting and writing and observing.

Working as a meatpacker after college, he sold a novel, *Pride of the Bimbos,* in 1975, and another, called *Union Dues,* about a factory union in Boston, in 1977, becoming a renaissance man in a tank T-shirt, with muscles bulging. (He acts, too: He played a mechanic in *Secaucus Seven,* one of the black-shirted alien enforcers in *The Brother From Another Planet,* and he has a cameo role as an anti-union fundamentalist preacher in *Matewan.*)

After the financing had collapsed two-and-a-half times, by his count, he finally went back to West Virginia last fall to small towns near Matewan. Using local residents, who brought their own passions and familial memories to their minor roles, he re-created a world in which people were willing to kill over the right to organize.

He and the producers are planning a limited release, with hopes of "good reviews, good word of mouth, that magical crossover to the people who run the malls with 16 screens to fill, to what William Goldman calls 'the snob hit of the year,' to reach people looking for the next *Killing Fields, Kramer vs. Kramer, Chariots of Fire*. That's the first step of the crossover, followed by the people who go to *Robocop*.

But the question remains, is there is an audience for a film with a union theme?

"We're going to find out," Sayles said. "Basically, I make the movie for anybody who turns it on by accident, who wanders in. There's got to be something for them on an entertainment level—walking the line between didactic and being dramatic."

He is currently living in Indianapolis, preparing his second "low-budget epic," his adaptation of Eliot Asinof's book, *Eight Men Out,* about the infamous Chicago Black Sox who purposefully lost the 1919 World Series to the Cincinnati Reds in a gambling scheme.

Sayles nearly shudders when somebody asks if he would like to be the next Spielberg or Lucas, whose work he admires.

"I don't want to do all that campaigning for money. You get tired of that. It's always a surprise when you get them done, although raising $300,000 for *Lianna* was as hard as raising $4 million for *Matewan*. You're asking people to pay for what you want to do.

"It's sort of a different world, where you worry about bank loans, about lines of credit. It's different from what you want to do. That's why I've never taken an advance for novels. I want the option of sticking it on the shelf.

"I don't want the economic pressure on things I do. I can take a lot of risks that studios won't talk about. I can talk about things in depth. I can make the audience uneasy.

"I'm always saying, 'Well, if I'd only let the dog live,' meaning I could have made another half million at the box office, but that would have messed up the script."

And what's next? This time Sayles sounded like the union organizer in *Matewan,* getting off a smoking train with danger all around: "It's kind of a wiseguy line, but Nelson Algren once said: 'I try to go where I'm needed.' I feel that way about my work."

# Director John Sayles Makes Films With Conviction

KATHY HUFFHINES/1987

THEY SAID IT COULDN'T be done, but director John Sayles has done it time and time again. With one clever scheme after another, he's made five movies grounded in his strong social or political beliefs.

He has paid for movies about '60s activists (*Return of the Secaucus Seven,* 1978.) He has used screenwriting profits and investment offers to produce films undermining sexual stereotypes (*Lianna,* 1982.) He has convinced Paramount to pay for a love story about class relations (*Baby, It's You,* 1983.) He has wrapped comments on race, drugs and immigration in sci-fi stories that would win an audience (*Brother From Another Planet,* 1984.) And now, after the financing fell through three different times, he has come up with the movie he wanted to make in the first place. *Matewan,* the story of a West Virginia town's struggle to unionize its coal mines, will open in Detroit Friday.

"During the late '60s, I hitchhiked through Kentucky and West Virginia several times and got a lot of rides from coal miners," said Sayles, 37, a few weeks ago, stretching his lanky frame over the couch in a New York hotel suite. "That was around the time Jock Yablonski was murdered, and there was a lot of discussion. Again and again I would hear, 'This ain't nothin' like it used to be, buddy. You should have heard my Daddy about the coal wars in these parts during the '20s.' That was an extremely violent period, and not much has been written about it. Did you know that at one point, Billy Mitchell, the World War I flying ace, was called in to help break a

From *Detroit Free Press,* 27 September 1987. Reprinted by permission.

miners' union? The first time America ever bombed anybody from the air, it was their own people!"

Sayles found the particular coal wars story he wanted to film while researching his second novel, *Union Dues*. "From my reading, I learned that in 1920, the mine fields in eastern Kentucky and southwestern West Virginia were totally non-union. The mine owners controlled political offices and the police, posted armed guards at the mines and coal camps and sent spies to infiltrate the miners. When the native miners complained, the owners brought in what they called a 'judicious mixture' of blacks and immigrants just off the boat, assuming the three groups would never rise above their prejudices to unionize.

"In Matewan (W.Va.), the company spy C. E. Lively, was so effective, he was elected president of the UMW local. But, with leaders like a giant black miner known only as Few Clothes, the strikers joined together and wouldn't back down.

"Matewan was Hatfield-McCoy country. And though lots of people think those guys were dumb hillbillies, their feud was another economic war that pre-dated fights between the miners and mine owners. It started because the Hatfields, who ran the lumber business, tangled with the McCoys, who wanted to control the elections. In 1920, the Matewan chief of police was Sid Hatfield. And the strike turned into a shoot out when he and the mayor, Cabell Testerman, refused a bribe from the Baldwin-Felts Detective Agency, the enforcers for the state's coal operators. Hatfield told the agents they couldn't evict striking miners. They did. And when he and Testerman met them on the town's main street, a shoot-out turned into a massacre that killed the mayor, some of the miners and almost all of the Baldwin men.

"The United Mine Workers made a silent short film just after the massacre. It was called 'Smilin' Sid.' But the only print was stolen by a coal company agent and never seen again. So I thought I'd do the remake."

In the movie, Sayles (who also acts in the film) has organized this true-life story into four stanzas, shaped like a mountain ballad. And he's added several fictional characters who give his story its core, addressing the miners' struggle between pacifism and violence.

"There's the union organizer, Joe Kenehan. I wanted him to be a genuine pacifist, not the sort of Western hero who pulls his gun in the last reel and wipes out the baddies. So I made Joe a Wobbly, an IWW guy. They weren't communists or socialists; they were Americans, populists, working stiffs—lumberjacks, longshoremen, railroad men and farmers.

"Since Joe's an outsider in that town. I invented an insider, Danny Radnor. He's a boy preacher who has both the Old Testament values of righteousness and retribution and the New Testament dreams of peace and justice. Joe's fight against the mine owners is also a struggle for Danny's soul: to help him see beyond the endless vengeance of blood feud country."

Sayles's determination to tell this union story isn't just theoretical. He's put his money where his mouth is. "I've been around unions all my life," he said. "In Schenectady, where I grew up, you had the big General Electric plant and the Electrical Workers. Basically, you got the minimum wage, and that seemed like good money to me, $2.10 an hour. But to guys with families, it wasn't so good. So you paid your union dues."

After graduation from college, Sayles worked at Boston's Genoa Salami factory. "Everyone but Crazy Manny and me and Joe Fontana spoke Italian, but we all belonged to the Meat Packers Union."

Sayles is the kind who would never dream of doing location shooting without trying to help out the people in the area. "When it turned out that we couldn't use the town of Matewan because it had been flooded three times since 1920 and every building had been modified with new fronts, fake mansard roofs and pizza parlors, we ended up in Thurmond (W.Va.), the area's Las Vegas. The Rockefellers used to park their train there and play poker. At one time, near the turn of the century, there was a continuous poker game for 14 years and a bar that never closed.

"About 60 or 70 people live there now, and we wound up hiring about half the town. Usually they were miners. The big guy with the beard was the editor of the local paper. The public defender of West Virginia was in the cast, too. So was the state's four-time fiddling and sheep-calling champion.

"At first, there was a lot of suspicion, a feeling of 'What's he getting us into?' But we were sensitive to the fact that we were guests and people figured 'This isn't some guy who's going to make us look like hillbillies.' They saw the story we were telling wasn't *Lil' Abner.* It was the story they'd heard all their lives. We'd keep hearing our story told back to us time and time again. One woman said, 'When I was a little girl, I remember hiding under the table and hearing bullets whistling by.' Another guy came in with Sid Hatfield's gun. With the notches on it."

To give you an idea of Sayles's determination to look at the social, political and economic underpinnings of his stories, consider the movie he's shooting in Indianapolis. *Eight Men Out* is about the 1919 Chicago Black Sox Scandal. And Charlie Sheen, John Cusack, Studs Terkel and D.B. Sweeney will look much more natural than Robert Redford did in *The Natural,* says Sayles.

"One of the things I'm trying to do is get right into the game. In *The Natural,* Redford never did anything but strike out or hit a home run. He never popped up or hit a single. So much of *Eight Men Out* is about who's trying and who's not. I *do* see the social and political elements in everything. I'm interested in *why* they threw the series. How did *they* see the world? If I were writing about a football team in the '60s, I'd probably be writing about how they were stacking the blacks," a practice whereby teams would meet racial quotas but maintain segregation by limiting the positions blacks could play.

Here's the big test. At the beginning of his career when he was writing Roger Corman screenplays with titles like *Piranha, Battle Beyond the Stars* and *The Lady in Red,* could Sayles have *possibly* managed to introduce The Deeper Message?

"Sure," he says.

"*The Lady in Red* was about the woman with John Dillinger. To me, what it tried to be about was *why* Dillinger and the FBI were shooting each other. To me, Dillinger was just a PR job. J. Edgar Hoover made stars out of the guys he knew he could catch. He never got anybody from the Mafia. He'd take smaller guys, bank robbers, and make them Public Enemy No. 1.

"In other words, to me that movie was about *why* Dillinger became Public Enemy No. 1 at a time when one-third of the women in Chicago between the ages of 15 and 35 were working as prostitutes."

# Sayles Relishes Independence

PHILIP WUNTCH/1987

IN THE MOTION PICTURE business, everything is relative.

In the canon of screenwriter/director John Sayles, *Matewan* has a blockbuster budget of $4 million. The average Hollywood film costs at least $15 million.

But Sayles doesn't make average Hollywood films. His movies—*The Return of the Secaucus Seven, Lianna, Baby, It's You, The Brother From Another Planet*—are independent in spirit and financing. They don't cost much, they play art houses and they earn a profit. The $4 million budget for the large-scale *Matewan* is minuscule by Hollywood studio standards, but it towers above the $60,000 outlay for *The Return of the Secaucus Seven.*

"Every time a film of mine makes money, the studios beckon, and I sometimes succumb to their call," Sayles says, talking by phone from Indianapolis, where he is filming *Eight Men Out,* his interpretation of the Chicago Black Sox bribery scandal of 1919.

"But things frequently don't pan out with the studios. Often, I've been asked to do one too many rewrites of my screenplays and to relinquish too much control."

So the 37-year-old Sayles remains one of the leading American directors of small-budget, independent films. He still maintains his offices in Hoboken, N.J. He knows how to make a $4 million film look like it cost at least four times as much. And, for the most part, he has few complaints.

---

From *Dallas Morning News,* 16 October 1987. Reprinted with permission of The Dallas Morning News.

*Matewan* tells the sad but true story of a group of courageous West Virginia miners who fight a powerful coal company to form a union in 1920. It has elements of *Joe Hill, Shane* and, in its climactic moments, *High Noon.* He got the idea for the story from conversations he had with coal miners while hitchhiking across the country during the late 1960s and early 1970s.

"I hitchhiked over several different periods in those days. I took different routes through the hill country of West Virginia, Tennessee and Kentucky. Coal miners were the most generous people about giving me a lift. They told me wonderful stories, filled with their own wonderful, strong opinions.

"Coal miners have opinions about everything. Even now, they have a difficult time convincing the authorities of the everyday risks they take. They even had struggles getting the union to recognize some of the hardships.

"But, to a man, they all said, 'If you think I've got it rough, you should hear about the way things were in my grandpappy's day.' They made me wonder just how hard it must have been."

One of the most fascinating characters in Sayles' script is a teen-age lay preacher named Danny, who uses scripture to save the life of the union organizer.

"He's a composite of several accounts I read of adolescent boys who were both apprentice coal miners and lay preachers. If you were a precocious kid, being a lay preacher was one acceptable way of getting yourself heard. You could speak out and say anything without getting shouted down by the grown-ups."

*Matewan* is one of the few Sayles films to boast a known actor in its cast. James Earl Jones, fresh from his stage success in *Fences,* plays the real-life character of Few Clothes, a scab who eventually joins the union.

"We never thought we'd get James Earl Jones. We were looking for a James Earl Jones *type.* I've always had trouble with known actors. They take forever to give me a simple yes or no. And then, when they've said, 'No,' and the film turns out all right, they always write me a note saying they would have been delighted to be in it, that it was their agent and not them who said, 'No,' and that if they'd only known I'd wanted them for the part. . . .

"Finally, after looking for various James Earl Jones *types,* I decided to try for the real James Earl Jones. He said, 'Yeah,' and he was just great to work with."

Sayles' films never have been shot in the order he wrote them. He wrote *Eight Men Out* 10 years ago and *Matewan* three years later. He wrote *Lianna,* an intelligent and compassionate look at a lesbian relationship, before he wrote *The Return of the Secaucus Seven,* a study of former 1960s radicals that many critics preferred to the trendy *The Big Chill.*

"There is a certain advantage in taking my time. Certainly, it gives me time to think about a project. People have commented on the unified sense of community there is in *Matewan.*

"But there was definitely a sense of status in the town of Matewan. People were judged according to how high up on the hill they lived. The higher up on the hill, the lesser their status. If they lived in the flatlands, they were considered the cream of the community. Notice that Bridey, the widow who becomes a prostitute, lives high up on the hill."

He has directed three music videos for fellow New Jersey native Bruce Springsteen—"Born in the U.S.A.," "I'm on Fire" and "Glory Days." Perhaps out of respect for Springsteen's penchant for privacy, he speaks sparingly of his association with the rock star.

"He and I got together through friends. My girlfriend's sister knows the manager of one of his musicians. That sort of thing. He was fine to work with. A total professional."

Sayles started his career as a novelist, publishing *The Pride of the Bimbos* in 1975 and *Union Dues* in 1977. He published a collection of short stories, *The Anarchist's Convention,* in 1979. He soon had a profitable career going as a screenwriter and script doctor. He wrote the offbeat screenplays to such exploitation flicks as *Piranha, The Lady in Red, Battle Beyond the Stars, The Howling* and *Alligator.* One of his less successful ventures was an attempt to turn the best-selling novel *The Clan of the Cave Bear* into a viable screenplay.

After *Eight Men Out,* Sayles plans to finish a novel about political intrigue within Miami's Cuban community.

He became a director because "I got tired of seeing things I had written turn out differently than I had planned. As a screenwriter, you have to relinquish control. Once you've written it, it's out of your hands completely. Believe me, that is not a comfortable feeling."

# Filmmaker Puts Message Before Money

DAN SMITH/1987

No filmmaker does so much with so little as John Sayles. He made his first film in 1978, *The Return of the Secaucus Seven,* a thoughtful precursor to *The Big Chill,* with only $60,000. Always working with a budget well below the industry average, Sayles has nonetheless managed to endow each of his films with a remarkably authentic, evocative look.

Take the film he's shooting now, *Eight Men Out,* a drama about the famous Chicago White Sox baseball scandal of 1919. Sayles brought his Indianapolis-based film crew to Louisville in mid-October to shoot scenes at Churchill Downs. After scouting numerous locations within reasonable access of Indianapolis, Sayles determined that Churchill Downs was the most authentic 1920s-era race track for the scenes of the gamblers who fixed the 1919 World Series.

"Robert Altman once said there's no such thing as a low-budget film, just an appropriately budgeted film," Sayles said during a break in the filming.

These days, Altman could take a cue from Sayles. With Sayles' newly released *Matewan* (which he wrote and directed) receiving near-unanimous critical praise, he is fast becoming America's leading independent filmmaker.

*Matewan,* which had been scheduled to open at the Kentucky Theatre until the recent fire temporarily closed it, is at The Vogue Theater in Louisville through Nov. 5. It plays at 3 and 7:30 p.m. today. For other playing

---

From *Lexington Herald-Leader,* 1 November 1987. Reprinted by permission.

times, call the theater at (502) 893-3646. *Matewan* will have its Lexington premiere at one of the USA Cinemas in the next few weeks, the film company says.

In 10 years of writing and directing his own movies, Sayles, 37, has consistently bucked the Hollywood establishment by making thoughtful films.

From his cult classic *Secaucus Seven* and *Lianna,* a sensitive 1981 study of lesbian relationships, to *Matewan,* a stirring drama about the 1920 coal-mining wars in West Virginia, Sayles has never wavered in his commitment to movies with a message.

Even before *Matewan,* Sayles' star was rising. In 1984 he wrote and directed *The Brother From Another Planet,* a clever, offbeat contemporary fantasy that has done very well in cable and home-video markets. Sayles, who lives in Hoboken, N.J., also directed three of Bruce Springsteen's music videos, "Glory Days," "I'm on Fire," and "Born in the U.S.A." *Matewan* meant so much to Sayles that he wrote a book about the experience, *Thinking in Pictures: The Making of the Movie* Matewan, published last month by Houghton-Mifflin.

But if Sayles is moving closer to mainstream success it's not because he's compromised his own individual vision. *Eight Men Out,* like *Matewan,* is what Hollywood calls a "difficult" film: it's serious, historical, and doesn't have a happy ending.

So from the beginning, Sayles knew that if it was going to be done at all—and most of the big studios wouldn't even consider such a film—it had to be done as a low-budget, independent film. *Eight Men Out* has a modest $6 million budget, less than half the standard Hollywood budget.

Sayles was first attracted to the story of *Eight Men Out* more than 10 years ago when he first read Eliot Asinof's 1963 book of the same name. Even though the rights to the book weren't available then, Sayles wrote a screenplay adaptation of it anyway, to use as a writing sample in Hollywood.

Enter producer Sara Pillsbury, who along with her partner Midge Sanford produced the risky but successful *River's Edge* and *Desperately Seeking Susan.* In 1980 Pillsbury and Sanford took an option on the book. Shortly afterward, Sayles got word of it and within weeks they joined forces.

"(Francis Ford) Coppola and (Robert) Altman were interested in the story," Pillsbury said during filming at Churchill Downs recently. "But John Sayles is one of the few filmmakers who can make a movie at such a price."

Pillsbury is convinced that the film's theme of corruption and scandal in professional sports is a subject that American audiences will care about. "It goes to the heart of the American experience," she said. "It's not just a baseball film: It has the strength of allegory.

"The players of the 1919 team were the nation's first media stars, almost as famous as Lindbergh. And when the scandal broke, it caused a sense of betrayal. The film is about character. And it's about morality and history," she said.

Morality and history are two of Sayles' favorite film subjects. Both *Matewan* and *Eight Men Out* deal with the difficult choices people have faced. In the case of *Matewan,* it's the coal miners' decision to form a union to take on the mine owners. In *Eight Men Out,* it's badly underpaid ballplayers who accept bribe money to fix the World Series. And in both cases it's not a single protagonist's story, but a richly textured look at whole groups of people.

Sayles acknowledges the similarity in the two films. "*Matewan* is about a whole town," Sayles said. "*Eight Men Out* is not just about eight people but a lot of others, different strata of society. It's about how people can corrupt each other. How they lose an ideal or a spirit."

Sayles is also aware that *Eight Men Out* will be compared with another recent baseball film, Robert Redford's *The Natural*. "*The Natural* is about a guy with great skills who loses them because of the money and the celebrity. *Eight Men Out* is like that, too," he said.

But there the similarity ends, Sayles says. "In *The Natural,* they went for something mythic. Redford either struck out or hit a home run. Here we're following the play by play of the game with no slow motion. We're simulating some real game situations."

To lend more authenticity to the baseball setting, *Eight Men Out* will feature actors who will perform the ballplaying scenes themselves. Sayles has cast the "Black Sox" team with young actors with baseball experience, including Charlie Sheen (*Platoon, Ferris Bueller's Day Off*), John Cusack (*Class, The Sure Thing*), and D.B. Sweeney (*Gardens of Stone*). Sweeney played some minor league ball.

The film also features Christopher Lloyd (*Back to the Future*), Studs Terkel as Hugh Fullerton, the journalist who first exposed the scandal, and Sayles himself as the writer Ring Lardner.

Does Sayles expect his young actors to pull off professional-looking double plays? Sayles smiled and acknowledged the difference between Hollywood and the major leagues. "In the big leagues you have to do it right all the time. In the movies you only have to do it right once."

Doing it right even once is not easy in a low-budget film. On a cold Saturday morning last month, only 1,200 extras showed up at Indianapolis' Bush Stadium—less than a third of those who had agreed to serve as extras for the game scenes. Sayles and the crew did their best to shoot around the sparse crowd, but everyone in the production is counting heavily on the two remaining Saturdays left on the shooting schedule for scaring up a large crowd in Indianapolis.

Despite such production problems, Sayles remains optimistic about the scene for independent filmmakers. "I'm encouraged at the possibilities. It's still possible to make a film under $1 million. There are many more theaters that will show that kind of film and many more who will come see it. Then there's cable and home-video possibilities. More people will get a shot (to see the film)—like Spike Lee's *She's Gotta Have It.*"

*Eight Men Out* won't be released until sometime next fall, perhaps during World Series time, Pillsbury said. But is Sayles worried about selling another "difficult" movie?

"Baseball is getting a lot more popular these days," he said. "If just half the men in America go see this movie, we'll be all right."

# Director Found History on the Road

## CAROLE KASS/1987

FILM MAKER JOHN SAYLES got more than a ride when he was hitchhiking through the West Virginia mountains in the 1960s.

"The people who picked me up in West Virginia were generally coal miners. It was when Jack Yablonsky was battling Tony Boyle to head up the union, and they would say, 'You should have been around when my father—or grandfather—was here.' And they'd tell me stories."

Sayles, who wrote and directed *Matewan,* the film playing at the Broad Street Cinema, was born in Schenectady, N.Y., and was graduated from Williams College in Massachussets. He adapted the screenplay from his second novel, *Union Dues.* It is the story of the first battle in the violent coal miner wars, an oral history based on the stories he heard on West Virginia's roads.

The independent film director is best known for his poignant and rueful *Return of the Secaucus Seven.* Another film, *Brother From Another Planet,* co-starred Caroline Aaron (Abady) of Richmond for whom he specially wrote the part. His *Baby, It's You* introduced Rosanna Arquette.

To earn a steady living Sayles writes screenplays. They range from *Piranha, The Howling* and *Alligator* to *Clan of the Cave Bear* and *Wild Thing.*

Sayles honed his style writing screenplays for Roger Corman. "He hadn't picked the directors when I wrote the screenplays, so I sat down and talked specifics with him and wrote shooting scripts. It was a kind of schooling:

---

From *Richmond Times-Dispatch,* 11 December 1987. Reprinted by permission.

I got to see what I had written put on screen, see how it could have been done better or why it looked so well.

"When I write screenplays for other people, none of them are original projects. They give me an idea, a book to adapt, a screenplay where I'm told, 'Keep the title and throw everything else away.' It's like I'm the carpenter.

"But then, I'm the architect when I write and direct my own work. I invest the money I make from the screenplays in my movies."

*Matewan,* for which he wrote the first draft eight years ago, was budgeted at $4 million. It is his most expensive film, wholly financed by Cinecom Entertainment Group.

"When we went down to Beckley, W.Va., where we shot, many in the cast and crew were locals. They came up with stories, some of which got in the script.

"The housekeeper at the Econo Lodge where we stayed remembered her Italian immigrant grandmother telling how they hid under the bed when the Baldwin-Felts goons—mercenaries hired to intimidate the miners and beat up union organizers—would shoot into the houses.

"John L. Lewis was in his first year as union president in 1920 when the Matewan Massacre occurred. It consolidated his position when the radicals were thrown in jail. He was a middle-of-the-roader.

"The union wars that followed, with airplanes dropping bombs, armies and men fighting in trenches, was the biggest uprising in America after the Civil War. We don't know about it, because history is written by the winners, and the coal companies didn't talk about it."

Sayles talked by telephone from the New York editing room where he was working on *Eight Men Out,* a film about the Chicago "Black" Sox scandal in 1919 when the team threw the World Series.

Editing is what he loves best about movie making.

"Screenwriting is speculative. Some screenplays I've written never get made.

"When I'm directing, the meter is always running. There's pressure to get a shot before the sun goes down, before we go into overtime. But with editing, the film is in the can. I've written screenplays to pay for editing and mixing machines. But I don't have to worry about the sun or overtime."

The time and place in *Matewan* are captured in the music: Hazel Dickens singing her special brand of folk music, as well as what Sayles calls, "the fusion of black music from Alabama, the mountain music and the squeeze box and mandolin of the Italian immigrants."

The cool look of the hot film is cinematographer Haskell Wexler's work. "It was serendipity. We had a limited budget and a limited time to shoot. Haskell had started as a documentary maker. He shot *Bound For Glory* and *Heat of the Night* [and *Reds* and *Apocalypse Now*]. He could have made more money working on something else. But I called him and he said yes. He gave a seamless look to footage shot when there were a lot of seams in the weather. He was the most experienced person I ever worked with."

# Breaking the Rules. John Sayles' Films Carry His Unique Imprint

LINDA BILLINGTON/1988

JOHN SAYLES BREAKS A lot of filmmaking rules—or at least, bends them into celluloid pretzels.

In horror scripts such as *Piranha, Alligator* and *The Howling,* Sayles' characters do indeed poke around in dark, lonely or inadvisable places—but, unlike folks in films penned by lesser writers, they do it with a certain flair.

Those less-than-A movies, along with *Battle Beyond the Stars* and even *Clan of the Cave Bear,* were written for a purpose: to finance his own, more personal, films. These he both wrote and directed—and in the process broke (or at least bent) a different set of rules: the rules that say how far a low-budget filmmaker can go.

"I think a lot of what we've been able to do is just say, 'Well, look, there's an ecology here, and there's a little niche that I bet we could get ourselves into,'" the 37-year-old Sayles said in an interview last week. "And if we can get ourselves into that niche we can make a movie and we can get it shown—and do it at least on our own terms as far as what the movie says.

"It may not look the way we'd like it to look or sound the way we'd like it to sound or get seen by as many people as we'd like to have see it—but at least it will say the stuff we want it to say."

Sayles started messing with the rules back in 1980 with *Return of the Secaucus Seven,* a story about the weekend reunion of a group of former '60s activists. It was short on camera movement and long on conversation; it cost an anorexic $60,000, and it earned back three times its price tag.

---

From *Anchorage Daily News,* 22 May 1988. Reprinted by permission.

He continued with *Lianna, Baby, It's You* (his first involvement with a big studio, which left him less than overjoyed with the results), *The Brother From Another Planet* and, most recently, *Matewan*. All show his distinctive stamp.

The big screen hasn't been his sole medium. Three novels, a host of short stories, a couple of television movies and three Bruce Springsteen videos are also part of his oeuvre, as well as a number of acting jobs. Now he's gearing up to release another of his own films, *Eight Men Out,* based on the Chicago White Sox scandal of 1919.

He says he hasn't had a vacation in two years. Nor, for that matter, has his longtime producer and partner, Maggie Renzi, with whom he lives in Hoboken, N.J. This week, they found themselves for the first time in Alaska, guests of Affinityfilms, a local non-profit film production company. They got to go fishing, but mostly it was work: a screening of *The Brother From Another Planet,* a reading of one of Sayles's short stories, a luncheon with the Alaska Division of Tourism's Film Office and a weekend in Rainbow Valley, where they told 15 Alaska filmmakers and scriptwriters how to film independently—and on the cheap.

Sayles—a 6-foot-4 tower of loose-jointed lankiness with pushed-up shirt sleeves—has had plenty of experience in that area. Over the years, his films have grown more complex, but their budgets, although rising, still represent the low end of the scale. *Eight Men Out* came in at a whopping (for him) $6.5 million. That compares favorably with a few other movies on tap for this summer: *Bull Durham,* cost $8.5 million, *"Crocodile" Dundee II* hit $14 million (described by one film magazine as "impressively low") and *Rambo III* tops the charts at $55 million.

In his book *Thinking in Pictures: The Making of the Movie* Matewan, Sayles outlined the "don'ts" of low-budget filmmaking: Don't set your picture in a historical period, don't shoot on location, don't have a lot of speaking parts. And so on.

*Matewan,* a 1987 drama set during the West Virginia coal miners' strike of 1920, broke all these rules, and then some. Its cost: a little less than $4 million.

"I don't think we break (the rules) in any big conscious important way," Sayles said. "But I do think that coming from the outside the way we did, we just didn't accept the rules or we never would've started . . . Sometimes we were surprised that we got away with it."

Social change is a major influence in Sayles' films. He's intrigued by it. "A lot of the history of America is the history of assimilation, of people coming here and gradually becoming whatever we are today or whatever they became in their lifetime," he said. "I've always been interested in how those bigger things, bigger political things, affect people, and how individual decisions can sometimes affect those bigger things."

Assimilation was the norm for Sayles, who as a kid moved around a lot in the area of Schenectady, N.Y. In 12 years and six or seven schools, he was the outsider, at least for a while.

He's still an outsider when it comes to the Hollywood studio system. He and Renzi tend to create their own films, find their own financing, keep a close eye on distribution and watch the myriad other aspects of filmmaking. It's a lot of labor—but the trade-off is having control of your work.

Although *Eight Men Out,* was made under the benevolent aegis of Orion Pictures, Sayles said, "Most studios are not interested in things that don't have at least the potential to be blockbusters."

Sayles has written a couple of scripts because he thought the subject matter was important. *Unnatural Causes,* a television drama about Agent Orange, won the Writers Guild of America award for original long-form television earlier this year.

Despite his low budgets, Sayles's reputation is such that he lures some high-powered and high-priced people to his projects. The biggest name in the *Matewan* cast is that of respected actor James Earl Jones. The film was shot by Haskell Wexler, the Oscar-winning cinematographer for *Who's Afraid of Virginia Woolf* and *Bound for Glory.*

Sayles and Renzi still didn't have a director of photography for *Matewan* by the time they had moved to the location in rural West Virginia, so they figured they might as well give the big-time Wexler a chance to say no. He returned their call—from his car phone—while they were out. The message: "Whatever they want, the answer is yes."

Later, during filming, Wexler—who got an Academy Award nomination for his work on *Matewan*—told *American Film* magazine, "My usual salary is four times what I'm making here. But I'm getting four times more in personal enjoyment. You seldom get to do something with your professional life that has character, dignity and significance."

Sayles's influence on his films doesn't just come from behind the camera. Moviegoers frequently see the man himself—as well as Renzi—in the cinematic flesh. Sayles was one of the deadpan extraterrestrial bounty hunters who track an escaped alien slave through Harlem in *Brother,* the local boy who didn't leave town in *Secaucus Seven* and the preacher in *Matewan.* Renzi turns up as an obstructionist social worker in *Brother* and an Italian coal miner's wife in *Matewan.* Her largest role was the hostess of the weekend house party in *Secaucus Seven.*

Sayles keeps Renzi in mind when he's creating a script, but roles for himself just pop up, he said. "I don't need to be in everything that I make. But as I'm writing, every once in a while I'll just"—he snaps his fingers—"Boom! There's one!"

In *Eight Men Out,* Renzi is a player's wife and Sayles portrays sportswriter Ring Lardner. "I started learning more about Ring Lardner just before we shot and learned that he was 10 years older than I thought he was, so he was my age in 1919. And he was 6 foot 2 and I'm 6 foot 4. And I realized, 'I can play this guy.'"

Although it was just filmed, *Eight Men Out* was actually the first screenplay Sayles wrote—about 11 years ago—so he could have something to show when he went looking for an agent.

The script was based on the 1963 book by Eliot Asinof, which recalled how the Chicago White Sox—who became known as the Black Sox—went down in a gambling scandal when most of the team threw the 1919 World Series.

Sayles, a former jock and all-time baseball fan, was intrigued by the subject matter. He was also drawn, as always, to a year and a place of change.

"If you think of America being an adolescent at the time," Sayles said, "(the scandal) was one of those things that made a big impression on that adolescence. Although there were a lot of corrupt things and a lot of cynical things going on in America, the official view, if you read the newspapers, was that it was still this kind of blue-skies, pure white Americana country. It was hard for people to ignore the fact that America's game, America's pasttime, was as corrupt as most other things were in American society."

# Real Big Leaguer Connects Again

CHERYL L. KUSHNER/1988

It was John Sayles's turn at bat.

The audience at the Center-Mayfield Theater had sat quietly while the screen credits rolled and then warmly applauded as the director of *Eight Men Out* was introduced to the 380 gathered at a benefit screening for the Cleveland International Film Festival.

The slightly tousled Sayles, dressed in a partly unbuttoned aqua shirt, stonewashed gray jeans and sneakers, was ready to answer questions about his new work, which focuses on the fixed 1919 World Series between the Chicago White Sox and the Cincinnati Reds. Based on the best-selling 1963 novel by Eliot Asinof, the film explores how eight ballplayers found themselves caught between White Sox owner Charles Comiskey and a cadre of gamblers, who swindled each other as well as the players.

Sayles offered a few comments and then took questions. The scene was a familiar one for the film maker, who had attended similar benefit screenings in Chicago and Cincinnati. From the audiences'—and critics'—responses, it appears that Sayles has hit a home run with *Eight Men Out*.

"Well, certainly as many people, just in number of bodies, have seen it already than most of my other movies and it's only in six cities," Sayles said during an interview earlier that day in his hotel suite at Stouffer Tower City Plaza Hotel. The film opened in six cities Sept. 2 and in Cleveland last Friday. "They (Orion Pictures) are not doing a wide release, but a wider

---

From *The Plain Dealer,* 25 September 1988. Reprinted with permission from *The Plain Dealer* 

release than anything else I've done, and it's actually out at shopping malls. And I go see movies at the Secaucus Mall—and there it is."

Certainly that's got to be gratifying for the independent film maker from Hoboken, N.J., whose first film, *Return of the Secaucus Seven,* was made for $60,000, and who since has caught the fancy of film critics and film buffs alike.

Yet, he's literally been ignored by the big studios.

"Most people in Hollywood still haven't seen anything I've done," Sayles said matter-of-factly. Does it concern him that he's considered a breed apart from the mainstream?

"It's important to try to make the movies you want to make, the way you want to make them," he said. "If you can't do it through the studio system, do it some other way; if you can do it through the studio system, do it that way.

"Our movies haven't done especially well in LA, but have been seen because they sit in one theater for a long time. And that just doesn't happen in LA. It's too spread out there... for the word-of-mouth to really do something."

Word-of-mouth has helped give Sayles's earlier efforts an almost cult following *Secaucus Seven* (1980) was compared to Lawrence Kasdan's big-budget *Big Chill* (1983) and the latter came up wanting. Critical response to *Brother From Another Planet,* (1984) about a mute, black extraterrestrial who crash-lands in New York and ends up wandering through Harlem, and *Matewan,* (1987) which concerns a union war in the coal fields of West Virginia, has made people sit up and take notice of the film maker. He's been, to borrow a football term, a successful triple threat in his films, and took the field as screenwriter, director and actor in *Eight Men Out.*

"As the screenwriter you have to do two things: You have to get the movie made so you have to write in a way that it reads like a story, 'cause other people have to read this thing and get excited about it and say 'yes we're going to give you the money to make it.'

"But you also have to tell the story so you don't have to do a lot of rewriting on the set. To me, that was really juggling a lot of characters and juggling a big story and also trying to tell it in two hours."

Sayles compared the pressure the director feels on the set to the pressure the manager experiences during a baseball game. Tension is high and concentration important. "As director, the difficulty is always trying to juggle all these logistic things. It's sort of like being in a cab where the meter is running except it's $50 dollars a minute instead of 10 cents.

"You have to make sure the actors don't feel the tension. If they have a different idea, you've got a take for them to try that different idea out. If their job is to hit a triple off the right field wall, they don't start getting nervous 'cause everybody is waiting and looking at their watches."

The director takes that pressure, he said. "You've got everybody pointed *just* at you . . . and you know how much it costs every time you foul one off instead of hitting it off the wall."

The actor's job is to know his character, Sayles said, and then to "forget everything else except the person you're talking to or the thing that you're doing onscreen."

Concentration can be difficult when a camera is almost on an actor's face, a light stand blocks his line of vision, a boom microphone hangs 6 inches above his head and a half-dozen people stand around and take notes.

But, said Sayles, you have to focus them out and really live that moment between you and that person. "The minute *I* say action and boom!—we're into it . . . and then until the scene is over and the last word is said and the last thing that's going to happen onscreen happens I stay there, and then it's like coming out of sleep—not a deep sleep but out of a sleep and I say, 'OK I'm a director again, and cut.' "

For this film, Sayles cast himself as sportswriter Ring Lardner, who had covered the White Sox for many years and later became famous with the success of his "You know me Al" stories. Lardner and Hugh Fullerton, one of the most popular sportswriters of the time, represent a Greek chorus of sorts as they sadly watched the talented Sox throw the Series.

"The role ended up bigger than I thought it was going to be," said Sayles, who bears an uncanny resemblance to Lardner. "As I was thinking about casting, I read more about him. Two things I learned: At that time he was about my age (Sayles is 37) and that he was 6-2 (Sayles is 6 feet 4) and towered over everyone.

"I realized I could play this role. And when you are casting 60 speaking parts, any actor who you don't have to to worry about or who you know is easy to work with, well, it's a relief.

"I had met Studs Terkel (who plays Fullerton) before . . . and I knew he had been a radio actor—he's certainly a performer—and as I read more about Hugh Fullerton, there was Studs."

Sayles had drafted a version of the screenplay about 11 years ago as an example of his writing ability. He got an agent, but learned that the rights to the book were in litigation. When the dust settled in the early 1980s, Sayles found out that Sarah Pillsbury and Midge Sanford had taken an option on the book. He called them up and the three agreed to join forces to get the film made.

"We made the run on the major studios and independent financiers and there was resistance," Sayles said. There were three strikes against them: Studios weren't anxious to sink money into another baseball film since earlier baseball movies weren't hits at the box office; they wanted to tell an ensemble story rather than focus in on one character; and because the subject was known history, the Sox couldn't win the Series.

"(The studios) realized this wasn't a *Rocky* kind of movie; it's a sports movie and who wants a sports movie about people who lose . . . and it's not a star vehicle, so how are we going to get a star to be in this thing."

But by the time the producers found Orion, there was a pool of young, male actors who had some name recognition. "A lot were jocks and had played baseball and found the idea of getting to play a major leaguer very attractive," said Sayles. "They helped sell people on the movie as much as the screenplay did.

"It was much more difficult to get the actors' *agents* interested in letting them do it, than it was in getting actors interested in first place. Then once you have a Charlie Sheen (center fielder Hap Felsch), John Cusak (third baseman Buck Weaver) or D.B. Sweeney (left fielder 'Shoeless' Joe Jackson) say yes, then all of a sudden it becomes an attractive project for them to get their clients into. So then they start calling you."

When casting the roles of the Sox players, Sayles relied on actors—like Jace Alexander and David Strathairn—he knew had athletic ability or he had worked with before. "Jace (pitcher Dickie Kerr) was in *Matewan*, and I played softball with him and knew he had a good arm." But Sayles needed someone to get the actors into shape. That fell to Ken Berry, a former major-league center fielder. Said Sayles: "We held a training camp before we started to get them loose so they didn't get hurt."

Sayles gave Berry a specific list of what each actor's character needed to do. "I told him, 'they have to slide; they have to hit a single to right field, and they have to turn a double play. And I don't care how, as long as it will look like it gets a guy out.' "

About half of the nine-week filming schedule was spent shooting the baseball scenes. The game action takes place in Indianapolis' Bush Stadium, doubling for the Chicago and Cincinnati ballparks.

"While we were shooting, Ken did a lot of fungo hitting (fly balls to the outfield) and hitting the ball to an exact spot in the infield. For pitching, well, there weren't as many fastball pitchers then as now," Sayles said. "Trick pitches were still legal, and there were a lot more junk ball pitchers. We didn't need somebody who could throw 90 mph; we needed somebody who could get it over and have the motion of a pitcher."

Sayles cast Strathairn (one of the bounty hunters in *Brother*) as pitcher Eddie Cicotte, who reluctantly joined the conspiracy after Comiskey wouldn't pay him a promised $10,000 bonus. "David turned out to be a good pitcher and he'd never pitched before," Sayles said. "James Read (Lefty Williams) looks like a pitcher, only he has to pitch bad. He had some control problems because he was afraid of hitting the camera. Eventually I just said, 'James, I don't care if you hit the camera, just throw it as hard as you can. I don't care where it goes. Just throw hard.' "

With all the work behind him, Sayles can bask in good reviews and press attention. He said he's going to take some time off from directing and work on a novel. He doesn't have a film project in mind, although he thinks "it will be something low-budget and contemporary.

"There's a lot of stuff I want to do that doesn't fit into the studio mold," he said. "I don't know if they're appropriate for big studios 'cause it's an expensive process.

"If you want to make gourmet food, you don't go to General Mills to distribute it because eventually what's going to happen is that they're going to have to take whatever made it special out of it to do it on that scale."

# Interview with John Sayles

DICK JOHNSON/1989

WITH HIS 1988 FILM adaptation of Eliot Asinof's *Eight Men Out* novelist-filmmaker John Sayles has crafted the most authentic baseball film released to date. His respect for Asinof's work, and for the look, language and rhythm of dead ball era baseball is evident in every frame of the film. Unlike any other baseball movie, *Eight Men Out* is nearly devoid of saccharine sentimentality, distracting extracurricular nonsense or embarrassing errors in its depiction of baseball and its surroundings.

I met with John Sayles on the morning following the Boston premiere of *Eight Men Out* to discuss the movie, the Black Sox scandal, and baseball in general. An avowed Pirate fan, Sayles answered my questions for nearly an hour over breakfast in the genteel confines of the cafe of the Ritz Carlton Hotel.

Q: *Describe your fascination with the book* Eight Men Out. *Did the screenplay emerge from your being a baseball fan or from being a fan of the story?*
A: I think the initial interest was hearing the story and wondering how eight men could throw the World Series. I had read a couple of other books that alluded to the scandal but didn't have many details. In 1976 I discovered Eliot's book, read it, and felt that it described the scandal in

---

Originally published in *The SABR Review of Books*—Volume IV (1989) by the Society for American Baseball Research, Cleveland, Ohio. Reprinted by permission of *The SABR Review of Books* and the author.

great detail. I found that my feelings toward the story changed after reading this book; it wasn't simply that these were bad guys and this was how they did it; it was why they did it. And they're not all necessarily bad. It was a very complex human situation. I also felt, and this happens when you read certain books, that this would be a great movie story. There were lots of great characters and a page-turning plot. At this point in my career I was turning from writing fiction to writing screenplays, and had just finished *Union Dues* and parts of *Pride of the Bimbos*. Interestingly the literary agency I got to sell *Union Dues* had a deal with an agency on the west coast who called them to represent my books as screen properties. I didn't really write them for the screen but told them I did want to become a screenwriter. In turn they asked me to send them something I had written at which point I got off the phone and decided maybe I would adapt *Eight Men Out*. I think I was under the mistaken impression that maybe because I was a novelist my entry into films would be adapting books. I was wrong. They don't really care if you're a novelist out there in Hollywood. They think novelists are people who write books that they buy, and then overcharge them to write bad screenplays, and then grouse about the movie once its released. In Hollywood you almost have to whisper that you've written novels.

So I adapted *Eight Men Out* and sent it out. It so happens that the head of the agency had been Asinof's agent back in 1963 and was familiar with the material. He said I had done a fine job but to forget about doing the picture; the rights were in litigation.

Q: *How involved was Eliot with you in writing the screenplay?*

A: I didn't meet Eliot or talk to him until he came to the set while we were shooting and he played a part. I felt that with the screenplay the job was to take that book and somehow make a two-hour movie of it. I was definitely interested in telling the story of *Eight Men Out*. So I didn't think Eliot would be too bent out of shape by it. I'm sure he had his trepidations because he had been through court and a lot of other troubles. And people had always wanted to romanticize the story, make it more of a vehicle for one or two stars where Eliot always wanted the story he had told to come out. I think he ended up being pretty happy with the screenplay because it tried to tell the story as he had depicted it. I'm sure, like everyone, he asked, "How is this going to work as a movie?" because the screenplay is very dense and complex. This is a movie that, until you see it with the music, crowd sound, and rhythm you really don't know if it's going to work or not. There's a lot of moviemaking to it.

Q: *What part did you think the 1920 White Sox team would play in your film adaptation of the story? After all, the team was better than the 1919 Champs, yet played the season under a shroud of controversy.*

A: If we had done a mini-series I could've covered that part of the story. It would've taken at least six hours. With only two hours to work with dramatically I couldn't take a side trip into the 1920 season. For one thing I would've had to introduce a couple of new characters. For one, Red Faber, a pitcher who had hurt his arm in 1919 and would've probably torpedoed the fix because the gamblers would have realized that bagging two of four starting pitchers wouldn't fix a nine game series (though it could alter an individual game or two), but not the whole series. It seems that during 1920 the gamblers were still into Cicotte and Williams or they were into the gamblers and games were thrown. It's very unclear as to whether they were getting a lot of money or just a few bucks and a lot of threats. Eliot told me that a lot of the guys he talked to were still afraid of the gamblers, even though the gamblers were long in the grave. The idea was simply that you just didn't mess with these people.

Q: *What did you talk about with Edd Roush when he came to the set?*

A: Well, some of the players were there, we were shooting the train interior scenes in Kentucky across the river from Cincinnati, and they mostly asked him questions about playing baseball in those days. What was the ball like? Who was the toughest pitcher? He was a crusty old guy, full of . . . "Oh, these guys today can't play." He told of catching balls that were flat on one side because the dead ball really was dead and he never tried to hit home runs because his only hope was a couple of inside the park jobs per season . . . balls bouncing through the fence or whatnot. He played extremely shallow center field and had to stay on his toes to avoid giving up any such homers himself. If you had a good day in his era you knew you'd end up on your ass the next. It was a much tougher game. Regarding the Black Sox he contended that he heard guys arguing in the hotel room next door and went to his manager who asked if he had been approached by gamblers. Roush hadn't but Hod Eller apparently had been approached in an elevator and told the gambler to get the hell away from him or he'd punch him out. Roush's contention was that the Sox only threw the first game. When I asked him why Lefty Williams got tossed out of baseball if they only threw the first game, he said, "Aw, I don't know, maybe he was in on the meetings." So he was still holding onto the notion that the Reds would've won anyway and the Sox only threw one game on purpose. He was on the way to the airport and didn't have much time to talk with us, but a bunch of the guys who were playing ballplayers got a chance to meet and talk with him which was nice.

Q: *What feelings do you have about the contention, held by some, that Joe Jackson belongs in the Hall of Fame?*
A: Well, that is really up to the Hall of Fame to define themselves about what they're about. If they're about character, he was actually considered a very good guy when he went back home to Brandon Mills, but he made a big mistake that had to do with baseball. If the Hall is just about stats then he's in, but if the Hall is about character as related to baseball then you have to realize that he did sell out games and confessed to the act and therefore shouldn't be selected. If he were enshrined there should be so many asterisks around his name that his plaque wouldn't be included in the same room with the others.

Q: *Have you ever contacted any of the relatives of the players?*
A: Not really, although the granddaughter of Swede Risberg was an extra when we filmed a racing scene down in Kentucky. But she really didn't know about it. She indicated that her father never talked about it. I also ran into a guy who had Swede Risberg's son, the woman's father, as a gym coach and he once asked him if Swede was his father. The coach, who was also a pretty hard guy, just clammed up. We did get a nice letter from a woman whose husband had just suffered a stroke and was one of the bat-boys for the Sox. The letter said that he didn't know about the fix but that the players were screaming at each other on the field which wasn't usual for that club. Even though many of the players disliked each other their

normal behavior was to keep their ill feelings to themselves and ignore one another. She also mentioned that he didn't attend a major league game for over thirty years following the scandal because he felt he was sold out by his buddies.

Q: *Isn't it true that Ring Lardner left the baseball beat in 1919 for much the same reasons?*
A: Well, he had already kind of left before 1919 because in many ways he had outgrown baseball. He wasn't a sports reporter anymore; he was writing short stories and musicals. He just returned to cover the series and maybe an occasional boxing match. I think what soured him on baseball even more than the scandal was the rabbit ball. He didn't think it was baseball.

Q: *What, if anything, would you have done differently if you'd had more money or time to spend on the film?*
A: Actually the only thing that I would change would be to make the coverage of baseball more three dimensional. Certainly if we had unlimited money and I felt like it was worth spending we could have paid extras enough that they wouldn't have stayed away and therefore we could have shot beautiful vistas of full grandstands from the outfield in. We only had enough money to pay extras twenty dollars per day and we never got more than one thousand people in a day. Usually we had around two hundred people. That limits your shots towards the stands. Then we couldn't take down all the light standards in Bush Stadium in Indianapolis; we could only take down the center ones. So we had to keep moving this stupid smokestack around to look like a factory in the background. If you really paid attention and stopped the movie on a video freeze frame, you could see that the stack was always moving around, in both ballparks. When we shot from the dugout there's always a coach blocking another light standard we couldn't take down. To top it off the Pan Am Games used the park and a field across the street so that even more light standards were erected that we couldn't touch. If we'd had the money we could've removed all the lights and had far more leeway in shooting towards the outfield. We couldn't move the camera that much, so we had to be very, very careful. Otherwise we would reveal empty seats and modern lights. It all turned out fine because we had time to consider each shot, but would have pre-

ferred to use wider lenses instead of long lenses. I wanted to avoid the telephoto look you get in modern baseball. There are no shots from center field, with the pitcher stacked up against the catcher. That was just too modern for me.

Q: *How closely did you and your staff work with historians and the people at the Hall of Fame?*

A: We had a researcher and I had been doing a bunch of research on the era since doing *Matewan*. We were already experts on subjects such as train interiors and things like that. Our researcher was in daily contact with the archivists at the Hall of Fame. They were able to send us information about the look of the uniforms if they didn't already have a 1919 version. They sent us a rule book, programs, newspapers, and the names and numbers of collectors from across the country who had access to loads of great items. We ended up borrowing a score of gloves, bats, shoes, chest protectors and the like in order to shoot the film. We even hired a shoemaker especially to make spikes for the players.

Much of the equipment used in the film was original stuff from 50, 60, 70 years ago. Needless to say, it was tough to keep everyone equipped all the time. We used a lot of safety pins and tape! Because of our research we also changed the script regarding topics such as mass communications. For example the scene where the boys are using a crystal set depicts the kids picking a crude morse code account of the games.

Q: *In the final scene of* Eight Men Out *you show Joe Jackson playing in Hoboken—did he actually play there?*

A: I imagine he did play in Hoboken in a Jersey semipro league. In Eliot's book he played for Bogota, New Jersey, which isn't far from Hoboken. If we had put Bogota on his jersey, seeing the short scene in which this occurs, I was afraid that people would've thought that he was playing in South America. I didn't want people to think... "Oh the poor guy... Why isn't he speaking Spanish?" or "Where are the palm trees?" Hoboken, better than anyplace else, puts his feet squarely in New Jersey.

Q: *What are some of your other favorite baseball stories? If you were ever to do another baseball film which story would you select?*

A: I think somebody should take another crack at the Jim Thorpe story. He certainly found the beginning and end of his athletic career in baseball.

I think Christy Mathewson would also be another great subject. There was a book which got sort of esoteric about Mathewson called *The Celebrant* which includes some interesting material. The dynamics of his relationship with John McGraw are especially interesting. Of course McGraw knew about the 1919 fix. This reminds me of an anecdote about Comiskey who was asked by a journalist after the second game of the Series if he had "seen anything" to which the Old Roman replied "what do you mean by anything?" I don't doubt that he had bets down on the Series too!

# Independent Sayles-man

NANCY SCOTT/1991

BECAUSE HE MAKES MOVIES about problems nobody knows how to solve, there is the expectation that John Sayles is going to be a forbidding kind of guy. Austere. Remote.

There is also the expectation, having seen him act in his own movies, that he is built on Paul Bunyan lines.

Well, that part's right—Sayles is 6-foot-4 and two ax-handles wide across the shoulders. For the rest—he is unassuming, amiable and plain-spoken. He shares the conversation about his latest movie—*City of Hope*—with his long-time companion, Maggie Renzi, co-producer of the film (with Sarah Green), and Renzi has at least as much to say as he does. If either owns an outsize ego, he, or she, left it at home.

Asked about "Shannon's Deal," the TV series for which he wrote a number of scripts—a show praised by the critics and killed by the network—he shrugs, makes a gesture of resignation, is more interested in talking about *City of Hope*.

His sixth movie as an independent writer-director, Sayles made it on a budget of $3.1 million, a puny price in today's movie market.

Set in a small American city (between 50,000 and 500,000, says Sayles), it boasts a cast of Dickensian size and variety, flesh and blood representatives of issues enough for three movies: education, housing, poverty, racism, homophobia, crime, graft, patronage. The plot encompasses urban politics

---

From *The San Francisco Examiner,* 23 October 1991. Reprinted by permission.

and corruption on a large scale, connects them to personal decisions and individual action on a small scale.

The hope of the title is an ambiguous possibility, not an inspirational statement.

Sayles has no answer to the question: What's to be done about our cities? He has no solutions. If he did, says Renzi, "He'd be running for office, wouldn't he?"

"Or I'd be making them up," says Sayles. "One of the problems we have, people say, is 'So what was your point with this movie?' I think that's because they're used to: 'The moral of this story is blank.'

"I just want people to be thinking about these things when they leave, and the difficulty of them, and possibly having some sympathy for the people who have to make those hard decisions . . . one of those decisions of loyalty—those are the most difficult decisions you have to make."

Sayles' conversation frequently sounds like a miniature screenplay, peppered with lines spoken by himself and by other people, real or imagined. " 'OK, I've signed on with this group,' " he says, inventing a decision-maker. " 'Or, I was born into this group, and here's a decision where I may have to go against their interests for the interests of the whole. What are my loyalties to the whole? What are my loyalties as an American citizen?' "

These are not questions posed by your ordinary life-in-the-city movie with its lonely hero amid the faceless crowd. Says Renzi: "It's not about anonymity, is it? But about, what tribe do you belong to? . . . Are you black, are you a councilman, are you a husband, are you a mother, are you a welfare mother, are you a concerned mother? Where do you want to team up?"

Says Sayles: "One of the important things about this movie was to show that within each of these camps, each of these tribes—whether it's the police department, which is its own tribe, or the black community or the Italian community—there are some very important, very extreme gradations of opinion."

Camp, tribe, community: To one degree or another, these ideas have informed each of Sayles' movies. His first, *The Return of The Secaucus Seven* (1980), an elegy to the ideals of the 1960s, won him a faithful following among the '60s generation.

Thereafter came movies that are wildly diverse in subject: *Lianna* (about a lesbian), *Baby, It's You* (middle-class girl, working-class guy), *The Brother From Another Planet* (a black extra-terrestrial crash-lands in New York harbor), *Matewan* (coal miners on strike in West Virginia) and *Eight Men Out* (the Black Sox scandal of 1919).

For Sayles and Renzi, the idea of community does not exist in an aesthetic vacuum; it extends to the process of moviemaking. "We try to get rid of rank as much as we can on a movie set," says Sayles. "We try to have function because that's how you move efficiently. So, definitely the cinematographer tells the first assistant camera operator what to do, but that doesn't mean that they live in different hotels and get different meals and you don't learn one's name and not learn the other's name.

"Also, I think, it gets into the style that we shoot and the style that I write, which is the idea that there are no truly secondary characters; there are people with smaller parts, but they are, you hope, three-dimensional people as well as the primary characters."

Says Renzi: "All of the movies are certainly communities; it's where our friends come from. . . . It's a very personal experience. It's how I met Sarah; it's why Sarah became my partner."

Of the 52 actors in *City of Hope,* 24 have worked with Sayles before, including Vincent Spano, Joe Morton and David Strathairn, and for each Sayles had a specific role in mind. He had a role for himself in mind, too, as Carl, a sleazy garage owner who runs a nice sideline in fenced goods and arson.

Says Sayles: "The joke on the set was, he was the guy who was going to get the spinoff TV series—'Carl's Place.'" Of his appearances in his own movies, often, though not always, as a villain, Sayles says: "I don't feel like I'm doing a Hitchcock thing. I have four screenplays written that I want to make as a director and there's not a role for me in any of them, but I was an actor before I was a writer or a director, and it's something that I like doing, and every once in a while there's a part where I feel like, 'Oh, I know how to play this.'"

A list of what Sayles has done over the years suggests that either he's really 63 years old, not 41 as listed, or a man of prodigious energy. In addition to his own screenplays, past and to come, he has written eight for other directors, a host of short stories, three novels and a nonfiction work on the making of *Matewan*. He has won a number of awards, including a MacArthur grant.

At present, he is writing a TV pilot based on *The Brother From Another Planet*—his one outright comedy—and he has a movie in the works to be filmed next spring in Louisiana.

Renzi says that it's about a soap opera actress who's paralyzed in a taxi accident—"after getting her legs waxed." When the laughter dies down, she says, "It's about her relationship with her caretaker, and it's a comedy."

Says Sayles: "We hope."

# Sayles Talk

DAVID BARON/1991

JOHN SAYLES'S PANORAMIC *City of Hope* is a raw and sometimes bitter drama of urban discontent. Its fictional metropolis of Hudson City, N.J., is beset with virtually every ailment currently afflicting urban centers: crime, official corruption, drug abuse and a failing educational system are some of the roots of a malaise whose symptoms include ugly racial and ethnic tensions and police brutality.

Yet while most of the lives he chronicles in the sprawling 2¼-hour ensemble piece are lives of quiet (or not-so-quiet) desperation, the maverick writer-director, a citizen of big cities for nearly all his 41 years, says he isn't ready to throw in the towel on behalf of urban America.

"Life involves compromises," Sayles said in an interview last week, "but I certainly didn't mean the film's title ironically. Yes, I believe there is hope in Hudson City."

Sayles proclaimed himself an optimist in spite of the smoldering conflicts his film details because he believes "every positive act of compassion" on the part of an individual attempting to cope with frustration or injustice "is magnified as its effects ripple out."

Ultimately, he feels, cities are organic entities whose citizens are interdependent in ways they may be utterly unaware of . . . and he explained that he tried to suggest this odd linkage in *Hope* via an editing style that reflects the seemingly random connections among 38 characters.

---

From *The Times-Picayune,* 26 October 1991. Reprinted by permission.

"I wanted the feeling that these were parallel stories that eventually converge," Sayles said. "The film is like a knot. Everyone is tied up together. I wanted people to be able to tell—in part by the way it is shot—that there's no way these people can avoid affecting each other, even if they've never met."

Sayles's editing technique "is hardly original," he elaborated. "Orson Welles used it in the opening shot of *Touch of Evil,* and Max Ophuls used it in such films as *La Ronde.* What I'm interested in in my movies is how the hero fits into his world, so I like to pay attention to the background of the story as well as to what's up front.

"That usually means making ensemble pictures," Sayles admitted, conceding that spurning time-honored studio formulas (like the one that frowns on ensemble casts) inherently involves taking risks.

"People hesitate at the notion of a lot of characters," he said. "They really do want to have it as simple as 'the hero, the girl and the enemy,' and when you ask them to do more, they resist."

Sayles, to his credit, consistently asks them to do more—in movies (such as *Return of the Secaucus Seven, Matewan* and *Eight Men Out*) that often defy conventional filmmaking wisdom. And his generally uneasy relations with Hollywood testify to the less-than-spectacular grosses those movies have tended to generate at the box office.

"We flirted with each other for a while, the studios and I," Sayles remembered. "We even went steady for maybe a week." The filmmaker chuckled, recalling for a reporter his 1983 battle with executives over the studio-backed *Baby, It's You.* But in the end, he said, both parties' attempts at seduction failed, and the Sayles of 1991 reported he's content to remain a lone wolf unless (or until) he reaches the point where a major studio is willing to allow him "total freedom"—i.e., the liberties a Spike Lee or a Woody Allen is permitted in shaping a movie (from casting to final cut) entirely according to his whims.

The Schenectady (N.Y.)-born, Williams-educated Sayles said he's lived in cities like the one depicted in the film for most of his life, including stints "in east Boston during the busing crisis, in Atlanta when they had their first black mayor, and in Albany, N.Y., near the end of the reign of the Democratic machine that had ruled for decades." He said he chose a densely populated northeastern metropolis for his fictional Hudson City "because push comes to shove a lot quicker in those cities where people are really crowded together."

Encouraged to create a metaphor for urban politics, Sayles expressed the idea that "a circular chain of race, class, family ties, personal ambition, past history and conflicting loyalties serve to force people apart, (while) romantic and familial love, idealism and shared hopes for the future bring them together.

"What I have found," he added, "is that once you get below the national level, politics is as much about family, personal connections and culture as it is about ideology. And one of the main points in *City of Hope* is that even within each tribe—Italian Americans, African Americans, whatever—there's a lot of internal dissension, a lot of differences of opinion.

"Not all black people, and not all Irish people or Italian people or Chinese, think or believe the same way," he said. "There are a lot of divided loyalties, and it's when you begin to recognize that people are individuals that you begin to get a handle on how a city works."

# John Sayles

## CLAUDIA DREIFUS/1991

JOHN SAYLES MANAGES TO do what no one else does in the world of the cinema: He calls his own shots, writing, directing, financing, and editing movies about the hidden corners of American life. In an industry in which *Terminator 2* is the money-cow ideal, the forty-one-year-old Sayles somehow pulls off wonderful small pictures on themes that the rest of movieland ignores. *Baby, It's You,* his only major-studio production, sheds warm light on the big American secret—social class. His classic *Return of the Secaucus Seven* looks at a group of 1960s activists at midlife, still grasping for their ideals. *Matewan,* his masterpiece, concerns a coal miners' strike in West Virginia.

And this fall, we'll see Sayles's newest offering, *City of Hope,* a brawny meditation on modern urban politics. Like most of his work, this new one is gritty, tense, and complex, discarding the Hollywood formula of likable characters and happy endings. In many ways, it's a companion piece to Spike Lee's *Do the Right Thing* and, as in Lee's films, there are few heroes.

Sayles also writes novels and short stories. HarperCollins recently published *Los Gusanos,* a broadly drawn epic about Miami Cubans who, like the characters in *Return of the Secaucus Seven,* are desperately clinging to their ideals. He wrote *Los Gusanos* over a twelve-year period in between film shoots. It briefly made several regional bestseller lists, and will appear in paperback next summer.

---

Sayles met me on a sweltering summer afternoon in an Italian restaurant in Poughkeepsie, New York. Long based in Hoboken, New Jersey, he and his companion, Maggie Renzi, had just moved to a farm in upstate New York so he could work in an atmosphere of serenity. He picked a restaurant for the interview because he is an insistent guardian of his privacy and wouldn't meet in his home. Or even near it. Over pasta and Diet Cokes, though, John Sayles was ebullient and open.

Q: City of Hope *is about the disintegration of a big-city political structure—and about the competing ethnic forces waiting to scavenge the spoils. It's a real 1990s kind of story, the kind of story being acted out in New York City as we speak. After spending so much time on movies rooted in the past, did you finally want to do a story more of this moment?*

JOHN SAYLES: No, I don't really think in those terms. *Baby, It's You* is supposed to be a young girl who goes from high school to college, from the 1950s to the 1960s in one jump. But in a lot of places, the 1950s never died. I go back home to where I grew up in upstate New York and there are people still listening to the current equivalent of Chuck Berry, which is heavy metal, and working on their cars. As to whether *City of Hope* is about the 1990s or not, I think it's about different cities at a different stage.

This city is in its Tammany Hall period. The main ethnic group is controlling the politics, but their numbers are gone. Their constituency has moved, and patronage has become a very ugly thing because it's a one-way street. There's no delivery anymore. For the Irish, the Italians, and the Jews, patronage worked, moving people into the system at the turn of the century. But then there comes the point where it's not working. They are stealing whatever isn't nailed down, and they know their days are numbered, and they are just stripping the city of whatever is left.

You see this a lot in Detroit and in Jersey. Look at Detroit. What's left of it? The old group is saying, "Now you [blacks] can have the city—what's left of it." The new group is always faced with the fact that the previous group took the office furniture. *City of Hope* is not about the 1990s. It's about a kind of system that's been going on since, I'm sure, the 1800s in this country of ethnic groups. What's 1990s about it is that, all of a sudden, black and Hispanic people are getting their shot at power. In *City of Hope,* the blacks don't have the numbers to take over the city. They will only get to take over their ward.

Q: *You are one of the few directors around who's telling these kinds of stories.*
SAYLES: Or who's getting to.

Q: *How do you feel about being one of the few who gets to make movies about coal miners, 1960s activists, academic lesbians, and now urban politicos?*
SAYLES: Well, it's unconscious. I'm not consciously saying, "This is what *they* are doing, so I will do something different." I'm a writer. I write stuff and then I realize, "This doesn't really fit into any genre." Usually, when I have to pitch a script to a potential backer, I have to tell the story. I find I can't say, "This is a cross between *Rambo* and *Missing*." My pieces tend to be in-between genres. They tend to be about characters, about situations, rather than, say, "an action-adventure-police story." So the stories that I happen to be interested in telling are that way.

Q: *How do you manage to be a man with a 1960s consciousness who is directing?*
SAYLES: I think I've been very lucky. For one thing, my bread job—writing movies for other people—was a lucrative one. So even when I first started and was getting "scale," that was $10,000 a movie. Most people's bread job is waiting tables or teaching in some form, where you make a base pay of $10,000 a year. I can write a genre picture and do a bunch of those a year—so even when I was just getting scale, I could make $50,000 in one year. It only took me two years to get up enough money to do *Return of the Secaucus Seven*. I financed that picture myself. I financed *The Brother From Another Planet* myself. I was one of the major investors in *Matewan*. So rather than making that one independent film and having to sit around for another five years till someone gave me the money to do another one, I've been able to put myself back into the game by financing my films myself.

Q: *So when there's a story you want to shoot, you'll write a TV movie and then, voila, you've got seed money?*
SAYLES: Yeah. Or I'll doctor a script for someone else. And that's fun as a technician. It's not something you're going to put your soul into—because it's somebody else's story. When it's done, at least I have the money to get my own film started. With *Lianna*, we started out needing to raise a budget of $800,000. We ended up making it for $300,000, of which I put up $30,000. Now most people I know, when they start to make movies, don't have

$30,000; $30,000 is as tough to raise as $3 million, if you're talking people into it. So that's one thing: I've had that economic advantage.

Q: *About* Return of the Secaucus Seven*: Were you yourself active during the 1960s?*

SAYLES: Certainly. But only as a foot soldier. I was at events with 30,000 other people. On marches and things like that. I went to Williams College.

Q: *Williams? I had the impression you came from a grittier background, that your family was more blue-collar.*

SAYLES: It's a long story how I went there. I really didn't know if I wanted to go to college, but I ended up there. I knew I really didn't want to be in the Army, whether there was a war or not. When the antiwar stuff happened, I would occasionally participate.

Williams was an elite school, but in a funny way. It wasn't very competitive. I had a guidance counselor say to me, "Here's two places I want you to apply—Williams and Colgate." I ended up feeling like, if I went to Colgate, they'd want me to play serious football, and I had played much-too-serious football in high school already. So my place of education was accidental. Williams was the kind of place that, when the black kids took over the administration building, the first thing the white college president did was make sure they had enough food.

Q: *Were you involved in a march on Washington where a deer got killed en route? "Bambicide," you call it in* Return of the Secaucus Seven.

SAYLES: No, but we did get stopped on a couple of marches by cops, on the general theme of "I know where these guys are going—let's stop them and search for drugs." The people the film is based on are not so much people I knew in college but people I knew afterwards, when I was living in East Boston. I knew a lot of people who were involved in the little city halls there, a bunch who had known each other in the 1960s.

Q: *No doubt you saw* The Big Chill*, which many critics noted was about a group of ex-1960s types getting together for a long weekend reunion, just like* Return of the Secaucus Seven.

SAYLES: It's a different movie. It's called *The Big Chill* for a reason. It's a film about people who have either lost their ideals or are realizing they never had them in the first place. *Secaucus Seven* is about people who are desperately, desperately trying to hold onto their ideals. That's a very different group. *Chill* people are more upper-middle-class. The *Secaucus* group is more lower-middle-class; some of them are probably the first people in their families who went to a four-year college. And they've chosen to be downwardly mobile. The movie I think *Return of the Secaucus Seven* most resembles is a French one, *For Jonah, Who Will Be Twenty-five in the Year* 2000. It was the precursor.

Q: *Come on, admit it. Surely you felt a bit... cribbed by* The Big Chill. *The structure and the idea seem so similar: A group of ex-1960s folks get together for a long weekend and wonder what they did with their lives.*
SAYLES: No. I actually didn't have any big problem with it. I thought it was a more-thoughtful-than-usual Hollywood movie. It's very much about people who do exist. It's just that they weren't my friends. It was not a rip-off. There's too much thought, and too much feeling, in that movie. [Director Larry Kasdan] sees the world differently. It was more: "Here's what happens when the people *I know* get together for a three-day weekend."

Q: *But again, you're about the only bona fide member of the 1960s generation making movies. How come?*
SAYLES: I don't think I'm the only one. Brian De Palma, Martin Scorsese—they were very much of that moment and then they grew into doing different things. What was one of De Palma's first films—*Greetings?*—about, the draft? Besides, I keep running into these people who used to be in the Weather Underground who are producers now.

Q: *You're often compared to Spike Lee. Is that fair?*
SAYLES: Well, he's doing things that nobody else was interested in doing for a long time. But he's been much more successful at getting out to a large audience than I have. He's doing pretty much what he wants to do and still reaching some kind of mass audience. It's not the mass audience that something like *Terminator 2* reaches, but he's working on studio budgets now, and that's a real achievement: to be able to do that and still make the movie you want to make.

We've talked about my being the only one making these kinds of movies. I find that in this country there's a real suspicion of content. Sometimes, a real resentment of content. Some of it came out of the *auteur* theory. There is a whole raft of movie critics who basically feel: Okay, what we treasure a film director, an *auteur,* for is his ability to put his stamp on any material. The minute you're talking about that, you're automatically talking about *style.* On the other hand, there's a much smaller group of people who only care about content and whether you're politically correct or not.

I'm sure that Sam Goldwyn Sr. said a lot of intelligent things, but the one that we always quote is, "If you want to send a message, call Western Union." Haskell Wexler and I were talking about this once. He said, "All films are political." I agreed. I said, "*Beverly Hills Cop II* is a political film." If you look at it, it's about attitudes toward women and violence, and it says a lot. But nobody would look at the director of *Beverly Hills Cop II* and say, "Hey, that's a political film." Because those are mainstream values, so no one notices them.

If you're working in the mainstream media, if you're going to story conferences, what almost always gets scarified is *content.* Because they distrust it. Because it almost always is secondary to making this great arcade ride that the people are going to pay money to get on.

Q: *You're still telling stories that no one else is, and you're constantly breaking formulas. In* Matewan, *the good guys lose and the community is shattered. That's against the Hollywood formula of happy endings for the protagonists.*
SAYLES: In *Matewan,* the hero does not pick up a gun, and that was a problem most mainstream moviegoers had with it. "Now wait a minute," they'd go. "The hero really is a pacifist. He's not going to turn out be a guy who's a great shot and who takes his gun off the wall."

In so many Westerns—*Shane*—that's the tension of the story. This guy has decided he's pacifist and there's this thrill in the audience when he finally straps his gun on one more time. It's a difficult thing to fight. When we were creating the film, it was hard to create a guy who is telling people something that might get them killed. We gave him a speech; he said, "Look, the way things are now, the coal owners are just waiting for a chance to tromp you. Yes. If you pick up the gun, you'll give them that excuse. If you do that, the war is going to start and you're going to lose."

Q: *And they do—and that's what happens in* Matewan. *But to change the subject, you've just published a novel about Cuban-Americans in Miami,* Los

Gusanos. *How is writing a book different? It must be a place where you have total control; after all, as the writer, you're God.*
SAYLES: Well, I don't have to worry about how we can afford extras! In *Los Gusanos,* I do the Bay of Pigs invasion and I don't have to worry about how we get the tanks and the extras—all those practical things that make a movie difficult. What you don't have in a book is all the fun of a collaboration, and I do think movies are collaborative, *auteur* theory aside.

Q: *You wrote* Los Gusanos *between movies. How did you keep your concentration?*
SAYLES: As far as research went, I never left the novel. Thirteen years ago, I had an outline, which I pretty much kept to. What I did was write the first few chapters and then I couldn't go on without much more research. So I did movies, and research while I did the movies. Whenever I'd run into people who were Cuban-Americans, I'd talk to them and that got filed. There were two long Writers Guild strikes and during them I worked on fiction. And then finally, after I finished *Matewan,* I took a year off and finished it.

But you know, nothing I've done is a career move. Every project, from the movies to the novel, were things I wanted to do. It's not, "How do I get myself to the point where I am going to be in the Hollywood system?" I never thought, "If I take a year off, I'll lose where I am." Being a fiction writer is a nice net to have. If I have to spend two years when I can't get a movie off the ground, I can always write novels.

Q: *About* Los Gusanos, *I had this feeling that one of the things that appeals to you about Cuban-Americans is their commitment to a cause.*
SAYLES: To me, the important spectrum in *Los Gusanos* is not right-wing or left-wing, because most of the people are right of center. It's between "believers" and "cynics." A lot of what I'm dealing with is how do you still act once you know too much to be a true believer.

I'm interested in commitment, in how do we still have commitment. I have a character in the book who was in the Lincoln Brigade, and I have a lot of respect for those guys. In this nursing home in the book, you have this guy who's a veteran of the Lincoln Brigade right next to this guy who was in the Bay of Pigs.

My question is how do you keep commitment once you *know*? How do you not get cynical?

Q: *Were your folks movie buffs?*

SAYLES: Readers. They really encouraged us to read. Both of my parents were teachers, and then my father became a school administrator later on. And both of their fathers were cops. The main way my parents were influential is just that they encouraged us to read a lot and they didn't lay on any big trips about, "This is what you are supposed to be or do." Enough people in my family did things they didn't like, and they didn't want us to do that. I wanted to be a pitcher for the Pittsburgh Pirates.

When I got out of college, it was a bad time to get a job. I ended up working in nursing homes and factories, because that was something I had done before. If I had gone into anything else that paid a little more, the employers would have said, "You know, you're signing up for the long run. We want people who will be here for fifteen years and be happy about it." I wasn't interested in that. I worked as an orderly because it definitely was not a career decision.

In the entertainment industry, when I went into it, I was only interested in it for the work. I wasn't interested in getting a big house. All I was interested in was, "I think it would be really great to make movies. This is the kind of storytelling that I really like. How do I get to do that and do that on my terms?"

At first I worked for [B-movie mogul] Roger Corman, and it was really fun. It was the equivalent of working in a hospital. You didn't have to take it home. Nobody took themselves that seriously. They worked hard. Nobody fought about, "What does this movie mean?" What you knew was that every ten pages, or every fifteen pages, you were going to have some kind of animal attack and it's meant to be fun.

Q: *You seem so nonchalant about what you do, as if it's as natural as breathing air. Most film directors I've met are religious about their profession.*

SAYLES: I'm *not* nonchalant. I'm interested in the stuff I do being seen as widely as possible—but I'm not interested enough to lie. There comes a time in any story when you say, "I know how to make this more popular." But then, it's bullshit. I have worked on movies that were basically fantasy movies—where you try not to say things you don't believe in and you can do it because the whole thing is really about the genre. For instance, read the script of *Alligator*, if it's about anything other than being a kind of monster movie in the almost classic Japanese tradition, it is about how social problems start in the lower classes and nobody is really dealing with them until they start eating the rich people.

*Battle Beyond the Stars,* to me, is about death, but finally it is just *The Seven Samurai Go to Space.* That's what was handed to me to write and that's why people watch it. That's what Roger gave me to do. *Battle Beyond the Stars* is about how these different creatures feel about death.

Conversation is what I'm ambitious about, being a part of that. To a certain extent, so many mainstream movies are just consumable items. They aren't things people can remember and apply to their lives. I think, in general, consciousness is a really important thing and that's one of the reasons I'm glad I work in the consciousness industry. In a cumulative way, movies do have an effect. If you don't like the effect they are having, maybe you can do something to counteract it. At least you can be part of the conversation.

To me, the important thing is the conversation. The important thing is to get that moment when someone in the audience thinks, "I have never spent time with the people in this movie," and then they realize that, because of the movie, they have.

# Where the Hope Is: An Interview with John Sayles

GARY CROWDUS AND LEONARD QUART/1991

CINEASTE: City of Hope *presents a bleak but realistic view of contemporary urban political corruption. What message would you like the viewer to take away from the film?*

JOHN SAYLES: To me, one of the most distressing things happening in the world today is a breaking down into tribalism. You see it in Yugoslavia, you're going to see it in the Soviet Union, and you certainly see it here. It's something that's been encouraged from above, the idea that, "Look, we can't take care of each other, it's everybody for themselves, and may the best man win. If a few of you fall out at the bottom, well, that's tough." That encourages a kind of tribalism which you see in old alliances and old tolerances breaking down, and so you get very strong movements within tribes. In *City of Hope* you see the black tribe, the Italian tribe, and the police force who are always their own tribe. I want people to think about those hard decisions of how you consider yourself. What I talked with Joe Morton a lot about in terms of his character was, "OK, am I a man of principle first, a black man second, city councilor third, and husband fourth? Or do those shift around? Is there a point where there are things more important than what's good for my ward? . . . because I'm also a city councilor who's supposed to be talking about the whole city."

I've lived in lots of cities with this kind of politics. I've lived in Albany, New York, which had the longest running Democratic machine, even longer than the Daly machine in Chicago. I've lived in East Boston, and

From *Cineaste,* December 1991. Reprinted by permission.

I've lived in Atlanta, right when they had their first black mayor. It's a very familiar idea that you can piece together coalitions among tribes and that within their little areas they will all get along and the whole will work. Well, it doesn't always work that way. People have to transcend that family blood, that tribal blood. What I'd like viewers to come away with is a sense of what has to be done, that help doesn't come from above very often—you know, at the end the homeless guy is saying, "Help! Help! Help!" People themselves have to find ways to make those bridges.

CINEASTE: *By the end of the film, Wynn, the Joe Morton character, seems to realize that he must master the art of politics as compromise. Do you feel that, in trying to deal with often conflicting demands for justice in society today, it's impossible for one to be an effective politician and at the same time remain a decent human being?*
SAYLES: It's really hard. That's what some of the Joe Morton characterization is about, that politicians are human beings, too, and the best of them do a balancing act between being a leader and being somebody who just listens to his constituency, including all their prejudices and fears and their reluctance to go forward and be progressive. Franklin Roosevelt, for example, did a lot of good stuff but he was also a machine politician. That's how he got in. If you look at most politicians who have been progressive in any way, you see points in their careers where they really just voted the status quo. Now and then you get a secure politician like Teddy Kennedy whose voting record is excellent, partly because he doesn't have to worry about being reelected. He had it in the bag and he knew it for so many years that he was able to vote his conscience.

Yes, it is a very difficult thing, and you hope that in ten years Wynn won't be the mayor [*laughs*], or at least won't be like Mayor Baci, whether he's the mayor or not. He's realizing what the former black mayor tells him on the golf course, that "This isn't about testing your personal moral fiber. It will be tested, but that's not all it's about."

CINEASTE: *The key incident in the film is a kind of riff on the Tawana Brawley affair. Did you feel that to be an important political point to make?*
SAYLES: The point of that—and I didn't actually follow the Tawana Brawley thing too carefully—is that, in today's overheated political climate, whether you're a black politician or a white politician, you have to

have an opinion about this kind of thing. It used to be enough to say, "Oh, that's a police matter. I'll let the police take care of that." Every time something happens now, the media call Dinkins, they call D'Amato, they call Spike Lee, and five other people who have to have an opinion, and they don't know shit about it. They weren't there, they haven't talked to the people in the neighborhood, and half the time they haven't even talked to the cops yet.

CINEASTE: *For some people that's not necessary.*
SAYLES: No, not at all.

CINEASTE: *They have prefigured judgements.*
SAYLES: Yeah, and one of the pressures on any black politician, as Wynn says in the film, is that, "At some point I'm going to be stood up in front of everybody and asked, 'Do you think those guys are lying?,' and that's a huge pressure to face, to realize I could lose votes over this."

CINEASTE: *Do you see the politics of the black community itself as an obstacle to progress?*
SAYLES: It's an obstacle and an opportunity. It's an obstacle to the extent that you have these factions fighting against each other. The film shows you the establishment politician, a guy who's in the middle range, and someone who's very much of a Muslim—a very newfound Muslim, so he's at his most doctrinaire. As I told Tom Wright, the actor who plays Malik, this is a guy who's really struggled in his life and he's just found religion, so he's at his most extreme. When people like that are pulling in different directions, it can be an obstacle to concerted effort or concerted voting, those kinds of things that help a tribe, a group, a minority, to develop some power within a majority structure.

The opportunity, on the other hand, is to take some of the energy and ideology from each of the factions to forge something very good. You say, "OK, we're stuck in this system, we have to learn how to work within it, but we can also use some of the militancy of these guys." You know, there's that line. "If you can't get respect, you settle for fear." That's what the Black Panthers were dealing with to a certain extent—"Hey, we're going to settle for fear at first, and maybe we'll get respect later." What they got was wiped out, but there's an opportunity there as well as a liability.

A more important factor than the fragmentation of the black community is just brute economic factors, and there isn't much chance for me to talk about that in the film. The mayor at one point says, "Look, this city is going down the toilet. Anybody with any brains is going to leave and let the blacks and Hispanics duke it out." If you look at Detroit and some of the other cities that now have black mayors, like East St. Louis, they're getting to run the city, but what's left?

CINEASTE: *There's nothing, no tax base.*

SAYLES: Yeah, and so the biggest obstacle to advancement of those people in cities is that, when they finally do get power, it's only because everybody else has abandoned the place, including the tax base. Another thing that is posited in this movie is that we can't expect each new group that takes power to reject patronage politics, to say, "We're going to be a meritocracy, we're not going to just hire our relatives and friends and the people who got us into office. We're going to hire some outside experts, even if they're white, you know, even if they're not from our group." It's just not going to happen and I don't think we can expect it to happen.

CINEASTE: *You have wedded the film's political mosaic to a family drama. What function do you see the relationships between Nick and Angela and Nick and his father playing in the context of the larger film?*

SAYLES: In a small city, and I've lived in lots of them, the tribalism gets to the family level. One of the most difficult things is to expect people to transcend family. When I was living in East Boston, it was "If the mayor doesn't get in, your cousin Louie is going to lose his job as a teacher's aide." In West Virginia, where we shot *Matewan*, half of the feuds were about that very thing, so if you got a sheriff in, all of a sudden you win the boundary dispute. Or if you get to be the vice sub-marshall or somesuch, then you get to collect graft from the guys who are moonshining. So it comes down to a family thing.

What's really awful about bureaucracy is that it's inhumane, and, on the other hand, there is this fallibility built into any kind of politics that includes personality, because people are fallible, and this is the reigning drama. What I wanted were these two countercurrents, with Wynn trying to get into something, trying to get more power, to become part of the establishment, in his mind to rise up, and then Vincent Spano's character,

Nick, trying to get out of it, but for whom there are these responsibilities. He's like a prince who's been born into this complicated Machiavellian society, and it's not that easy to get out.

CINEASTE: *In most of your films you usually don't go in for this kind of melodramatic confrontation. Why did you use it here?*
SAYLES: Well, it's what we kept calling the Arthur Miller part of the movie, which is that, once it gets down to family, things tend to be unavoidably melodramatic. There's a point where there's so much personal drama going on, which, although it's related to the larger story, is finally family drama, and it seemed artificial not to have some kind of resolution between these people. It's very emotional and very much tied into each other's business. This is more like *Lianna* in that it's more about the personal drama of power relationships—you know. "This is what he wanted me to be, but I'm not going to be that to punish him for what he did to my brother"—and all those kinds of things where you realize that there are bigger forces that Nick is fighting with. And those forces do eventually come down to two people who are related to each other battling it out.

CINEASTE: *Do you think that perhaps the character carries a little too much moral weight, that you're demanding too much moral resonance from him?*
SAYLES: Well, I don't know, because he's so confused. I see him as representing the third generation, where people work in the factory but they don't believe in the union anymore, or they're in the mob but they don't believe in the mob anymore. They don't have the drive that the generation before them or the original immigrant generation had. The first generation ended up with just enough to feed themselves and the hope that their kids would get educated so they could become more than their parents. The second generation is the one that said, "I'm going to prove that my pop was right," and they kill themselves to establish a business. With the third generation, you either get these disaffected people or you get somebody like Mario Cuomo or Doug Wilder, these guys who can say, "I had a lot of adversity and my parents had even more than me, but we're still moving forward." Well, Nick is someone who doesn't feel he's moving forward, this is the decay of that kind of politics. When that kind of politics has been in for a certain amount of time, you get that Tammany Hall period which produces a lot of moral casualties, and that is what I think

Nick, and to a certain extent his father, are. His father's still in the game, and he's doing things that he's realizing now are wrong, but his son is the moral casualty. Nick's not articulate enough or active in a sense of what he's going to do, he's just kind of reacting, and all he knows is that he wants out.

CINEASTE: *The only time he really seems to come alive with a sense of purpose is when he's courting Angela.*
SAYLES: Yeah, and the whole thing with that is that he's desperate for somebody who's taking responsibility, to be part of that. The things that she says that usually scare guys away—"I have this awful life, I have this crazy ex-boyfriend, I've got this kid with cerebral palsy"—make her even more attractive to him because she's a serious person. At first, she's just beautiful and then he realizes, "Wow, she's somebody who's taking care of business, which is what I haven't been doing for ten years."

CINEASTE: *You have a special gift for capturing the way sensitive but inarticulate people communicate to each other. There are two sequences with Nick and Angela that work wonderfully. Where does you ear for dialog come from?*
SAYLES: I think just listening, really, and having been in a lot of places. Somebody was talking to me about Cassavetes recently, and that's the one thing that he always worked for. He'd have a little improvisation, and then write it down, then improvise it some more, and write it down again.

CINEASTE: *He worked more from theatrical roots.*
SAYLES: Yeah, and mine I think comes from my novel writing, so I was doing it on paper when he was working it out theatrically.

CINEASTE: *What was your conception of Carl, the character you portray?*
SAYLES: My basic character thought for playing Carl was Jackie Presser, who was simultaneously working for the mob, the Teamsters, and the FBI. He had to keep juggling those interests, but he survived. And Carl will survive because he'll always be useful to the cops and he'll always be useful to the mob. Unless he pisses off someone like Vinnie, who just shoots him, he's politically put himself in a perfect position as a conduit for information, deals, and other stuff that gets done.

CINEASTE: *How would you compare your perspective on the police and the white working class to that in other recent urban movies like Spike Lee's* Do the Right Thing *and* Jungle Fever?

SAYLES: I like Spike's movies. I really think they're getting at stuff that needs getting at, but I always feel like I'm making movies out of my own experience and what I know, not reacting to other movies. The neighborhood in *Do the Right Thing* could be in *City of Hope*, and if I had chosen to be on just one side of L Street, I could have made something very much like that. From that perspective, the cops do look very much like they do in *Do the Right Thing*—as invaders who don't live in the community and who don't know anything about it. I'm trying to do a wider thing, so I want to get in the car with those guys and see where they're coming from. Both my grandfathers were cops, and I have lots of relatives who were cops. The police are a tribe but they do have disagreements among themselves.

CINEASTE: *There'd probably also be a diverse range of responses to the police among various members of the black community. Not everyone would see them as an occupying army.*

SAYLES: Sure, there'd be those people who say, "How come it takes so long for them to show up?" You know, the 911 is a joke idea. Why aren't they on our side and when they do come, why do they leave so many dead bodies?

CINEASTE: *But what we're getting at is that while Lee's is a black perspective, you're operating out of a different notion. The police are not shown as stereotypes, there's always a sense of ambiguity. If they're not fully individuated as characters, you at least get them in the round as nuanced social types.*

SAYLES: I have one older cop who says, "My father used to live in this building." And there are cops who say, "People steal stuff because they're poor, period. Not because they're bad, not because they're genetically predisposed, but because they're poor, and if they weren't poor they wouldn't steal stuff. My job, unfortunately, doesn't have anything to do with curing that, it just has to do with sorting out the survivors and making arrests."

When I had friends of mine from Jersey politics see the movie, the one thing they didn't believe was the cop in the car who refuses to go along with a coverup.

CINEASTE: *You mean the Hispanic cop?*
SAYLES: More than that he's Hispanic, he's a newcomer. These are new partners and it's an uneasy marriage. But the only thing they said is that, "I don't think that would happen," and that's a sad commentary.

CINEASTE: *It's reminiscent of Lumet's* Prince of the City, *where those codes are broken.*
SAYLES: The Italian guys I know say, "That's a bullshit movie. The only guy I had any respect for was the guy who shot himself." It's the idea that you don't rat on your friends, you take care of your own business. *City of Hope* also brings to mind *On the Waterfront* which deals with the same kind of divided loyalties, family vs. the greater good. *On the Waterfront* basically tries to have it both ways. First he rats, then they have a nice slugout so it looks as if he's not just a rat. He's also somebody who'll go in there and face physical danger and he gets to throw the guy in the water.

CINEASTE: *He also finds in some vague way a moral alternative to Johnny Friendly.*
SAYLES: To pure violence as the only way to do it. The message at the end of *New Jack City*, where the old guy shoots the drug dealer, is that what we need are better vigilantes. Most urban movies deal only with making it in the business world—the *Working Girl* type movie—or crime. *City of Hope* tries to deal with a lot of other things as well. Crime is one part of it but it's not the main part. You can't separate crime from urban life, especially because of what some of these characters are into, but it's not a gangster movie.

The only other American movie that this reminds me of more than *On the Waterfront* is *Force of Evil*. That's about numbers running, but it's about that sense of one guy who squeezes another who squeezes another. I think American filmmakers tend to be afraid of politics. I certainly find that in most of the reviews that I read. There's a whole raft of American film criticism that's anti-content, whether it's political or not, because they feel that it's a betrayal of pure film.

To get back to your other point, one thing that we tried to do with the Italian family is that the guys I know in construction do fairly well, if they're working, so we gave him a nice house. You know, everything isn't covered in plastic. The mother and father have a fairly good relationship, so they're not screaming at each other all the time, and waving their hands around and stuff like that. They're really becoming kind of upper middle class in income, and their roots have been sold in some ways, they've made these deals with the devil, and that has to come back to haunt them.

CINEASTE: *In your scripts for hire—like* Alligator *or* The Howling*—you do your best to deliver the genre goods, but in your own films you do your best to subvert or at least go against the grain of genre conventions. The result is a much more politically and emotionally challenging kind of work.* City of Hope *is not the feel good movie of the year.*
SAYLES: Yeah, we were thinking of calling it the feel bad movie of the year.

CINEASTE: *In this regard, have you resigned yourself to being a more socially conscious version of Woody Allen—with a smaller, more discerning, better educated type of audience—or do you think that Hollywood has sold short the mass moviegoing audience and that they can respond to and appreciate a higher quality film?*
SAYLES: What I know from having worked out there in various capacities is that if you want a mass audience for something like *City of Hope*, you hire stars. There's a selling aspect to all this, it's a product, and you want to get people into the theatre during its theatrical run, rather than insidiously creeping into their lives through video and cable TV, which is kind of the way that *Matewan* and some of our other movies got seen. The problem with trying to use stars is that there are very few of them who are also right for the part. Once you've started to invite people to the party who shouldn't be there, it changes the movie, and it's no longer what you wanted to make in the first place. There's usually a short list of stars who are right for the part—it may be two deep or only one deep—and we usually go through that list very quickly.

We've been lucky to get actors who don't necessarily sell tickets but who are considered names that people like to see, such as Tony Lo Bianco, James Earl Jones and Gloria Foster. These people could make a lot more money doing something else but they're willing to work with us because they think it's a good part and a good project.

CINEASTE: *What prognosis do you think your film makes for the future of the city?*

SAYLES: I think that some cities, because of the economic factors I mentioned, are doomed, especially small cities like Chelsea, Massachusetts, or Camden, New Jersey, or East St. Louis. There's just no money there and the federal government, which has taken a very Darwinian attitude toward their survival, is making no effort to help them. What's been happening—just kind of mindlessly in the economy but also with the support of people in power—is that since we need less and less people to run the things we really care about, the attitude toward those kind of body jobs is, "Let 'em go to Haiti, let 'em go to Costa Rica, let 'em leave." I think you pay for that eventually, because stuff like that just doesn't take care of itself, and in about five to seven years there's going to have to be some kind of conscious effort to find purpose and employment for people.

CINEASTE: *Do you see a kind of de facto apartheid?*

SAYLES: Well, what you're seeing is more and more communities which, out of their own pockets because they have the dough, pave their own streets, send their kids to their own schools, and start their own security forces. It's like the Philippines. If you move there, you're told right away that you have to have servants, a guard, and Dobermans, period. Because everybody else is so poor, and the government doesn't want to know about you, you've got to take care of protecting yourself. And if you don't have servants, people will throw shit at you on the streets, because it's your job to provide some employment.

I do feel that that is happening. If you go around some of those dying cities, you find communities like that. But you can't keep that down forever, and the hope is that the disenfranchised within those communities will have the energy and the talent and the intelligence to say, "OK, they abandoned us, but we'll run the show, we'll do something here. Things are fucked up, but we can take care of this block." If you go to the South Bronx, there's a couple of blocks where people just said, "Fuck it, we're going to make something out of this."

CINEASTE: *Like Kelly Street and community organizations like Banana Kelly that involve sweat equity efforts to restore buildings.*

SAYLES: And you wish there were more of these people and that they got more encouragement when they're starting out.

CINEASTE: *So you wouldn't say that the cities are beyond redemption?*

SAYLES: No. There is hope. The title is not only ironic. They're not getting any help from above, but there are those connections that people can make, so there is hope, and the hope is coming from within. Nobody came down from the heavens and tapped them on the shoulder and gave them the idea. It came from themselves, and that's where the hope is.

# John Sayles: "Fish" Out of Water

JANE SUMNER/1993

THE AMERICAN FILM BUSINESS started on the East Coast. And for at least one independent film maker, it's still there.

Writer-director John Sayles, currently winning praise for his new film *Passion Fish,* lives in Hoboken, N.J. Thirteen years ago, his *Return of the Secaucus Seven,* about '60s radicals turning 30, established him as the American independent film movement's point man. Made for $60,000 from his own screenwriting earnings, the film anticipated *The Big Chill* and President Clinton.

Mr. Sayles, 43, could have set *Passion Fish* anywhere. But the textured plot about a daytime television star turned paraplegic (Mary McDonnell) and her strong-willed nurse (Alfre Woodard) thickens in Louisiana's sweet-water swamplands like ground sassafras in gumbo.

"When I was thinking about this story, I wanted May-Alice (Ms. McDonnell) to be from a place that definitely wasn't New York City," the Schenectady native says. "She's gone up there from somewhere and gotten a lot of armor and become a pretty abrasive New Yorker, probably because she had to in order to survive. I wanted her to come back to someplace and realize 'How did I get this way?'—it's not appropriate behavior anymore."

A few years ago, the film maker took what he calls "a kind of rock 'n' roll tour of the Southwest" with friends from Australia. "We started in

From *The Dallas Morning News,* 30 January 1993. Reprinted with permission of *The Dallas Morning News.*

Austin and went all the way to New Orleans. Just going through that part of southwest Louisiana refreshed in my mind how unique it is:

"The music is different and the food is different and there are still people speaking French. There's a kind of way that people are with each other that's very attractive." *Passion Fish* is a serious film exploring complex personalities, but Mr. Sayles also lets the *bon temps roulez.*

Snaring Ms. McDonnell, in demand after her role as Stands with a Fist in *Dances With Wolves,* and two-time Emmy-winner Alfre Woodard for his leads was a coup for the independent.

"It was a triumph of casting work that we could get them both free at the same time because they both have a pretty full dance card. They're both people I had worked with before and I wanted to work with again."

Ms. McDonnell played the boardinghouse keeper in *Matewan,* Mr. Sayles' quietly powerful film about a 1920 miners' strike in West Virginia. Ms. Woodard was a crusading nurse in his script for *Unnatural Causes,* a TV film about the effects of Agent Orange on Vietnam veterans. Both played in *Grand Canyon,* but had no scenes together.

"Every movie, maybe a third or half of the actors I've worked with before," the film maker says. "It helps me, especially with a big cast. They know how I work, and I know how they work so a few question marks get erased. Every film shoot for a director is millions of questions, millions of variables. You don't want to eliminate all the variables because that's boring, but if you can eliminate a few of them, that's great, especially with personalities."

Mr. Sayles got interested in the "forced marriage" between patient and caretaker while working as an orderly in high school and college. Brushing up for the film, he talked with a therapist in New Orleans.

"She said there are limits as to what she can do for patients. I asked what kind of limits. In order, she said: 'How good their insurance policy is; how good their attitude is; and then the nature of their injury.' "

This weekend, Mr. Sayles goes back to the bayous for a special showing of his film. His company headquartered in the former Jeff Davis Beauty College in Jennings, La., and shot in Jefferson Davis and Vermilion parishes. "We shot in April, May and the very beginning of June 1992. After that, it's so steamy that you spend all your time wiping sweat off the actors."

At first, Mr. Sayles says local residents were wary. "They said, 'This isn't going to be one of those movies where the Cajuns shoot everybody, is it?'

I told them, 'No, the Cajuns are going to come off fine in this.' I don't think the people were too fond of *Southern Comfort* (Walter Hill's survival-of-the-fittest thriller pitting a handful of Cajuns against National Guardsmen in an allegory of America's role in Vietnam)."

In an era of big-budget films, *Passion Fish* cost $3.1 million to make. "For me, that's a pretty healthy budget. We shot for six weeks. My last two films were financed by presale to home video. Two of the movies, *Eight Men Out* (about the 1919 Chicago White Sox scandal) and *Baby, It's You* (about a middle-class Jewish girl and her relationship with a working-class Italian boy), were basically studio movies, financed by the studios."

In *Matewan* and *Lianna,* about a woman's coming to terms with her lesbianism, he was a major investor—but only one of many. "They were pretty much financed by putting together independent financiers—people's friends and relatives, a pre-sale here and promise of a pre-sale there and some foreign rights. You can piece it together. You look at Carolco movies. Very often they're financed with many hands in the pot, but it's a $28 million, $32 million pot."

Acting for Mr. Sayles is a labor of love. Nobody gets an obscene amount of money. It's all very equitable. If any actor gets scale plus $20, all the actors get scale plus $20, he says.

"What that does is give actors' agents an out—so that it's clear everybody gets the same. And the signal doesn't go out that 'Oh, this actor must be in trouble since he's working for less than his price.'

"It's almost worse to pay an actor half of what he usually gets than to pay him scale or something close to scale. If the industry understands the actor wanted to do this and got nothing, that's one thing, whereas if they take half of what they usually get, they can't command their price anymore."

Because of such low wages, Mr. Sayles says he sometimes has trouble getting his scripts to actors. "That's because agents don't want their actors working for that little or don't want them tied up for five and six weeks on a low-budget shoot. Often agents will hold us off until the day before we shoot if we let them—just in case something better shows up."

Despite the vicissitudes, he says American independents are cranking out films. "They find a way to make nice little movies and as soon as one source of funding dries up, they find another one. The people who run Sundance say every year they get more independent first features. The bottleneck is that there's just so much entertainment out there. I think the country could use another 20 percent independent screens."

Overseas, the film business is more depressing, he says. "Except for maybe India, everybody's industry is less healthy than that of American independents. It's harder for world-class guys such as Bill Forsyth or Neil Jordan or Pat O'Connor or some of the Australians to get a movie made than for an American independent.

"That's why I always feel lucky. If only a fraction of the people who go to movies in this country go to our movies, we make our money back. If 10 to 15 percent of the moviegoers in Australia go to see their movie, they pay for their parking tickets."

# A Filmmaker with "Passion"

ROGER EBERT/1993

THINGS MIGHT BE EASIER, John Sayles sometimes thinks, if he were just starting out—if he had no track record. Then investors might be quicker to roll the dice by putting money into one of his movies. But he has made eight films, establishing himself as a leading (but not often profitable) independent director, and that makes it harder. That's why the success of his newest film, *Passion Fish,* comes as such a relief.

"My track record," Sayles was explaining, "is like this. I've made eight films. None of the previous seven has grossed over $20 million. The average Hollywood film now costs over $20 million. So to somebody looking at the bottom line, what that says is, lightning is not likely to strike in this place."

And yet lightning has struck with *Passion Fish,* the story of a touchy relationship between a paralyzed actress and her live-in companion. The movie (now playing in Chicago at the Fine Arts) is performing strongly at the box office, and seems likely to win Academy Award nominations for Mary McDonnell, who plays a bitter accident victim, and Alfre Woodard, the black woman who puts up with her because she needs the job.

For Sayles, talking during a recent visit to Chicago, the movie comes just in time. He received probably the best reviews of his career for his previous film, *City of Hope,* which starred Vincent Spano in a network of stories about crime and corruption in a New Jersey city, but the movie did poorly at the box office before turning into a hit on video.

---

That was the latest in Sayles' series of critical hits with uneven box office records, such as *Return of the Secaucus Seven, Lianna, Brother From Another Planet, Eight Men Out,* and *Matewan.*

Yet Sayles keeps plugging along, making uncompromising films and financing their roughly $3 million budgets by acting in other people's movies. His latest performance is in the John Goodman comedy *Matinee* (now playing in Chicago); he's the tall, lanky stooge working for the sleazy exploitation sci-fi producer. Now comes *Passion Fish,* which matches good performances with a depth of writing that makes even the supporting characters seem to have rich lives of their own.

The movie first opened in December and January in New York and Los Angeles, to qualify for Academy recognition, and then it was supposed to close again until late January. But it made a number of year-end Top 10 lists, and business was good enough in those theaters that Miramax, the distributor, decided to keep it running all the way to the national opening date.

Sayles thinks the Oscar hopes for McDonnell and Woodard are better because both have been nominated before—McDonnell for *Dances with Wolves,* Woodard for *Cross Creek*—and because their performances are strong in a generally weak field.

"First of all," he said, "they *are* outstanding performances. So that helps. And it wasn't a particularly strong year for women's parts in American films. Looking at the usual suspects—the women who have been nominated numbers of times—some of them didn't get to work at all, and some of them didn't work in strong films or get very good parts to play."

If the film does win a couple of nominations, it will be helped more than the typical big-budget film might be.

"For a film like ours, which is not going to have a $10 [million] to $15 million advertising budget, getting an Oscar nomination legitimizes the film in the eyes of the mass audience. It's free advertising. Just put the Oscar in the ad. So, yes, there is a cold financial aspect, but you hope there's also part that's fun.

"I love the Oscars. I get together with my friends, and everybody says nasty things about people's dresses and the movies they didn't like, and we cheer for our favorites."

Sayles writes most of his own films, and *Passion Fish* was inspired by his own experiences. In the film, McDonnell plays a New York soap opera actress who is hit by a taxicab and paralyzed from the waist down. After rehabilitation, she returns to her family home in the bayou country of Louisiana, and goes through a string of paid companions before finally settling on Woodard. McDonnell's character does not adjust cheerfully to her new state, and sits around brooding on negative thoughts and sipping white wine. Woodard will take only so much—which leads to a struggle of wills between the two strong women.

"I worked as an orderly in hospitals and nursing homes for several years," Sayles said, "and I had a lot of nurse friends who would moonlight as home-care companions. I got fascinated by the relationships between people who spend eight, 10, 20 hours at a time together, and yet don't necessarily have anything in common. They're stuck together; one needs the job and the other needs the care.

"Often, it's a power relationship—one has the power to hire and fire and the one has the power of being physically able to get up and leave the room. And that balance of power might switch during the day. It's not just upstairs/downstairs; downstairs can become upstairs at some point."

In a typical TV disease-of-the-week docudrama, the two women would be best friends by the end of the first act. But it doesn't work that way in *Passion Fish*. Sayles writes particular characters and is true to them.

"Even at the end of the movie," he said, "even though the women are almost to the point where they're friendly with each other, Chantelle [Woodard] still hasn't told May-Alice she's having a romance. There are things she keeps private; there are things May-Alice keeps private from her. So although they are helpful to each other, they are still very distinct people. It doesn't end with an embrace and a freeze frame."

Surrounding the two women is a gallery of well-written supporting actors: a gay uncle, two gaggles of friends, a son and a local handyman (David Strathairn) May-Alice had a crush on in high school. Each is onscreen only briefly, but somehow has a role much deeper than the screen time would seem to indicate.

"I think some of the depth in my writing comes from having been an actor," Sayles said. "When I finish a screenplay, I look at every part as if I had to act it, and ask, is there enough here to be a three-dimensional character? Or could it use maybe one more line or one more relationship or one more indication? No matter what your part is, you have to believe that you have a life outside of the movie. When a supporting character walks offscreen, we should feel like it would be neat if the camera could follow him, and see what he's up to next."

The secret of *Passion Fish,* he said, is that the movie isn't really about paralysis or paid companions or any of the surface things. It's about the personalities of the two women.

"Using science fiction for *Brother From Another Planet* was a way to get the story into Harlem; it was a way into what's basically a very naturalistic story. The paralysis in Mary's case and the drug addiction in Alfre's case is a way into getting these characters together. The story is about their personalities, not their disabilities. This isn't a movie that finds happy solutions. Mary doesn't walk at the end of it. You don't overcome being a paraplegic; you learn how to live with it. But even more important, you're the same person before and after.

"Preparing for the role, Mary worked with a woman who had been a nurse and is now a paraplegic and she said, 'Well, yeah, here's all the mechanical stuff I'll show you—but let me tell you, if you've got problems before you're hurt, you're gonna have the same problems after, and they're just gonna be a little bit worse.'

"A lot of the point of Mary's character is she had hit a dead end before she got run over by a taxicab. She'd had a bad marriage, and her career had stalled before it got to her dream; she was getting a little cynical about that. She had gotten to be this bitter, tough, agitated, aggressive New Yorker even before she was hit by a taxi. That's what forces her back into Louisiana—where all of a sudden, a person who would be totally acceptable in New York doesn't fit anymore. At one point, she says, 'Then how did I get this way?' It wasn't by being run over by a taxi; it was other things, other choices she made, other things that happened to her."

Sayles' films have often taken a left-wing viewpoint, as in *Matewan,* the story of a bitter labor strike, or *Return of the Secaucus Seven,* which preceded *The Big Chill* and was a similar story of friends from the 1960s holding a reunion; the friends were more political in the Sayles version.

You'll have a better chance of getting invited to dinner at the White House now than you've had for a while, I told him.

He smiled. "And a much better chance that I would accept the invitation."

# Sayles Talk

TREVOR JOHNSTON/1993

AS THE LATEST YOUNG turks fight to see who can make the cheapest "guerrilla" feature, John Sayles' position as the doyen of American independent film-making seems more than ever assured. Having started his career as a novelist and learned his screenwriting craft at the Roger Corman school of exploitation graft, Sayles' 1980 feature debut as writer-director with the seminal 'reunion' picture *Return of the Secaucus Seven* proved it was possible to finance your own movie, get it released and capture the attention of the Hollywood majors into the bargain. The $60,000 price tag gained as much notice as anything else, but in its ensemble structure, broadly liberal sympathies, tart dialogue and willingness to focus on the concerns of the over 30s, the film now stands as a fair record of the forms and questions its maker would continue to address. His subsequent output remains poised in both creative and budgetary terms between the mainstream's dollar-intensive factory product and the indie sector's modestly resourced pioneer activity.

Sayles' latest offering, *Passion Fish,* marks an effective honing down of his concerns to date. The film is founded on a wry, clearly delineated script and close attention to the performance of Mary McDonnell as an injured television soap star coming to terms with her new-found physical handicap under the care of Alfre Woodard's equally troubled nurse.

Where Sayles' earlier union conflict chronicle *Matewan,* baseball corruption story *Eight Men Out* and contemporary urban survey *City of Hope*

---

From *Sight and Sound,* September 1993. Reprinted by permission.

pored over wider social and historical frescoes to pick away at the land of the free's obfuscatory ideological myth-making, the new film is scaled down in approach. Yet, as a wise spin on the problem pic, it still cloaks itself, like many of its predecessors, in approachable generic garb. From his earliest commissioned screenplays, Sayles has been nothing if not resourceful in his mastery of sundry genre formulae. His own films have injected familiar stylistic routines with a greater sense of thematic commitment—as in the science-fiction *The Brother From Another Planet* and the sports picture *Eight Men Out.*

In this light, it is easy to read Sayles' films as issue-led, each presenting the particular challenge of finding the right package in which to box a relevant social ill or question. While *Return of the Secaucus Seven* mines the insecurity of the 60s angry generation, *The Brother From Another Planet* tackles racial problems. Even Sayles' horror scripts for *Piranha* and *Alligator* are imbued with a whiff of eco-conscience, while the films where the genre element is less pronounced (*Lianna*'s lesbian coming out, *City of Hope*'s state-of-the-nation address) tend to leave the mechanisms of their ideological apparatus more vulnerably exposed.

To his detractors, Sayles' too-perfect liberal conscience can feel like over-earnest PC point-scoring, yet with *Passion Fish,* his human and societal insights are earned by the progress of the drama rather than willed into it from above. What's more, Sayles' unpredictability from project to project—who'd have guessed his next movie might be an Irish-set kids 'n' animals adventure—while still managing to retain an identifiable signature stands firmly in his favour.

TREVOR JOHNSTON: *After* Eight Men Out *and* City of Hope, *were you intentionally looking to do a more intimate piece like* Passion Fish?

JOHN SAYLES: I never make the movies in the order that I write them or think of them, and *Passion Fish* harks back to when I worked in hospitals 20 years ago. People had seen *Persona* by that time and would go on about the symbolism. I thought it was about a nurse and a patient, and I always reckoned it would be a good idea to do a comedy American version. What influenced me more was not going from the social to the personal, but the fact that I'd done three "guy" movies in a row, which is basically what politics still consists of. Maggie Renzi, my producer, asked me if I had any stories for women, so I thought we'd do the hospital one next. A lot of things clicked together: we were traveling down South and hooked up with a friend who plays in a zydeco band, we stayed in his parents' house and both the band and house ended up in the movie.

*As in previous films you seem to be dealing with an area of American experience—the Cajun culture—that could be seen as peripheral.*
There are specific reasons why I chose that place. I wanted it to be very much somewhere that wasn't New York, so that it was evident that May-Alice, the Mary McDonnell character, had to change herself to make it in the city. And there aren't that many places left in the US that are different from McDonald's shopping mall America. In that part of the South people still speak French on the radio, they have their own food, their own music. I also needed a place where if you came back as an unmarried woman of 30 people would know about it and you would know they knew. I needed a place that was sensual in nature: here are two women denying their senses or closing them down—Alfre Woodard's Chantelle has decided to become a nun and keep herself away from temptation. May-Alice is drowning her senses in alcohol and soap operas. It needed to be fleshy and sensuous, so there are more dissolves in that movie than I've ever had before.

*Your films seem to run counter to McDonald's shopping mall America in their examination of social, cultural or political specifics.*
A lot of my movies are about community. Their culture is an attempt at community culture rather than mass culture. May-Alice is an exile from the mass culture of the soaps, but it's still coming at her through her TV. It's only when she turns that off that she's able to appreciate what's around her.

I'm aware of mass culture, and I'm aware that I'm part of it. The stuff I do goes into theatres, it's advertised. I do interviews. But I want my work to be about it, but not necessarily of it. What I do in film is not just another meal at McDonald's, it's more a case of opening a funky little restaurant that becomes a cool hang-out. One week you do Cajun food and the next you do something else, on the understanding that most people aren't going to eat there. The bottom line is that they don't like that kind of food: it's too spicy, it's too foreign, they can't find the address. Most people don't see our movies in a theatre because they can't get to them. We don't get played in the chains.

*The film could be summed up in a soap opera way—alcoholic wheelchair-bound ex-soap star recovers with the help of ex-junkie nurse—but one of its aims seems to be to bring out the difference between the clichéd soap opera treatment of these issues and your own more sensitive approach.*
One of the things the movie is trying to be aware of is people's desire to have an easy answer and not slug through things. To be able to place someone right away, to resolve a conflict that's not resolvable in a half-hour television slot. Even though they have the time, soap operas don't have the patience to have characters who develop in an organic way—instead, it's forget about the fact that you're only 16, the ratings are dropping so you've got to have a long-lost son.

So much American culture is market-driven. Demographics and research are getting everywhere. I can make my movie and sell it to Miramax, telling them that this is the final cut and if you don't like it, don't buy it. But they still bring in their marketing people, who say this is what people have said and this is why we want to cut this, and this, and this. What I'm hoping is to use that system to carry what I want to carry, but not to get eaten up by it. It's like surfing—the wave could kill you, but it could also give you a great ride.

*Do you find it frustrating that people don't see your movies in cinemas?*
I wish they could. Usually the cinema is a fuller experience, though the television screen is an experience too—it may not be like going to a rock concert, but I still like records. It's certainly much better than there being no video, the movie playing in 15 cities for two weeks and then hardly existing. Most of the places I've lived, like Jersey City, have never played one of my movies. People there have seen them because of video, and both *City of Hope* and *Passion Fish* were financed by home video pre-sales. That money has been vital for the independent American film movement.

*Has that situation given you a greater feeling of security for the continuance of your film-making career?*
I would say that the continuance of my movie-making career rests on whether I can write enough screenplays and make enough money to finance or be a major investor in my next film—which will still have to be made for very little money. Right now I'm broke—the last couple of movies haven't done very well. Who knows whether I'll make back the

money I put into *The Secret of Roan Inish,* the one I just shot? I've made eight or nine movies, but none of them has gone platinum. What I have is a track record that's very good in some ways, in that I attract good technicians and actors because they think my stuff is good and interesting to do. And then I shoot fast, so it's only five or six weeks out of their lucrative schedules, which means that sometimes their agents will even allow them to work with me.

But as far as financiers are concerned, it's problematic; they see me as a guy who's had nine chances at bat and lightning still hasn't struck. I've kept being a director because I always had money to put back on the table. Right now I don't have any money left, so I'm looking for work as a screenwriter. Maybe my next picture will be shot on 16mm for $500,000. When we finish one movie, we almost never know if we'll be able to do another.

*Do you rule out writing the kind of pieces that might require studio backing?*
I write things because they're fun to write, because I want to tell the story. Then I look at them and think, "How the fuck am I ever going to get to make this?" So rather than writing studio movies, I do movies of a certain ambition. It's a mutual thing: they're not all too interested in what I want to do and I'm not too interested in what they want to do. Every once in a while there's something close, I run it by them and the answer is "Gee, I wish we could make movies like this! I really wanna see this movie!—but I'm not gonna give you the money to do it." That's fine, that's a legitimate answer. As far as being a director-for-hire, I don't get many offers. I usually get asked to do things I'm writing, television movies or cable movies mainly. After *Secaucus Seven* Roger Corman offered me *Mutiny on the Bounty in Space*... I sometimes wish I'd written that one!

*In terms of writing, what gives you the confidence to connect with individuals whose experience is completely alien to your own? That's a common thread in many of your screenplays.*
First of all, I'm not afraid of failure. I don't get upset if people don't like it: I'm doing it because I'm interested. Second, you build up your confidence by doing your legwork. You spend time with people, you read more than one source and you always remain suspicious about anything anyone else has written. When I wrote *Los Gusanos* I had to learn Spanish to get to the

books I needed that weren't translated and to get to the people I needed to talk to. It's like being a reporter in some ways: I'm a conduit for people's voices. Like the disclaimers the networks put on some of their documentary programming, the views expressed in the movies may not necessarily be mine. Often some of my wackiest dialogue is verbatim—for instance, most of the dialogue in the car shop in *City of Hope* is just the flavour of the garage in Jersey City where I go to get my car not fixed—including my favourite line: "Benny, you fat fucken haemorrhoid, get in here!"

*For me* Passion Fish *is successful because of a combination of that kind of authenticity, and the fact that it is extremely well constructed. Do you think the early part of your career—whether it was writing novels, theatre or exploitation pictures—was a good school for learning your craft?*
It all contributes. Certainly acting helps in that it forces you to think about point of view, so when you write different characters they don't talk in the same way or want the same things. Novel-writing helps in a lot of ways too, because it makes you think about rhythm, though instead of it being a matter of words on the page, in film you establish rhythm in lots of different ways: there's camera movement, the way characters speak, cutting, music, the variation in framing and so on.

I learned a lot from the directors who made the Roger Corman movies, because they'd be straight on the phone to me, screaming for help: "I've got $800,000 to shoot this epic you've written. It's set in 1933, we've got 68 speaking parts and we start filming in two weeks. Do you know anything about the movie business? You're killing me!" Then I'd do a freebie rewrite so the movie could be better, rather than them just tearing out pages of the script at will. That way you learned what was capital intensive and what was labour intensive: what you had to throw money at and what you could overcome by ingenuity.

*Do you have work that you're more proud of as a director than as a writer?*
It's not that interesting to me. You just try to tell the story as best you can, using all the weapons you have at your disposal. For each movie you have a different team, different demands, different logistical problems. At every point I try to zero in on the most important thing in the scene—sometimes it's the camera, sometimes it's the actors. When it's the acting I tend to keep things simple and I don't cut very much. I don't make movies

because of some technique I want to try; I try a technique because there's a story I want to tell and that seems the way to do it.

*When you started out as a novelist, what kinds of movies led you to want to write screenplays and eventually direct?*
I have wide taste. I like everything from *Cries and Whispers* to *Enter the Dragon*. I like different things in those movies, obviously—the acting in *Enter the Dragon* isn't my favourite thing about it, and the karate in *Cries and Whispers* is like nothing, whereas the storytelling grabbed me. Whenever a movie could get me into the story so I'd stop thinking about how it was made, that interested me.

*Has your career turned out the way you imagined?*
I didn't know anyone in the movie business and I didn't know anyone who was a writer, so I had no role models. When I first went to Hollywood, I did think it through: I want to write movies and I want to direct the movies I write. How do I get to do this? They're not hiring theatre directors, they're hiring producers' sons, stars, people who work their way up through TV, and writers. Hey, I'm a writer, I can write my way to it. I'll do original scripts and assignments and if any of them make any money maybe I can suggest that I direct the next one. It was clear after writing three movies for Roger Corman that those were not the kind of movies that got any attention, so I went the Stanley Kubrick route and made my own fucking movie with *Secaucus Seven*. That was the start, because even if I hadn't got it released, at least I'd made a movie I wanted to make.

# A Man and His Myth

## KENT BLACK/1995

FILMGOERS WHO HAVE SEEN John Sayles' new film, *The Secret of Roan Inish,* no doubt settled into their seats expecting this master of gritty realism and champion of the American working class to apply his unsentimental brush strokes to a Gaelic canvas.

In scene after scene, however, expectations have been jolted. In one scene, a seal sheds its skin and becomes a beautiful woman. In another, a young girl races after a little boy she believes is her brother, lost years before. Just when she is about to catch him, however, he leaps into a magic cradle that floats away.

Could this be the work of the independent writer-director who, more than any director since John Cassavetes, has explored and portrayed slices of everyday life in films such as *The Return of the Secaucus Seven, Passion Fish* and *City of Hope*? Has Sayles really given up on reality and turned to fairy tales?

The 44-year-old Sayles snorts at the idea. "All fiction stretches reality to get at truth. In all my films, I've explored questions of identity and community. In *Secaucus Seven* the community are these people who are glad to be around others they don't have to explain all their jokes to.

"In *Matewan,* there is a short-lived community that happens when there's a common enemy. And *Roan Inish,* it's the children who realize that by abandoning their homes on the island, they've also abandoned their

---

identities. In *Roan Inish* the use of magical elements is simply a way of pushing the metaphor one step further."

The novella on which the screenplay is based, *Secret of Ron Mor Skerry* by Rosalie K. Fry, was first brought to Sayles' attention by his live-in partner and producer of 20 years, Maggie Renzi. Originally set on the Scottish coast, the story is moved by Sayles to the stark and wild western islands of Ireland of 1949; he adds several new characters and plot lines to flesh out the story.

His version tells of 10-year-old Fiona, who is sent away by her failed, widowed father to live with her grandparents in a remote fishing village. She learns from her grandfather the sad history of her family: How during World War II, they were removed from their ancestral homes on the mysterious island of Roan Inish and how during the evacuation her infant brother, Jamie, asleep in his cradle, was carried away by a strong current and never seen again.

From a strange cousin she hears how one of her ancestors on Roan Inish captured and married a "selkie," a mythical, half-human, half-seal creature and comes to believe the selkies may be responsible for her brother's disappearance. Obsessed with the idea that by returning to Roan Inish, she will appease the forces that stole away her brother, she persuades her adolescent cousin to help her restore the cottages on the island.

*Roan Inish* is a textbook example of "magic realism," a literary label attached to such works as Gabriel Garcia Márquez's *One Hundred Years of Solitude,* Juan Rulfo's *Pedro Paramo* or Laura Esquivel's book and Alfonso Arau's movie of *Like Water for Chocolate.* In this form, the lines between the real world and a magical world are indistinct so that the fantastic walks hand in hand with the everyday. "It is the common belief in South American cultures," says Arau, "that we live in two worlds at one time."

Though magic realism is most often associated with Latin American artists, Sayles points out that it was a widespread system of storytelling from the pre-Christian Irish to Native Americans. "A lot of these myths have an instructional as well as spiritual aspect to them," says Sayles. "It not only tells you about the spirit of something such as an animal, but also its habits and its importance to the life of the community. In Native American myths, there is always an important, practical lesson in the tale of the crow or the coyote."

Sayles says his interest in making a film of the *Secret of Ron Mor Skerry* intensified as he got deeper into the tradition of Scot and Irish storytelling.

"I found there was a period in which stories about hunters feeling remorse over the killing of seals began to appear... and like *Roan Inish,* many were stories about 'selkies.' I realized there was a generation of hunters who no longer had to kill seals to make a living, but continued to do so as part of their tradition. Obviously, there was tremendous emotional conflict and guilt which led to the creation of these myths and stories."

Like Latin America, Ireland is a land where Christianity was grafted quickly onto an indigenous populace that never quite relinquished its animistic roots. Like Márquez's characters who exist in a gumbo of African, Indian and European Catholic cultures, the classic character of Irish stories is a God-fearing, Rome-facing devotee who, nonetheless, has a healthy respect for the powers of "the little people" and anthropomorphic entities. "One of my favorite scenes," says Sayles, "is one where [the grandmother] scolds her husband for his superstitious tales and then turns right around and uses the old Druid practice of blessing the fire in the hearth."

Though the film is chock-full of magic imagery and inexplicable occurrences, Sayles never resorts to any special effects more dazzling than a slow fade. Says Arau. "In *Erendira* [a film adaptation of a Márquez novel], the movie didn't work because they drew attention to the magic with the use of special effects. The whole point to magic realism is that the magic must coexist seamlessly."

"One of the reasons I set the film in 1949," says Sayles, "is so that the little girl, Fiona, imagines the events we see through her eyes in a way that is untouched by film or television. When her grandfather tells her these stories, she sees them literally... without special effects."

Another reason Sayles set the film in postwar Ireland was to focus on his recurring theme of community and identity. "This was the period when a lot of people in western Ireland and Scotland left the islands for an easier life on the mainland and in the cities... and, of course, there is a long tradition dating back to the famine of them having to leave their homes. And, of course, what happens is that when this generational tie to the land is severed, so is the sense of identity. You're suddenly uprooted and living in Australia or America and who are you? My purpose in *Roan Inish* is to show how these characters come to re-establish their identities."

It might be postulated that the Schenectady, N.Y.-born Sayles, whose parents were both half-Irish, was drawn to the project in a quest to establish an identity relative to his own Gaelic roots. Ethnicity, however, is the least of Sayles' interests. Familiar Sayles themes such as questions of community and identity, class struggle, the power of myth, the value of hard work and environmentalism make *Roan Inish* part of a continuing body of work that is consistent with the filmmaker and novelist's leftist-humanist vision.

Though he was educated at Williams College in Massachusetts, Sayles is quick to point out that he "came from a working-class family [both parents were teachers; his grandfathers were both cops] and went to a working-class high school in a working-class city." Like many aspiring artists fresh out of college, Sayles took a number of jobs—including meatpacker and construction worker—before getting his first breaks as a writer.

In person, Sayles gives the impression that the Directors Guild hires right out of the teamsters. At 6-foot-4, with biceps the size of most people's thighs, Sayles possesses a fashion sense that would make a Pic 'N' Save buyer cringe. It is a disarming contrast for a man whose intelligence and education disqualifies him from the working class.

Two generations ago, Sayles probably would've been leading Wobblies, the socialistic labor union from the turn of the century. Unlike other artists who struggled, he does not look at his working-class stints as menial or transitional. Rather, he maintains, such experience taught him the value of hard work and the value of workers.

In the '70s, Sayles was a screenwriter for Roger Corman, turning out scripts for films such as *Piranha, Lady in Red* and *Battle Beyond the Stars*.

It was with the money he earned on *Piranha* that he financed his first independent production *Return of the Secaucus Seven* in 1980. The story of a reunion of '60s radicals (sometimes referred to as the "original *Big Chill*"). Sayles and Renzi brought the film in for $60,000 by commuting to Boston from New York on weekends where he had the use of a free editing machine. Money was so tight that Sayles remembers more than once "running out of gas in some New York suburb and being stuck until we could score more gas to keep going."

With the modest success of *Secaucus Seven,* screenwriting fees from films such as *The Howling* and *The Clan of the Cave Bear* as well as $32,000 a year for five years from a MacArthur "genius" grant in 1983, Sayles was able to secure backing for two more films: *Lianna* (1983), the story of a housewife who falls in love with another woman, and *Brother From Another Planet* (1984), about a black extraterrestrial who finds himself in Harlem.

Twice in his career, Sayles has attempted to work within the studio system. But the experience of *Baby, It's You* at Paramount in 1983 and *Eight Men Out* for Orion in 1988 convinced Sayles that the easing of the financial burden wasn't worth the curtailing of his artistic freedom.

"It's extremely important for me to have the final cut on my films," he says. "And that's not something the studios are willing to give."

Though the absence of Big Brother has severely limited the distribution of Sayles' films, he maintains that being able to "see a project through from its inception to its completion" is well worth the price. Indeed, Sayles' uncompromising vision has won him not only the adulation of independent filmgoers but the gradual respect and admiration of the more mainstream film community.

*Matewan* (1987), the gripping, true-life story of a West Virginia coal miners' strike in the early part of the century; *City of Hope* (1991), a finely structured drama of urban hope and despair, and 1992's *Passion Fish,* a drama of a woman who returns to her Louisiana bayou home after being paralyzed, have established him as a visionary force. (He was nominated for an Academy Award for best original screenplay for *Passion Fish.*)

Sayles has also gathered praise and recognition in other forums as well. He has published a collection of short stories (*The Anarchist's Convention*) and three novels (*Pride of the Bimbos, Union Dues* and *Los Gusanos*) and written two plays (*New Hope for the Dead* and *Turnbuckle*). He was the creator of the television series "Shannon's Deal," and as an actor he has appeared in several of his own films as well as *Something Wild* and *Malcolm X.*

Still, as the production of *Roan Inish* has proved, such accolades don't necessarily mean people will line up to throw money at your independent production. Sayles and Renzi had to invest a considerable amount of their own money to keep the production going when their partners, Denver-based Jones Intercable, waited nearly two weeks into the production to finalize the deal.

Renzi was quoted during the production as saying that the financial situation was "a really ugly experience" and that she was close to giving everyone a severance check and sending them home. Luckily, their passion for the project won out and despite the potential for coming out considerably poorer than when they'd started, they pressed on.

Filmed on the wild Irish northwest coast of County Donegal, *Roan Inish,* Sayles' first foreign location, had a few other odd bumps along the way.

"One of the first things we had to do was to call a town meeting to dispel the widespread rumor that we were Mormons who'd come to kidnap all the local children," he said.

Along with a navy of only partially trained seals that rarely followed direction, weather which changed quickly and dramatically made the shoot schedule difficult. Some of the film's other problems included a mentally unstable local who burned down the set and an irritating cash-flow problem. But the production also had its high points, such as the precocious debut of Belfast schoolgirl Jennifer Courtney, who along with 1,000 other Irish girls auditioned for the role of Fiona.

Sayles credits his Irish cast and crew, especially veteran actor Mick Lally, with the authenticity of the production. "Being Irish was not a big part of my childhood, though being Catholic was," he says. "Still, I'm sure I was influenced on some level, particularly in terms of the rhythm of story-telling. I had several people—such as Mick Lally and another man who owned one of the local pubs, who are both [Gaelic] speakers—go through the script and point out problems in idiom or dialect."

A near fanatic when it comes to detail and authenticity, Sayles involved local fishermen in teaching his crew the method of fishing employed in the late '40s and located craftsmen who also taught them to build authentic cottages.

"In some ways we weren't really part of the rhythm of the community because our schedule was so dependent on light and tides," he recalls, "but in other ways, we moved right in. Because of the budget, we had to board everyone at the little bed and breakfasts... which are just private houses. Though I think some of the locals might've been a little tentative at first, a lot of people really got into what we were doing because they liked the story so much. At that first meeting, I had a big pile of scripts and told the locals to help themselves. By the end of the production, everyone in town was telling us about their selkie experiences."

# Sayles and Service: Prolific Movie Director Tries to Keep His Customers Happy

DAVID KIPEN/1995

IT'S HARD TO PICTURE John Sayles sitting on his hands at the beach.

After all, since the late '70s the Hoboken, N.J., novelist-screenwriter-producer-director-actor-editor has written more than 20 produced screenplays, directed nine, acted in quite a few, and written three novels, one of which won the National Book Award. He's also won a MacArthur Foundation "genius" grant.

But now after having just written, directed and edited a new movie, *The Secret of Roan Inish,* Sayles seems to have no problem sitting in an office on Sunset Boulevard and talking about loafing.

"Sometimes I've written a script and just not sent it in for another week," he said, "just so people won't feel like, oh, this guy just dashed this thing off. If you just hand it in in two weeks, they feel like they didn't get their money's worth. So you sit on your hands, go to the beach, whatever."

Here's a guy who wrote his first script draft of the modern-dress samurai picture *The Challenge* over a long weekend, wrote the *Jaws* knockoff *Alligator* in the peace and tranquility of the New York Port Authority Bus Terminal, and directed his first movie, the acclaimed *Return of the Secaucus 7*, with the $40,000 he made writing B movies like *Piranha* for Roger Corman.

In short, Sayles writes fast and well enough to make all but the most prolific scribe hang his head in shame.

---

From *Los Angeles Daily News*, 7 February 1995. Reprinted by permission.

"I'm very capable of wasting time," Sayles said a little defensively. "It's just that once I start writing, I can concentrate fairly easily. I can write in bus stations. I can write on airplanes. That helps. I don't have to sharpen a lot of pencils to get into it.

"I can also skip," said Sayles, whose *Matewan* and *Eight Men Out* treat the dignity of work with a genuine, heartfelt populism. "Some writers, if they don't have a word, they have to stay there until they get the right word. I'll write the scene and write in the margin, 'Must be better,' and go back later."

His new film is adapted from a Scottish children's book. *Roan Inish* is Gaelic for Seal Island, the setting for a mythic story of a young city girl who goes to live with her Irish grandparents in the fishing village where her little brother disappeared years before.

"It's a more direct movie than some that I've made," Sayles allowed. "This movie is much more hooked into an oral tradition, and simple visually in the way that children's illustrations are simple. There's hills, sea and sky. Now and then, you'll see a satellite dish over a pub."

*Roan Inish* also may be the least green movie ever filmed in Ireland.

"Green is a tough color to control," Sayles said. "It bounces on skin tone and doesn't look very good. Green can take over a frame and be a little oppressive. Sometimes that looks good, if you're making a jungle movie.

"In this one, the sea is much more a character than the land. Sometimes the sea is a beautiful blue, and sometimes it's a really angry, almost black color. When Haskell Wexler, the cinematographer, would choose a filter, we always talked about whether the ocean is supposed to be blue and inviting or cold and a little threatening."

It might surprise a few critics to hear Sayles talking so knowledgeably about the visual aspects of film. Like many writer-directors, Sayles has chafed against his reputation as a talky, static, "uncinematic" director.

"It's interesting," Sayles said. "Critics listen to each other more than they listen to movies. There was a period when any new phrase that Pauline Kael said went through the critical community like the whooping cough.

"So writers and directors get typecast, same as actors. My second movie (*Lianna*), people said, 'Well, this is a real departure for you.' My third movie (*Baby, It's You*), they said. 'This is a real departure for you.' *This* movie, people say, 'Well, this is a real departure for you.' "

Early on, Sayles' unornamented visual style was dictated by economics. Then things changed—somewhat.

"Since my third or fourth movie," Sayles reflected, "I've had the wherewithal, the money and time and the experience, to get more visual storytelling into a movie. My first two or three movies were written very specifically not to need that. On $40,000 there's a limit to what you can do."

Even if his every film is a departure from the ones that came before, there is one thing that this extremely prolific worker's movies have in common.

"I realized the other day," he marveled, "there's a bar scene in every one of my movies. And I wondered, how did that happen? I don't drink. I spend more time in bars in my movies than I do in real life. I think it's just because it's a place where people meet. Somebody should write a doctoral thesis about this."

Sayles definitely was kidding. He had a run-in once with a doctoral candidate hoping to get tenure out of a thesis on Sayles' work, and it sounds like only one of them had a good time.

"There was a guy who interviewed me once," he recalled, "and I had him convinced for about 10 minutes that *Piranha* was an allegory for the Cultural Revolution in China. The piranha were the Red Guard, the four villains were the Gang of Four. It was starting to sound good to me.

"Then he said, 'Is this really true?' I said, 'No, but it sounds good.' "

# The Secret of John Sayles

## KENNETH M. CHANKO/1995

GOING THE IRISH-FABLE route might be the least likely career course you'd predict for John Sayles, one of this country's most uncompromising independent filmmakers. Not only does his new movie, *The Secret of Roan Inish,* which opens Friday at the Coolidge Corner Theatre, feature a mythological creature, but this hard-edged realist has also made a "family film," involving children as lead characters and seals and seagulls in key supporting roles. *Roan Inish,* which Sayles shot on Ireland's west coast, is also the first the filmmaker has set outside the United States.

The veteran Sayles, stretching out on the sofa in the Manhattan office of the public relations firm that's handling the release of his ninth film, says he doesn't see *Roan Inish* as a great departure for him. But then Sayles, who is not exactly a publicity hound (he's never employed a personal publicist), is the last person to go around trumpeting the fact that his latest film represents several firsts.

"In terms of the fantastic elements of the story, it's probably most like *The Brother From Another Planet,*" says Sayles, whose more recent films include *Matewan, Eight Men Out, City of Hope* and *Passion Fish.* He continues: "In *Brother* it was science fiction; here it's folklore. In both films, though, there's this realistic core, and the fantastic elements of the story serve the realistic story, rather than the other way around."

---

From *The Boston Globe,* 19 February 1995. Reprinted by permission of Kenneth M. Chanko.

Based on a short Scottish novel by Rosalie Fry, the 1950 *Secret of the Ron Mor Skerry,* the new movie can accurately be called a children's fable. But one shouldn't expect a special-effects-laden extravaganza or dollops of sentiment. Sayles, in fact, would rather not label the film at all, precisely because he thinks it would mislead moviegoers.

"The term 'children's movie'—and even 'family film'—has come to stand for something syrupy and sentimental," says Sayles. "If you want to use the 'family film' label, then I'd say *Roan Inish* is a 'family film' in the same way that *Treasure Island* or *Tiger Bay* or *The Member of the Wedding* or *To Kill a Mockingbird* are family films. *Mockingbird* starred this 8- or 9-year-old girl, and she was my way into the movie. I loved that film when I was a kid. As an adult, of course, you get it on a different level. I wouldn't really call any of those movies family films, but certainly kids and adults can watch all those movies and enjoy them."

*Roan Inish,* which was shot in Donegal almost two years ago, is the story of 10-year-old Fiona (newcomer Jeni Courtney), who is sent to live with her grandparents, Hugh (Mick Lally) and Tess (Eileen Colgan), and her 13-year-old cousin, Eamon (Richard Sheridan), on the west coast of Ireland. One day Tess tells Fiona the story of how Fiona lost her younger brother, Jamie, when his cradle was swept away and he was carried off to sea while the family was preparing to move off the island of Roan Inish. Later, Eamon tells Fiona of the rumors that Jamie is still alive, sailing in his cradle around Roan Inish. Further stoking young Fiona's imagination is the story she hears from her father's cousin, Tadhg (John Lynch), who tells her the legend of the Selkie, a creature who is half-seal, half-woman, to whom Jamie—and Fiona herself—might be related.

Sayles himself has no Irish ancestry; he says he simply wanted to make a genuine Irish film—and certainly not one in the style so many Americans think of as "Irish."

"My casting director in Ireland would have the word 'DOG' next to certain actors' names," the director recalls with a laugh. "I asked her what that was about, and she said it stood for 'Darby O'Gill'—meaning that that actor tended toward a stage-Irish character, especially when an American is looking at them. So, if I used them in the film, I'd have to direct them away from that broad, almost vaudevillian Irish-American view of what the Irish are."

While seeking to avoid stereotypical Irish whimsy, *Roan Inish* is steeped in the Irish storytelling tradition, with long stretches in which characters, well, talk. That, plus the fact that the filmmaker purposefully set the film in pre-television days, might make it tough going for some kids raised on cartoons and MTV, Sayles admits.

"If I were a marketing person and not a filmmaker, I would never have made this movie," says Sayles. "It's a tough sell. The style and rhythm of the movie is closer to the unfolding of a story from a book. Kids who are read to a lot by their parents will have an easier time getting into it.

"Also," Sayles continues, "I wanted the character of Fiona to experience and visualize these stories she's hearing in a very particular way. I didn't want the movie to seem so archaic that it couldn't possibly be happening today, but I also didn't want the girl to be of the television age. The way she imagines these stories she's hearing is very much nontechnological. It's very literal and, in some ways, creative. So she imagines the seal's skin literally peeling off to reveal a woman, rather than some sort of morphing technique."

Thematically, the original story appealed to Sayles because "I've always enjoyed stories like *Pecos Bill* and the Native American creation myths, which usually involve elements and questions about how animal or unanimal are we. The original story was set in Scotland, but I knew that myth from a similar Irish story. I'm much more versed in Irish literature and culture, so I knew I would only have to do half the research if I made it Irish. It's interesting that so many archetypical American stories are about the yearning to move on, about getting on your horse and riding out of town, while so many Irish stories are about the yearning to go back, to return, and whether that's truly possible."

Sayles, who will turn 45 this fall, can be considered a patriarch in the world of independent cinema—a fact that was brought home to him during his visit last month to the Sundance Film Festival, where *Roan Inish* had its debut. At one point, says Sayles, a young filmmaker came up to him, noting that Sayles' book *The Making of* Matewan was required reading in his film class one year, and told Sayles that he was inspired by the fact that Sayles was still around making movies outside the studio system.
"I kind of had mixed emotions about that," says Sayles. "Not least because I remember I never wanted to read anything that was assigned to me by any of my professors when I was in college."

The mix of writing-for-hire for Hollywood (Sayles writes and rewrites mainstream studio movies that he doesn't direct), writing novels (his most recent was *Los Gusanos,* about exiled Cubans living in Miami's Little Havana) and short stories (his third collection will be published later this year), and writing and directing his own films keeps Sayles a lot less frustrated than some of his screenwriter friends, he says.

"I'm glad I have these other things going on, because very rarely is it that what I want to do, in terms of writing-directing, coincides with what Hollywood wants to do," Sayles says. "I'm still often an investor—too much of an investor—in my own films." Sayles has used the payments for his Hollywood writing jobs, as well as money that came with a MacArthur "genius" grant he received in 1983, to finance his own decidedly personal projects.

Sayles is still based on the East Coast, splitting his time between Hoboken, N.J., and a farm in Dutchess County, N.Y. He has never sought to embrace Hollywood (the feeling has been mutual), but there are moments of convergence. He has made a deal with Ted Turner's Castle Rock production company, makers of *In the Line of Fire* and *A Few Good Men,* to direct a low-budget film, *Lone Star,* from his own screenplay.

To be shot on the Mexican border later this spring, *Lone Star* will have a shorter shooting schedule and will cost even less than the $6 million that went into *Roan Inish* ("No kids, no animals, no tides or bad weather," Sayles points out—though the budget will reportedly have to include salaries for Joe Morton, Frances McDormand and James Earl Jones). The film, a contemporary story with flashbacks, is about a sheriff trying to solve a murder committed 37 years ago, a murder that might have been committed by his father. "It gets into the weird history of Texas, including the many conflicts among Mexican-Americans," says Sayles.

This deal aside, Sayles says that raising money—from outside sources or from "mini-majors" like Castle Rock—has become harder, rather than easier, over the years. Of his nine films, only *Baby, It's You,* which Paramount picked up, and *Eight Men Out,* which Orion financed, have had Hollywood ties.

"This might sound strange, but I've become too much of a known quantity over the years for most executives to take a chance on me," says Sayles, who fully appreciates the money-man's position. "Look, a movie company executive might take a chance on a second- or third-time director, giving him $5 or $7 million, but a big part of a gamble like that involves the possibility of locking into a relationship with the next Tim Burton, someone who might eventually make this movie executive and his company a lot of money.

"But I've got a pretty established track record, and not only have I never gone platinum with any of my movies, but each movie has been with a different company. The only good thing about being this established is that people know who I am. I get my calls returned quickly."

Sayles pauses, then adds with a smile, "More often than not it's a 'no,' but at least I'm not in the dark for half a year about whether there's any interest in my project."

# *The Secret of Roan Inish* Revealed

DAVID HEURING/1995

HASKELL WEXLER, ASC AND John Sayles first collaborated on *Matewan,* the gripping saga of coal miners, labor unions and Pinkerton's agents that won an Oscar nomination for Wexler and critical acclaim for Sayles.

Their new effort, *The Secret of Roan Inish,* isn't nearly so politically charged. The story is based on a 1957 novella by Rosalie K. Fry and follows the spiritual fortunes of an Irish fisherman's family. The story takes place on the windswept west coast of Ireland, and that is where it was filmed.

Celtic myth often deals with the lure of the natural spiritual habitat, whether it be the land or the sea. *The Secret of Roan Inish* is about what happens to people when they lose an old way of life; it's about rekindling one's relationship to nature; but it's also about myths, legends, and their place in the real, "modern" world. Wexler and Sayles were recently asked about the production of *The Secret of Roan Inish.*

AC: *With all the unpredictable elements in this film—children, animals, weather, tides—what steps did you take to ensure consistency?*

WEXLER: We took a number of steps to anticipate the elements that were out of our control. To simplify, I decided to limit the stocks to 5245 and 5293. I chose 5245 because of the extremely fine grain and the excellent definition on landscapes. Long wide shots are almost like having a bigger negative. If I needed greater depth of field, we'd break out the 93.

---

From *American Cinematographer,* February 1995. Reprinted by permission.

*There were some low light situations; why not take advantage of faster film?*
WEXLER: In very low level mystic hour and fire shots I pushed 93 one stop. From tests before shooting I could see there was not noticeable deterioration rating it at 400 ASA. I did have to remember that 93 is more contrasty than 96, so I had to give a little more fill.

*Since* Roan Inish, *you've done testing of the new 5287 stock. What were your impressions?*
WEXLER: I would have loved to have had 87 in Ireland. It improves certain aspects of 93 by digging in the shadows, and being more forgiving on the underexpose side without sacrificing grain.

*The budget was modest?*
WEXLER: A very low budget by Hollywood standards. For sure, on a John Sayles film all the money goes towards putting it up on the screen. I often think of the waste in studio projects, where people who don't understand filmmaking do their budgeting solely by the numbers. Their economy contributions center on false savings. The philosophy is 1.) cut below the line; and 2.) cut below the line.

*How did the budget affect the equipment package?*
WEXLER: Well, we couldn't afford great toys: Akela crane, Technocrane, Ray Beams, 13 to 1 zooms—I love that stuff. Fortunately, I own a few goodies like the Preston Speed Aperture Control and a Weaver Steadman, which John rents at super bargains.

*Where did you use the Weaver Steadman?*
WEXLER: There was a shot of twenty or so live crabs crawling on the fisherman's floor. The Weaver in conjunction with a prism on the lens let us dolly on the deck like a vacuum cleaner.

*What kind of prep time did you have?*
WEXLER: About a week here in Los Angeles just going through my equipment and working with Scott [operator Scott Sakamoto] on customs lists.

*How did you prepare on location?*
WEXLER: I guess you know that our location was not the typical Irish location we're used to seeing in films. We were in the northwest, which is

rugged, rough, rocky country. John had spent time there writing the script and getting to know the locals, observing and noting the tides, and just settling in like the old documentary flickers.

*But what about your prep?*

WEXLER: Well, I was trying to say that John had already done a lot of it for me. During the scout we walked and climbed to every spot he had in mind. John had my compass and finder and we talked about the shots.

*Why the emphasis on tides?*

WEXLER: Working around tide changes was part of John's critical prep because the tides in the area are tremendous. The whole look of the place would change drastically. Shots in a certain place would look one way, and then bing!—the tide would go back a hundred yards, and it looked like a different place.

*You used mostly zooms?*

WEXLER: Practically all the exteriors were shot with zoom lenses, either the 18–100mm Cooke or 25–250mm Angenieux. We didn't take lenses on and off much because there was salt spray and salt air; the salt and the spray is pretty tough on the equipment. The clean-up job after every day's work had to be painstaking and thorough.

*The landscapes all seem to consist of green rolling hills, the sea and the sky. How did you control the light?*

WEXLER: Maybe, on the subject of nature, control is too strong a word. We roll with it, we enhance what we see, and we think about the range of printer lights. In Ireland we enjoyed and utilized some of the northern latitude light. It extended mystic hour to maybe three hours of light hanging in the sky. Sometimes when nature didn't do it all we helped with graduates on top, side or bottom. I had a set of color graduated filters that were used only once.

*Did you just luck out with the great sky over the animatronic seal?*

WEXLER: The sky was good and susceptible to accepting a Panchro mirror 90 neutral going 30% down the frame.

*What about diffusion? I didn't get the impression of a lot of filtration.*
WEXLER: I'm not sure I remember exactly what we put in front of the lens. Pretty much Ultra Cons, double fogs, and Mitchell B mostly to take the edge off the extreme sharpness of the new lenses. I was thinking of using some of my old favorites like the Angenieux 20–120 or a beat-up 25–250 from *Bound for Glory*. I figure they would look about the same as the new lenses with filtration.

*How did you handle the flashbacks to Ireland in the 1930s—for example, the scene where a teacher is trying to make the students speak English rather than Gaelic?*
WEXLER: I did some tests with a sepia 3, which has a fog combination. John liked it—I mean he didn't say he didn't like it. The sepia is in a number of scenes. We were careful to give a good gray scale so the lab wouldn't erase what we'd put in.

*Aside from the scenes in Donegal and a few shots with wildflowers, the colors are earthy, muted, and from a limited palette.*
WEXLER: It seems obvious, but a lot of that has to do with what we were photographing—I mean we have a lot of control nowadays, but we're all photographers. (Laughs.)

Also, there's a timer at Du Art with whom John has worked. His name is Gene Zippo. He timed *Matewan* and *Roan Inish*—a very creative person. The timer is an essential person in the chain of our work, and I know they're not spoken of very much. I value their input as creative people.

*Your dailies were done at Technicolor in London?*
WEXLER: Yes. We had some problems with the film—we were seeing flecks of white on the print and it was driving us nuts. Technicolor said, "Don't worry about it, we'll take it out and reprint it," but we wanted to know what the hell it was. It was appearing in both cameras. Apparently the lab talked to Kodak and they couldn't determine what it was. Kodak and Technicolor eventually determined what the problem was—a combination of the relatively new 93 stock and the drying/cleaning mechanism they used at Technicolor. It's a brush system, and it allowed little flecks to come off the sprocket holes on the film.

What was most impressive to me about it was that both Technicolor and Kodak immediately sent representatives to us on location—from London, a day and a half trip—to try to get to the bottom of it. It was interesting to watch these two big companies trying to find the source of the problem. It was sort of like Rolls-Royce—you know, if you have a problem with your Rolls-Royce, and you call up, no matter where you are Rolls-Royce will come and fix it for you—and then deny that there was ever any problem. (Laughs.)

*What makes you decide to operate on a shot?*
WEXLER: I did less of my camera-hogging on this film. Scott Sakamoto is my operator and he's excellent. We've been together a long time. When I take over a camera to operate it's because I have to see. When there are close-ups I generally operate, simply because I just have to see it through the lens at that time, mostly for the lighting. On the framing we have video assist and I can double-check that. And Scott's ideas about framing are excellent. I think that's one of the advantages of working with people you've worked with before. The assistant I worked with, Paul Englefield, a British guy, I had worked with on the Imax film [*Rolling Stones At The Max*], and he was a very good focus puller, very careful, cautious and meticulous. He's one of these guys that—I don't care if the tide is coming in and the sun's going to be covered up in the blackness—he would do his proper thing.

*Did you work under the British crew system?*
WEXLER: All of the crew except for Scott were either Irish or British, and they work in a very different style than we do. We know about how the operator normally works more closely with the director. But there were times that their system was frustrating. If the camera's on a tripod and you want to move it five or six feet over, the grips take charge, and they pull out all the cables, all the connections to the video assist, and the batteries, and take the camera off the tripod, move the tripod over six feet, and then put it all back together. It was driving me and Scotty nuts—it's so overtly inefficient.

A couple of times when the tide was coming in rapidly, Scotty would grab the camera, put it on his shoulder, set it down, level it, and shoot.

The first couple of times we did that, they really were insulted. We had a little meeting and hammered it out, but they felt that Scott picking up the camera and moving it was a slap in the face. They were just trying to help.

I must say that all of the technicians we had were really excellent. That Irish gaffer, Louie Conroy—I'd take him anywhere.

*A good portion of the film takes place on the water. What method did you develop for working in boats?*

WEXLER: For our "camera boat" we found an old, beat-up World War II "Duck," an amphibious vehicle designed for the armed forces. It was ironic because I hadn't seen one since I went ashore in one in World War II, when we invaded Sicily. The advantage was that we could operate it in the water, on the land, or any combination of the two caused by the tides.

For one water shot, John wanted it to appear as if the boy were riding on the back of a seal. Before we went to Ireland, I asked Garrett Brown how we could do it, and he didn't think any Steadicam application would do it, so he suggested making a little arm on the bow of the boat. We were thinking about putting an underwater camera on the arm, so the camera would alternately go under and emerge through the surface of the water, the way seals swim along the surface. We rented an underwater camera from England but it was cumbersome and awkward to work with. They may have better ones, but we didn't find one.

Instead, we found a waterproof periscope, which worked great. We were able to put the Arri II on the arm, which was mounted on the Duck, and Scotty would operate by looking at video.

We were out in a rather heavy storm when we did this particular shot. It really took some doing to get it right. We had a bilge pump on the Duck that barely worked, so we had to bail and pump because the thing was about to sink. Of course it was very cold, and John is very macho—he was there in shorts. We were all freezing, but we wanted to get that shot.

*According to John Sayles' book on the making of* Matewan, *there was some tension on the set between the two of you.*

WEXLER: It's true; it was because I thought I knew about that period and those coal miners, and so I had strong opinions. On this one, I didn't. John knows Irish history, the Irish tradition of storytelling, and he knew it was a very, very low budget. Since he knows and I don't know, I made a conscious decision to be his "obedient servant," like the old Orson Welles sign-off says. I decided to be as open as I could be and see what happened. I did that pretty well on certain things. Of course I gave some suggestions, but then John responded in kind. It was not the kind of artistic combat that we had on *Matewan*. We were both more respectful, and it was a good atmosphere all around.

*Sayles has racked up a lot of experience since* Matewan.
WEXLER: That's absolutely true. That's what's so smart about John—when he gets into something, he wants all the information, on any subject. You can talk to him about anything in the world, and he can come back with full knowledge on all subjects. He has a fantastic mind, but cool—he doesn't throw it at you.

I feel John is a very emotional guy, but on the surface you'll seldom know exactly what he's thinking. He'll seldom say "Gee, that was a great shot, I loved it." That's okay—a lot of times that love stuff is so "Hollywood"—but sometimes we need it.

*Sayles is director, writer, producer and editor of this film. How does that affect the photography?*
WEXLER: What you're doing is out in the open. So often in films now the director has to say "Well, you know, they're going to see this back at the studio. We'd better shoot it this way." They're not going from their gut creative decision. They have to wonder what someone else will think—like on a commercial. So the advantage of John's position, for all of us, is that we know exactly what he wants and what he believes.

*Sayles said he hoped that his control over the film—knowing on the set how things will cut together—allowed you to take a few more chances.*
WEXLER: That was one of the most difficult things—dealing properly with what will cut and what will match. It was difficult to retrain myself. All our training as directors of photography tells us to make things match, try to make it cuttable, to try to deliver footage so the cutter, who is somewhere else, can have his options. With John, when he said, "I don't care if she exits the frame here," it was like giving me a shot in the heart. I would feel panic, and he would say, "Don't worry, don't worry, I'm cutting it, I'll take care of it, I know." I'm very pleased with what he did with the film,

and I'm very much in admiration of his ability to do things we don't normally do in films and make them work.

*I understand you had animatronic as well as live seals.*

WEXLER: We worked very long hours under very rough conditions, but the seals were treated properly no matter what. If the water was going to be too cold for them, or the tide wasn't going to be right, we had to make adjustments. There are apparently all kinds of psychological things about seals. We would hear that "Well, she doesn't really feel right because Scotty was shooting it standing over there before, and maybe she's a little upset. Maybe we should use the other camera, it's a little quieter." We were very sensitive to the seals' psyches.

*What did you learn from making this film?*

WEXLER: The film is a narrative with a lot of words, with a very literary feel. There's really no action in it to speak of; certainly there's no violence. There's not one gun anywhere. One of the things the film revealed to me was how far we've come from this kind of film—for whatever reason, without making a value judgment, good or bad. I felt strongly that the storytelling pace that I'm accustomed to in a movie theater is different from what it used to be. But I've also seen the film with children, and some respond and some don't. It depends a lot how deeply they are into video games and TV.

I also learned a lot from the atmosphere of the place and the filmmaking, and the Irishness of it, I guess you could say. It was very, very rewarding personally for Scott and me, who are very close. We were among people who take the time to talk. You always hear about the Irish drinking, but there wasn't a lot of drunkenness or anything, there was just time taken to talk about everything, to laugh, just to have three or four people visit and talk with no agenda. We felt we were rediscovering human beings.

Scott and I had a little house with a sheep wall around it. We got very adept at building fires with peat. It was cold, and a number of times we came back and the whole place would be so full of smoke we couldn't breathe.

*Did your rediscovery affect the film?*

WEXLER: We felt like it would fit in with the mood of the film. It didn't make us have to work slowly. Often modern life detaches you from nature.

Being closer to nature and being more conversant and having more interaction with humans in a sense says you're more alive, and your life is not controlled by things, is not defined by objects, it's not described by what you have. The opportunity to be in touch is very great when you're on a project like that.

*Did you regret leaving?*
WEXLER: No. I'd had about enough of it. (Laughs.)

*How was what you saw in the theater—the finished you originally imagined it?*
WEXLER: After we looked at the locations I began to get a picture in my mind of what the movie would look like. In reading the script I didn't, and it was probably at that point that I decided that I was in over my head, and that I should put myself at John's command.

At times when I was photographing it, I was afraid it was going to be boring. Quietly, to myself, I was critical of the way John was directing the young girl, because she didn't seem childlike to me, she seemed flat and boring. I was afraid the movie would be that way. In fact, I did say something to John, and he said "Look, this is the way it should be." And again, with my new "obedient servant" persona, I said, "Okay, this is the way it should be."

In the theater, John's cut just excited me so much. Inside I felt I was getting credit for things that were only a very small part mine. I was pleased for it, I was glad, but I still said, "Damn it, John, *that's* what you had in mind."

## Q & A: John Sayles

AC: *Tell us about the genesis of the film.*
SAYLES: Maggie Renzi, the producer, had always loved the book from the time she was young, and found it again in her thirties, read it again and felt it would make a terrific movie. I actually wrote an adaptation just before we went down to Louisiana to shoot *Passion Fish*, so that she and her co-producer Sarah Green could go to Ireland and start to look at locations.

*Why did you ask Haskell Wexler to photograph the film?*
SAYLES: We came upon the choice of Haskell because of a combination of reasons. Since we were not shooting in the States, we were considering a

European cinematographer, but the more I thought about the look at the movie, and the fact that we were shooting a very ambitious movie—I guess it was a small budget by Hollywood standards, but we had small children and animals, and weather and boats and tides, a lot of logistical tangles to sort through, and not a lot of money—I felt that Haskell's experience and sensibilities were perfect for the project.

On a tight schedule, you can't wait around for the light. Haskell's very, very good, even if you're shooting outdoors a lot, at helping with the schedule—figuring out what time of day we should shoot which material, so that we'll get the most out of what's naturally there in terms of light and other elements.

*How did you prepare for the film?*
SAYLES: The woman who wrote the book, Rosalie K. Fry, originally illustrated it. I drew a couple of imaginary maps—an overhead view, and the view of the island into shore and the view of the bay from the shore. They tried to find something like that. They started down by Galway and searched up the entire west coast of Ireland to Donegal before they found the perfect spot.

*Your approach to the Irish folk-tale material was very simple—just present it to the camera, really.*
SAYLES: The budget had a lot to do with that decision, but also, you're dealing with a little girl, in postwar Ireland, in an extremely remote area. This child has never seen television, or even a movie, for that matter. She's never seen morphing or any other special effects. So when she's being told these stories about what happened long ago, the way she pictures things should reflect that. So the transformation of the seal was very low-tech. All the effects in the film are done very simply, animatronically or mechanically, the same way you might have done it in 1920.

Tied in with that idea is the fact that from day one, we tried to give everything a certain weight. We didn't want things to float away, so to speak. There's a point at which special effects—morphing especially—can make everything a little lighter, a little more cartoonlike. We wanted everybody and everything in the movie to have physical weight, to have a solidity and a texture. It's something we tried to do in *Matewan* as well. We didn't use too much filtration, which tends to gauze things up and make things a little lighter. Even though there's the magical realism aspect, and parts of the film are not literal, the kids still have to work. So Haskell was careful not to take the edge off too much.

*What is your working method?*

SAYLES: I break the movie down into sequences, which look like a step outline. I give one to each department head, with specific notes. The music breakdown, for instance, might include a comment like, "I'd like a reel here or a vocal there." It'll just give them an idea of where I'd like cues, and the emotional quality of the cues. And I'll do the same thing for the photographer. The breakdown doesn't say anything about lenses or equipment. It'll say, for example, "Night, tense, fades into a dream sequence, spooky."

*What is your storyboard/scheduling method?*

SAYLES: I had storyboarded, but the only ones that were really tight were the animatronic shots. The seal people have to know exactly what angle, and how far away. I had a 3 × 5 card for every shot in the movie. Each card included things like day or night, interior or exterior, whether there are real animals in this shot, puppets, cameras in boats, people in boats, et cetera. I also included what day it was to be shot, what time the sun rose and set on that day, and the tides.

Haskell and his guys became experts at making estimates, saying, "Yes, I think we can get this track laid and get two takes in before the water is up around our ankles." And sometimes we were wrong. But Haskell was able to stay flexible, and never painted himself into a corner. We always had something to shoot. And we would know that a particular shot would be much easier and take a quarter of the time if we did at the right time of day. And I think that's just Haskell's experience showing.

*So logistical abilities and experience were the most important factors in your selection of a cinematographer?*

SAYLES: To get a consistent-looking movie—or even a consistent-looking sequence—when it's been put together from four different shooting days, you really need somebody who's outstanding with the planning. Certainly Haskell understands the emotional content and has a sensitivity. That's the beginning of the conversation. But the important second part is that I get the movie done on time and on budget. That's the toughest thing.

For example, the same cottage appeared in the film in several different eras. So in one scene the fireplace is a scooped-out hollow in the wall. Later, the fireplace provides the only light source, and still later on the kids have fixed it up and whitewashed the inside. Sometimes it was just the late afternoon sun coming in through the door or the window. So you have three or four very different types of light quality, and each has to be matched regardless of conditions.

We had all kinds of sequences that were spread over weeks. Every Saturday, we would shoot a half a day with seals in various situations. But each of those shots was to be plugged into a different sequence. We were just struggling to get the seals and a boat in the same frame doing a certain thing, and Scott Sakamoto, Haskell's operator, would be in his wetsuit, trying to grab semi-documentary stuff. And Haskell would be watching the sky and juggling seal scenes in his head.

*It sounds like the emotional content of the scene is established first, so that on the set you can concentrate on execution.*

SAYLES: Every once in a while there's a shot where you can just kind of see Haskell winging it—where he's getting ideas as he's doing it. We've already talked about the feeling of the scene. He'll walk around, remember the conversation we had during the scout, and talk some more; you can see him getting the feel of the room again. There may be some interesting natural light that he makes use of, or he may blow the light in. But that's where it happens.

We probably do the most talking in those walk-throughs. Can we have this person go through some dark, and then back into light? What's the next scene going to be and what can make the transition visually? Because I'm also the writer and editor, I'm doing a lot of editing as we're shooting. Thus, we avoid the situation where you plan one kind of visual transition and then six scenes get cut out of the final version. My original cut of this was maybe five minutes longer than the final version.

*Do you stay near camera during takes?*

SAYLES: I tend to stay on the set. I don't usually go away for long periods of time while the director of photography is lighting, partly because it's fun to watch him work, and because that's where you put a lot of feelings into things. I try to make the blocking rational, so that it's not x-marks, instead, it's "You're gonna go over and pick up this brush." And because the brush is in a certain spot, Haskell knows where the person is going, the person knows why they're going there. Rather than looking for their mark, they just go to the right spot.

And then what you do—Bob Richardson and Haskell both do this—is what Haskell calls "f—ing up the frame." The idea is to affect it so that it doesn't look so rehearsed if you can manage it. Not to the point of the jerky stuff, which has its place, but you throw a few more extras in the way. You take a couple more turns, so that it seems much more "found." Of course, this is tough on your operator and tough on your focus puller, but it's necessary when things feel a little too "setpiecey."

*Do you ever operate?*

SAYLES: No! I can barely look through the lens. (Laughs.) One of the nice things about video assist is that I don't have to ride the dolly anymore. Haskell's an excellent operator, so he'll jump in when we need two cameras. Scott, who worked as an AC on *Matewan*, was operator on this. Bob Richardson [*Eight Men Out, City of Hope*] is an excellent operator, as is Michael Ballhaus [*Baby, It's You*], so I've also had the benefit of some really great operators.

*You mentioned video assist. How do you use it?*

SAYLES: I don't like to get in the way of the cinematographer's eye when they're setting things up. I use it much more when we're setting the camera up than when we're actually shooting. I try to stay close to the actors if possible when we're shooting. I find it's real hard to get the heat of the performance from the video screen.

*Filming in such a remote place, did you begin to feel isolated? Did the isolation have an effect on the film beyond the visual?*

SAYLES: Yes, and it was good. We never had to stop sound for cars or airplanes. This was a joy. It's a very, very small town. It's mostly sheep farms.

And because you hook so much into the natural world, I think you have a better eye for it. When your day really does depend on the tides, you get into that rhythm and you begin to have a feeling for how long it's going to be before that tide is up around your ankles.

*According to the production notes, "John Sayles will never call himself an artist."*
SAYLES: To me, "artist" is one of the terms that belong to professors and critics. I don't think in those terms. I tend to think in terms of "What do I want to say with this story; what will make it more fun to watch? What will make it a better story?" I don't think in those artistic strokes, and that's fine. They can label it anything they want to.

# Seeking a Sense of Community

PHILIP WUNTCH/1995

IN EVERY JOHN SAYLES movie—a collection that ranges from *The Brother From Another Planet* to *Matewan* to *Passion Fish*—a sense of community is important.

But never has that community been so exotic as the rough-hewn Irish coastal village of *The Secret of Roan Inish,* the enchanting mixture of folklore and reality that opened Friday at Landmark's Inwood Theatre.

"Community—or the lack of it—is very important," Mr. Sayles said during a Dallas visit this week. "The people in *The Secret of Roan Inish* are close to the land, to the sea, to the weather. Their livelihood often depends on it, and I find that appealing. When I grew up, I had the good luck to be around members of an older generation who still lived to a certain degree in the Old World.

"Americans have a sense of restlessness. We're nomadic. Very few of us live where our ancestors lived. But we find our sense of community in other things—sports-car racing, the Dallas Cowboys, belonging to a religious group, being members of an elite economic circle. But it's a created community, not a natural one."

Tall, brawny and vigorous, Mr. Sayles has the look of a jolly lumberjack. But he's also America's leading independent filmmaker and an author whose novel *Los Gusanos* inspected Miami's Cuban-exile community.

Whether on film or page or in private life, the sense of community is apparent. Mr. Sayles, 44, grew up in Schenectady, N.Y., and now spends

---

From *The Dallas Morning News,* 18 March 1995. Reprinted with permission of *The Dallas Morning News.*

much of the year in Hoboken, N.J., where he lives with producer Maggie Renzi, who has been his companion for 20 years.

Ms. Renzi, who read the Rosalie K. Fry novella *The Secret of the Ron Mor Skerry* when she was 10, brought it to Mr. Sayles's attention, knowing that as a boy he had loved stories about children raised by animals. The story, whose title was changed for the movie, deals with a motherless 10-year-old girl who lives with her grandparents, becomes attached to a group of seals and tries to unravel a family secret. That bit of family folklore relates to her ancestors' marriage to creatures who are part-human and part-seal.

"All that fascinated me, but the subtext of the story fascinated me too," Mr. Sayles says. "The young heroine and her cousins discover the truth, but they pay a price for learning the truth. It's not a tragic movie, but they discover there was tragedy in the family's history. And that discovery will prepare them for dealing with the tragedy that's inevitable in every person's life."

*The Secret of Roan Inish* is the first time Mr. Sayles worked extensively with a child actor. Ten-year-old Belfast native Jeni Courtney was chosen from 1,000 applicants to play the lead. She gives a remarkably poised performance.

"Kids basically want to please adults," the filmmaker says. "My responsibility was to see that they were still kids at the end of the movie, that they had not turned into adults before their time. Jeni never had acted in anything outside a school pageant. She was surprised that she had to do the same scene over and over, maybe do it five times from each angle. But she never under any circumstances wanted to admit she was tired."

Mr. Sayles is now in Texas, filming a drama tentatively called *Lone Star*. The film stars Chris Cooper, Kris Kristofferson and Elizabeth Peña and tells the story of a sheriff who attempts to solve a 30-year-old murder that may have been committed by his father. Again, the sense of community is important.

"It's set in a town on the Texas-Mexico border, and it gets into the culture of border towns. Those cities really are a Berlin situation. And I do think that Texans really carry the legends of the Texas Republic in their heads. Wonderful people, but unlike any other people in the United States."

Mr. Sayles loves acting and frequently plays parts in his own films and those of his friends. But he never considered a full-time acting career.

"I love being in control, and actors have a complete lack of control over their lives. Working actors take what they can get, and a lot of them wind up making movies they would never want to see. An actor has to wait to be tapped on the shoulder and told that he is wanted. That's not the kind of life I want."

One of his idols, John Cassavetes, spent time acting to finance his own independent films. Mr. Sayles, who avoids Hollywood when making his projects, has a similar moneymaking sideline as a Hollywood "script doctor."

"I guess 'script doctor' is accurate. I basically do rewrites. Sometimes I spend a weekend on a project, sometimes several months. I did rewrite work on *Apollo 13* late in the process," he says, referring to Ron Howard's upcoming astronaut epic that stars Tom Hanks, Gary Sinise, Kevin Bacon and Bill Paxton.

"Ron works really well with actors, and Tom Hanks was in on the rewrite sessions. That was the first time I had worked so closely with an actor, and Hanks, Ron and I really workshopped together. But Tom has a very strong film sense, and it was a good experience.

"The funniest experience I had was rewriting *The Challenge* for John Frankenheimer before it started filming. When Frankenheimer found out he could get Toshiro Mifune, he changed the background from Chinese martial arts to Japanese martial arts. They're completely opposite forms, but he said no one would know the difference. We changed all the martial arts scenes and all the background story because he was able to get Mifune."

Mr. Sayles recalls his script-doctoring experiences with humor rather than rancor.

"Basically, I'm called upon to provide background stories for various characters, which I enjoy doing. In that sense, I'm an employee of the studio system, but in a way I don't find objectionable. I've turned down rewrite jobs on scripts I've really liked because I felt I had nothing to bring to them. But if I can help others tell their stories, I'm glad to. And it pays enough to give me the freedom to tell my own stories my way."

# Borderlines

MEGAN RATNER/1996

JOHN SAYLES'S NEW FILM, *Lone Star,* is set in Frontera, a Texas border town shaped by two strong personalities: the bullying, violent, racist Sheriff Charley Wade (Kris Kristofferson) and his successor, Sheriff Buddy Deeds (Matthew McConaughey), who is said to have booted Wade out of the county one night in 1957. Wade, hated by the community, was never seen again. But the film is set in present day when Buddy's son Sam (Chris Cooper), who has reluctantly assumed the role of sheriff, finds his every move eclipsed by the achievements of his father. One day, a skeleton turns up on the outskirts of town, its only relics a ring and a sheriff's badge from 1957, and no one but Sam seems to want to investigate.

Like Sayles' earlier feature *City of Hope, Lone Star* weaves a complex pattern of overlapping stories, but this time the historical canvas is larger. Each of the characters must reach his or her own resolution with the intrusive, inescapable past. This heightens the sense of independence and interconnectedness *City of Hope* introduced; these characters form not only a community but also a sort of extended family.

This social and historical intercourse finds its most effective expression in the blues, Tejano and country music that underlays the action. Little Water, Big Joe Turner, Chelo Silva, Lydia Mendoza, Lucinda Williams and Patsy Montana are only a few of the featured performers. It's Sayles's smartest move: like the images on screen, the songs refute the easy cate-

---

From *FILMMAKER Magazine,* Summer 1996. Reprinted by permission. Subscriptions: 1-800-FILMMAG.

gories of Anglo, Hispanic and black. By allowing the music to carry the story forward, Sayles frees the narrative from its potentially politically correct, earnest overtones.

Sayles has his own take on movie genres: he's used sports (*Eight Men Out*), coming-of-age (*Baby, It's You*), period drama (*Matewan*) and sci-fi (*Brother From Another Planet*) to question fundamental aspects of our culture. In *Lone Star,* he plays with detective and western film conventions (no one particularly wants Sam to solve the murder, and his interest centers on undermining the town mythology rather than upholding it) to prod notions of good guys and bad guys, of history and legend—and ultimately of America itself.

FILMMAKER: *Like* The Secret of Roan Inish *which preceded it,* Lone Star *is about a search for a personal past—a search with mythic overtones. Did these concerns lead you to set the story in the borderlands?*
JOHN SAYLES: Well, it's kind of the other way around—the story and the border were intertwined. I see that whole area and its cultures as this kind of dysfunctional family. There are all these secrets that go way, way, back. It didn't used to matter what side of the river you were on, but now it's a big deal because of something totally artificial that somebody did. I was thinking about what's sometimes called revisionist history. This country was never just one culture; it was a whole bunch of cultures. Being a country is something that you manufacture. And there's some choice involved. It wasn't inevitable; there was a lot of struggling and killing involved.

FILMMAKER: *The feeling in* Lone Star *is similar to* City of Hope*: a small town that's a world unto itself but influenced by outside events, current and historical.*
SAYLES: I wanted a small town where the media would be a small part. If you're in a big city, the national media change the story. It's like having a monster movie when the army shows up. I wanted to keep things more personal, on a small scale.

FILMMAKER: *You've used flashbacks before, but in* Lone Star *it felt as though the past and the present had nearly equal weight. They actually play off each other.*

SAYLES: Like *City of Hope*, we used a lot of master shots to tell the story. Both films take place over three or four days, but *Lone Star* is so much more about history. I used theatrical transitions so that there would be this feeling [that] there wasn't a big seam between the past and the present. Orson Welles did things like that every once in a while. Basically, you get a background for your tight shot from 1996, you pan away, and when you pan back to where the guy telling the story was, it's somebody completely different, and it's 1957. There's not a cut or a dissolve. I wanted to reinforce the feeling that what's going on *now* is totally connected to the past. It's almost not like a memory—you don't hear the harp playing. It's *there*.

FILMMAKER: *The past is really part of the present for all the characters, especially Sam Deeds.*

SAYLES: It's in every relationship—racial history, personal history. In all of those histories, you have that question of—how much do I want to carry this? Is [the history] good, or is it possible to say, "I'm going to start from scratch? Do I still live my life in reaction to—for or against—my father?"

FILMMAKER: Lone Star *draws on the tension between what* was *and was supposed to* have been. *Do you think it addresses the larger question of what it means to be an American?*

SAYLES: Kris Kristofferson looked at the three sheriffs and was reminded of the Israeli general who said, "Well, I was a warrior so my son can be a poet." Charley Wade is the Teddy Roosevelt-era guy who says, "Hey, there are dark people and they're inferior. If you're going to get anywhere in the world, you have to be bold, so I'm going to kill them and take their land." The next generation says, "Oh they're not bad; let's give them a little something back and we can all live together. But *I'm* still in the driver's seat." And then there's the third generation that reached its fruition in this country in the '60s, where people said, "What have we done? What a terrible legacy we have—we stole this land" or, "We brought these people over in slavery." They question everything and can't really enjoy being in the driver's seat—they don't want to be there.

FILMMAKER: *That's certainly true for Sam—he doesn't even want to be sheriff.*

SAYLES: He realizes his accommodation is going to have to be a personal one. And on a personal level things are possible that aren't on a social level. You can have a relationship with a Mexican girl in a fairly racist border town, as long as you're discreet about it. I think there are a lot of white and black people who are friends, but that doesn't mean things are cool. Eventually it might carry over into something larger, but it takes a long, long, long time.

FILMMAKER: *Your characters usually offer a good mix of likable and unpleasant qualities, but Charley Wade is just plain evil. What made you decide to make him all bad?*
SAYLES: Basically, I've run into evil in the world. You read history and there's just really nasty shit. I've been reading a lot about the slave trade, and you just can't say, these were o.k. guys. What they did—and you base character on what people do—was monstrous. And there were monsters on that border. The problem is that Wade is an official monster who's maintaining the minority of Anglos in power. Even when we were shooting, every time we wanted to get to the river we had to go on some fairly rich Anglo's estate because that's the good land. Even on the other side, a lot of land is owned by the Anglos. That wasn't the way it was when the war ended. So it had to be taken somehow, and it was taken by bandits—sometimes by bandits who in their spare time were Texas rangers—usually with the help of local police and judges. And that's what the politics of the post-Mexican-war period were on the border. That's who Charley Wade is; he's a kind of a concentration of all that nasty history.

FILMMAKER: *Music always figures prominently in your films, but* Lone Star *relied on an unusually large number of existing recordings. What made you decide to do this?*
SAYLES: Whenever I start a movie I sit down with Mason Daring, the composer I work with, and talk about the philosophy of the movie. Because I wanted to deal with three different cultures in two or three different time periods in *Lone Star*, we decided that these are people who listen to music and it would often be a bridge. For instance, when Delmore Payne [Joe Morton] first walks into his father's bar, you're hearing Ivory Joe Turner singing "Since I Met You Baby." When Sam and Pilar [Elizabeth Peña] dance, you're hearing "Desde de Conosco"—which is "Since I Met You Baby" [in Spanish]. This great black piano crooner had a hit with "When I Lost My Baby I Almost Lost My Mind" on the black charts, but really that

was kind of chump change. Then a country-western guy covered it and made a fortune. Then Turner covered his *own* song with a sound-alike song ("Since I Met You Baby") that crossed over to the white charts. Then Freddie Fender had the first really big rock 'n' roll hit in Latin America with "Desde de Conosco." You don't have to know the history to feel it underneath. Music and sports are very often where cultures meet first, where they blend.

FILMMAKER: *There were a few scenes that seemed to be shot with a particular piece [of music] in mind, especially the sequence where Wade is killed. Did you go into production knowing what you'd use?*
SAYLES: I had the soundtrack before we went on location. That scene is set to a Little Walter song called "Blue and Lonesome." There's this great internal violence to it, a pounding rhythm and a kind of inevitable feeling. We went in with musicians and recreated it without the vocal. It's an old blues record, so you couldn't just take the vocal out. The original timekeeping was all over the place, and I cut it to the original song and didn't want to recut. It was really hard for the musicians—they had to make the same mistakes as the original, but they did a great job.

FILMMAKER: *Your films have a strong sense of control, a kind of novelistic feeling.*
SAYLES: People say that because [my films] are more complex than a lot of movies are, but [they are] not necessarily literary. It's really pretty hard to improvise too much on a low budget—you just don't have time. On *City of Hope,* we only had five weeks to shoot. We did 40 locations in 30 days. We actually planned all of the camera movements and described them in the script. We made it for a lower budget because postproduction was very short. There were so many master shots that I probably cut a total of five minutes out of the whole film. Sometimes I'll be able to cut something—I've already made the point, or an actor is so strong in the part that you don't need a scene that was there to reinforce part of the character.

FILMMAKER: *What was your budget and shooting schedule on* Lone Star*?*
SAYLES: About $4.5 million. One of the big reasons it was that much was that we bought a lot of music, [and] music costs have quadrupled since I made *Baby, It's You.* Back then, we would get three Motown songs for $25,000. Now one Motown song will cost you $25,000. So there were some

songs we just couldn't get. I had to cut down on the music; it went down from about 27 songs. But that's all right, it was never meant to be *Casino,* where the soundtrack album is a great double album. The schedule was seven weeks of shooting, which was a little more comfortable. There were only a couple of different locations, so not too much of our time was spent driving. We shot a lot of stuff in the town of Eagle Pass itself.

FILMMAKER: *How did you finance this one?*
SAYLES: *Lone Star* was financed by Castle Rock. They automatically sell to cable for a couple of million, so that limits their risk. They'll decide how to distribute it depending on who they're affiliated with. Basically, you can't fart in this country without working for Rupert Murdoch or Ted Turner. I've worked with them both but never met either of them.

FILMMAKER: *How much effect do budget restrictions have on what kind of movies you make? And on the process?*
SAYLES: The more movies I make, the better I am at getting a lot out of the budget. With a $3 million budget, I can be a little more ambitious than I used to be. Even though it's still hard for us to raise money, we *can* get really experienced people, both actors and technicians. That translates into a high talent-to-time ratio. The budget affects everything that you do. You try not to let it affect the actors.

FILMMAKER: *Does editing your own work help? Do you find yourself editing in your head as you go along?*
SAYLES: Yeah, it helps. If you're going to cover from four different angles and one of them is kind of a wide shot, you can move the camera—the actor may wonder why, when we didn't even do a whole take where one of us didn't blow a line, even though it felt good emotionally. I know where I'm going to cut it, and I've got what I need, trust me. It's one of the advantages to controlling the final cut. It's a deal you make with the actor: I'm going to use your best acting take—and it won't be based on some focus group.

FILMMAKER: *You don't always make the films in the order you write them, but do you think of them as forming a continuum of some sort?*
SAYLES: They really aren't a continuum. They're like short stories, all over the place. I'm just interested in a lot of different things. So what you

try to do is to make the style of the film, the look of the film, the music of the film, who is in the film fit with the story you're telling.

FILMMAKER: *You work with a lot of the same actors and crew from film to film. What's the motivation?*

SAYLES: When you're making something with a lot of story lines, a lot of actors, and all these technical problems, and it's very ambitious for the budget, you're juggling a lot of things. Anytime that you've worked with an actor before, you can eliminate a question mark. That's just that much emotional energy and time that you don't have to spend working something out with that actor. You know, I've worked with Chris Cooper a couple of times and I know he can take care of himself. Poor Chris! So many of his scenes in *Lone Star* involve asking for information. He's so consistent and such a deep actor; we could come to him with only two hours left in the day and say, "O.k., now we're going to do your angle," and he wouldn't feel panicked. He would have been doing good stuff with the other actors all day, but he still had what he needed left.

FILMMAKER: *There's a strong pragmatic streak that runs through your conversation and your method. You seem bent on telling the story, whatever it takes.*

SAYLES: I'd say the most pragmatic of all my movies was *Return of the Secaucus Seven*—we had the budget before we had the movie. I had to think, what can I do well for $40,000 to get it in the can? The difficulty is that it takes a while to think of a way that you can get the same result with less money, time, whatever it is. Some of your best ideas come out of that—I don't necessarily think getting handed everything is the best thing for you.

FILMMAKER: *Do you see yourself as part of an independent film community? Is there such a thing?*

SAYLES: I'm not sure how much community there is—it's not like [we] hang out at the Tribeca Film Center together; it's more like a bus station. All kinds of people pass through the bus station, and some are never going to come back. And some end up there day after day—they get stuck there. People have a different relationship to the station, but I'm someone who keeps going back. Not every single trip—sometimes I'll fly—but that's mostly where I end up. So I don't think that there really is a community.

To a certain extent, there is a group of people who act in and who work in—and produce—independent films more often than other people. A few of them have long-term relationships, like the Coen Brothers and Jim Jarmusch, who's worked with the Japanese quite a bit. But for an awful lot of people like me, each time out is a different bus. We've made ten movies, and I'd say seven of the companies that distributed our movies are no longer in business. I don't think there's any causality there—but that means that the next time out, we're just looking for somebody else.

FILMMAKER: *What's your next directing project?*

SAYLES: It's always a question mark, but I hope to make this movie I've written called *Men With Guns* (*Hombres Armados*), a very dark road movie. It will be shot in Latin America in Spanish and Indian dialect, the first time I'll work outside the English language. I don't know where we'll shoot. It depends on the stability of governments, and I need permission to shoot at some ruins. It has to do with where I can get a crew and what will be the cheapest place, because it's got to be very low budget. It's a subtitled movie with no big American actors—or even small American actors. And then there's the rainy season—when they say rain there, they mean it.

# Borders and Boundaries: An Interview with John Sayles

DENNIS WEST AND

JOAN M. WEST/1996

*John Sayles describes his new film,* Lone Star, *as "a story about borders." It is set in Texas, which Sayles explains "is unique among the United States in that it was once its own country. It was a republic formed in a controversial and bloody way. And its struggles didn't end with the Civil War. There is a kind of racial and ethnic war that has continued. That continuing conflict comes into the clearest focus around the border between Texas and Mexico." But this geographical boundary is only one aspect of the film's concern with borderlines. "In a personal sense," Sayles comments, "a border is where you draw a line and say 'This is where I end and somebody else begins.' In a metaphorical sense, it can be any of the symbols that we erect between one another—sex, class, race, age."*

*In an even larger sense, Sayles adds,* Lone Star *is also concerned with "history and what we do with it. Do we use it to hit each other? Is it something that drags us down? Is it something that makes us feel good? You can get six different people to look at the Alamo and they have six different stories about what actually happened and what its significance was. The same goes for your personal history. At what point do you say about your parents, 'That was them, this is me. I take responsibility for myself from this day.'"*

*John Sayles discussed his approach to these themes in* Lone Star *with Joan M. West and Dennis West in May at the Seattle International Film Festival.*

---

From *Cineaste,* 1996 (Vol. XXII No. 3). Reprinted by permission.

CINEASTE: *Borders and boundaries—geographical, social, ethnic, and personal—are a central theme of your film. How did previous border films such as* Touch of Evil, The Border, *or* The Ballad of Gregorio Cortez, *influence your approach?*

JOHN SAYLES: I was very aware of borders and the way they can be geographical or manmade. Within the movie there are lines between people that they choose either to honor or not to honor. It may be this enforced border between Mexico and the United States, it may be one between class, race, ethnicity, or even military rank. There's an important scene where Joe Morton's character, an army colonel, says, "I want to know what you think," and the private says, "Really?" She has to say that because privates do not get to say what they think to colonels and you have to have a special dispensation.

On the other hand, once you cross that border, you may find out things you don't want to know. You may find out that the streets of America are not paved with gold. You may find out what Joe Morton's character finds out, which is that this is not a gung-ho private, this is somebody who's going to say things that make him question himself. His character is having a crisis of faith—although it's not in the church, it's in the military—about what he's done with his whole life.

When you cross the border and go into some kind of new territory, you don't necessarily have the power that you had on your side of it. When Sam Deeds crosses the border, the Mexican guy says, "You're just some gringo with a lot of questions, I don't have to answer you. That badge doesn't mean anything down here." I think that's one of the reasons that people like borders—they can say, "South of this line, I'm a big guy, and I run things here." Or it may be as literal as, "This is my land and, if you come on it, I can shoot you."

A lot of imagery in the movie was taken from the Alamo. The bartender, for example, says, "This bar here is the last stand, Buddy." When Sam goes down to Mexico, the Mexican guy draws a line in the sand, which refers to a famous moment from the history of the Alamo, when Travis drew a line. Of course, the Mexican draws the line with a Coca Cola bottle, but it is still a line drawn in the sand. During the Gulf War, George Bush used that same imagery of drawing a line in the sand.

In the other movies you mentioned, I'd say Tony Richardson's *The Border* was more about drugs and identity. It was also a little more romantic, with Jack Nicholson as the border patrol guy falling in love with the

Mexican girl he saw on the other side. That film made it seem a lot harder to cross the border than it really is. She could have come across a hundred and fifty times with her brother. It wasn't very realistic that they would ever catch him. It was also a little bit more of a shoot-'em-up than I wanted to do. *Lone Star* is not a thriller. It involves a murder mystery, but nobody ever pulls a gun on Chris Cooper's character, so it's not a thriller in that way.

*Touch of Evil* was influential in just thinking about that idea of a legend. Orson Welles's character is a legend in his own time, but the first time you see him he's this monstrous character. He's the kind of legend who didn't die in time, he's hung around and now he's going to ruin his own legacy. As for *The Ballad of Gregorio Cortez,* both the movie and the song, as well as the *corridos* in general, were important to me. There are dozens of these songs and many of them have to do with people who probably were pretty bad guys but because they fought the *rinches,* which is what the border people call the Texas Rangers, they became heroes. Fairly early on in my research I read a book called *With His Pistol in His Hand*...

CINEASTE: ...*by Américo Paredes.*

SAYLES: ...right. I also read an unfinished novel of his which was published recently. But just going back and finding more *corridos* and reading the lyrics of them was very useful for me in understanding that long history of conflict on the border.

CINEASTE: *How would you explain your continuing interest in Latinos and Hispanic-American cultures?*

SAYLES: My feeling, basically, is that I've made a lot of movies about American culture and, as far as I'm concerned, it is not revisionism to include Mexican-American culture or African-American culture or any of the many other different groups. If you're talking about the history of the United States, you're *always* talking about those things, from the get-go. As Sam Deeds says, "They were here first." And then the other guy reminds him, "Yeah, but the Native Americans were there before." So I don't see those as specialties. As far as I'm concerned, they're just part of the picture, just part of the composition.

I've lived in a lot of places in the United States and the odds are that sooner or later you're going to live in a neighborhood where people don't necessarily speak English, which I think is one of the things that makes the United States an interesting place to live. Where I'm coming from, in fact, is pretty much the opposite of Pat Buchanan's idea of this monoculture which is being invaded. English-speaking culture is just one of many cultures. It has become the dominant culture or subculture in certain areas, but it's a subculture just like all the others. American culture is not monolingual or monoracial. It's always been a mix. As one character says, "We got this whole damn *menudo* down here."

CINEASTE: *Does* Lone Star*, then, represent your vision of the U.S. as an increasingly multicultural society with more and more bicultural couples?*
SAYLES: I would say no to the first part and yes to the second. As I said, it's not *increasingly* multicultural, it's always been so. If you go back and turn over a rock, you find out, for example, that maybe a third or more of African-Americans are also Native Americans and a much higher percentage of African-Americans are also white Americans. You know, as they used to do in New Orleans, if you're 1/64th black, you're black, and it doesn't matter what you look like.

I do think there are more interracial couples nowadays. One of the interesting things I noticed during the Gulf War, seeing so many people interviewed on TV, was the large number of interracial couples, both of whom were in the military. There were also many black officers interviewed, including Colin Powell and people like that, who were asked, "What do you think of this war?," and they'd say, "Well, it's my job to go." They'd be asked, "Why are you in the army?," and they would say, "It's the best job I could get." I was fascinated by the idea that the United States Army, which used to be a bastion of segregation and racism, has gotten to the point where, although it's not the most liberal place in the world, it has become more liberal than the private sector. As a black person, you have a better chance of getting a job there and moving up if you do a good job than you do in the private sector.

CINEASTE: *History is a central theme of* Lone Star*, and your seamless transitions in some scenes between past and present seem to represent the continuing weight of the past.*
SAYLES: It is kind of an obvious conclusion because there's not even the separation of a dissolve, which is a soft cut. The purpose of a cut or a dissolve is to say this is a border, and the things on opposite sides of the

border are meant to be different in some way, and I wanted to erase that border and show that these people are still reacting to things in the past. There is a preoccupation with history in the film, whether it's Sam Deeds wanting to find out the personal history of his father, or the grandfather looking back into the roots of the black Seminoles. Pilar is a history teacher for a purpose, including that meeting about how they're going to teach history in the textbooks. Even Joe Morton's character is dealing with the history of black and white relationships. When he asks himself, "Am I just a mercenary?," it's not only because of his personal feelings, it's also in a way a historical question, asking, "Can I be a black soldier in the United States Army and not be a mercenary like one of those black Seminoles who just chased Indians for the whites?"

CINEASTE: *Many of* Lone Star*'s important characters—Sam, Delmore, Chet, Pilar, and Bunny—are examined in terms of their relationship to a father figure, and even the town and county themselves are seen in relation to their sheriffs. How does this relate to your treatment of the theme of history and to the patriarchal Hispanic tradition of the* caudillo, *the strongman figure?*

SAYLES: Something that was very much in mind was taking a story and being able to move in both directions with it, of taking something that's a little more particular and being able to spread it out to the political—taking a story like Sam Deeds's and, as he does with his investigation, looking into what is basically his own family history. It tells you something about the whole community, but sometimes that becomes a metaphor for personal history. For me, very often the best metaphor for history is fathers and sons. Inheriting your cultural history, your hatreds and your alliances and all that kind of stuff, is what you're supposed to get from your father in a patriarchal society. Both Texas Anglo society and traditional Spanish society were patriarchal societies, especially on the border, which had a history of *rancheros*, with 'Don' this and 'Don' that, who had these big spreads with *peons* working for them. It was very pyramid like, whereas in other parts of Mexico it was much more influenced by Indian hierarchies, which are not pyramid like, where men and women have separate roles but it's a little more circular. There may be a village chief but he might change every year, so it's more about communal ownership rather than one guy owning the land, and whose eldest son is going to own it in turn, and it's going to be passed on that way.

It was also important for me to include the story of Pilar and her mother. I think people generally take the same-sex parent as their role model, and so here's Pilar finding out about her family history very, very slowly. She may not even know that her mother was born in Mexico. Her mother may have said, "My people are down there, but I was born here," or "I married your father and he was a citizen." Who knows what legend she's been told. Her mother is very closed about that because in the culture in which she lives, there's a certain amount of shame in being a *mojado,* a wetback.

CINEASTE: *Pilar's mother represents a conservative Mexican-American attitude concerning contemporary immigration issues. I assume you did that very deliberately.*

SAYLES: Yeah, not only to show that factor but also to show that, when talking about borders and lines between people, very often when people cross those borders they want to slam the door behind them. They may have been banging against that door themselves, but because they have internalized the system and given it value, their attitude changes once they get on the other side of the border. The army is a perfect example of that. You may start out saying, "Officers are stupid," but once you're made an officer, you probably change your mind and you definitely don't say, "Now that I'm here, I'm going to abolish rank." That's been the tragedy of the Mexican revolution—you get Porfirio Diaz, who does these great things, and after they get rid of that old guy, somebody else becomes the *caudillo* again. That has been repeated time and time again in Latin American cultures, where revolutions have turned into just a change of *caudillos.*

CINEASTE: *Would you comment on Sam and Pilar, the last couple seen in the film, who have crossed their borders, and, if you care to deal with a related question, will their children be born with a pig's tail?**

SAYLES: [*Laughs*] Well, their children won't be born with a pig's tail because, as Pilar says, "I can't get pregnant again." One of the things I wanted to do with that is ask, "OK, what actually is that rule?" I'm interested in the difference between when people do things because of good practical and emotional human reasons, and when they're just following the rules. So here are Sam and Pilar—they were raised separately, they're adults now, there's no question of one being the older brother or the older sister and in some kind of position of power over the other one, so it's a fairly equal relationship in that way. They're not going to have children, so they're not going to pass on any horrendous birth defects, so what is that rule about? She says, "If that's what the rule's about, I'm not going to have children." What they're left with is the realization that, "OK, we have this chance to do something that is going to be seen as enormously antisocial but it's good for us," and they choose to cross that border of moral opinion.

But it is only an individual accommodation, and that was a lot of my point with the ending, it's not going to change society. They're going to have to leave the society they're in, they can't stay in that town. You may be very very nonracial, you may be married to a black person, but if you're in the middle of the Watts riots, that's not going to help you. That individual accommodation you made has not changed the social situation, or hasn't changed it enough so that what society is still doing is going to honor your change. Interracial couples that I know are careful about where they go. If it's a black and white couple, for example, there are places with white people where they don't go, and there are places with black people where they don't go. Only on the edges of those societies is there a place for them and their kids. In the hearts of those societies, sometimes, they're just not welcome.

CINEASTE: *I understand* Lone Star *is a Texas produced brand of beer. Why choose* Lone Star *for the title of your film?*

SAYLES: Well, the same reason, I think, that Lone Star chose it as the name of their beer. Texas is the Lone Star state. Texas chose the lone star because they were an individual who wanted to become part of a group. Once they broke away from Mexico they said, "Well, we are a republic," and choosing a lone star for their flag was a wannabe gesture toward the United States. I associated that with the character of Sam Deeds, who is an individual who stands very much outside of the group, looking at it, and who is supposed to eventually join it, but in this case he decides not to. You feel at the end of the movie, no, he's not going to run for sheriff again.

CINEASTE: *Would you comment on Wesley Birdsong, the Native American roadside merchant figure?*

SAYLES: As long as I was portraying the other people down on that border, I figured, well, I cannot leave this guy out. What I found interesting in that area of Texas is that although the reservations cover a lot of land, there isn't a huge amount of political fighting going on between the reservations and the state the way there is in the Dakotas, Montana or Wyoming. In Texas, they really have been relegated to reservations that are out of the way and out of mind, so that Native Americans you meet off the reservation are very likely to be enormously outnumbered in the general population and therefore somewhat isolated.

CINEASTE: *Is the Native American merchant a Kickapoo and was he a veteran of the Korean War?*

SAYLES: Yeah, he would be a Kickapoo down there. I didn't get into their history in the movie, but those are people who have been everywhere, including both sides of the border. It's a very split tribe right now, with about four different outposts, stretching from the Midwest to Kansas to Oklahoma to Texas to Mexico. The idea is that he was a friend of Buddy Deeds, who was a veteran of the Korean War, so Wesley may or may not have also been a veteran. It's not unusual to go into an Indian reservation and find that most of the guys have been in the army just for something to do. There are an incredible number of VFW posts on Indian reservations.

For me, what's important is when Wesley says, "I tried living on the reservation but I couldn't take the politics." Reservations are extremely political, with very tough infighting, and what he has decided to do, once again, is to take that individual accommodation. Where you see him is, as he says, "between nowhere and not much else." He is extremely isolated and he happens to like that, but that's where that choice can take you. The choice to escape the politics, to escape history, to escape that struggle and to do the antisocial thing, can leave you enormously isolated.

He is very self-possessed and he seems fairly content, so he is the upside of that kind of isolation, whereas Bunny, the ex-wife of Sam Deeds, is the opposite of that. She's kind of like the Ghost of Christmas Future, she's the person who has not escaped her family history. She's somebody who is a warning to Sam. In twenty years she's going to be in that room, bouncing off the walls, talking about how, "I loved my daddy, I hated my daddy." He'll be five years dead in the ground and she will still be living in his shadow and she's never going to get out from under it.

She's almost like a throwback to what would have happened to Mary McDonnell's character in *Passion Fish* if she hadn't come back to the world of human relationships. Her strongest personal relationship, other than the one with her father, is going to be with the Dallas Cowboys, who are always going to be there for her. They are cyclical, and, in a way, outside of history. They will always be there, and they don't have to know that she's there for her to feel like they care. So she has escaped in that way. I've often used the metaphor, in *Brother from Another Planet, Passion Fish,* and *City of Hope,* of television as a drug. Some people are addicted to alcohol or crack, but for others that fantasy world, that received world of soap operas or football or whatever, becomes a constant electronic drug that's available to you.

CINEASTE: *This is the first feature that you have shot in Super 35mm format. How did that decision relate to the visual style of the film?*
SAYLES: Super 35mm basically is just a different way to get a widescreen look. We shot widescreen on *City of Hope,* and, in that case, it was a practical decision because we had to switch between all these characters. We were very crowded sometimes, with two people in the foreground and three people in the background, and we needed more room for them so the image size didn't get too small. We could keep the image size fairly big on them and fit more people on the screen because we were doing so much trading in the master shots, which was a stylistic thing which distinguished *City of Hope.*

One of the things we wanted to do in *Lone Star* was to show the horizontal look of the border. It's not mountainous, it is a very long, absolutely flat horizon line, and we wanted, at least in the beginning of the picture, to isolate people in that flat, wide land. It takes about a county's worth of acres to raise a hundred head of cattle down there, and widescreen gave us that feeling of just a few people fighting over that little thin strip of river where the good land is and which is surrounded by scrubby desert. Super 35mm is just a different way to get a widescreen look where you use regular lenses, but because you use more of the frame, you don't have to hang quite as much light. Making an ambitious movie on a low budget, you have to move a little faster.

# *LONE STAR:* Maverick Director John Sayles Makes Films His Way

TIM MILLER/1996

BOSTON—SOMETIMES, THE STORY comes first and the themes come later. Sometimes, it's the other way around.

So says maverick filmmaker John Sayles, a cult favorite since his super-low-budget *Return of the Secaucus Seven*—a kind of pre-*Big Chill Big Chill*—hit art houses in 1980. Since that time he's made a wide variety of low-budget independent films that have been met with wide acclaim, including *Baby, It's You, The Brother From Another Planet, Matewan, Passion Fish* and last year's *The Secret of Roan Inish.*

His latest film, *Lone Star,* currently playing at the Cape Cinema in Dennis and Hoyts Nickelodeon Cinemas in North Falmouth, is set in a border town in Texas. Chris Cooper, who starred as a union organizer in *Matewan,* plays Sam Deeds, a sheriff who is investigating a murder committed decades earlier—a murder he suspects his legendary lawman father Buddy Deeds may have had a hand in.

That's the story on the surface. Through it, Sayles, who wrote, directed and edited the film, delves into themes involving racial, cultural and generational boundaries. He also deals with how history affects our lives.

In the case of *Lone Star,* theme came before story. Sayles says over lunch during a stopover in Boston to promote the film.

"It was a theme that I had first, and I was just thinking about 'What story could I tell that would get all these things that I want to talk about—history and cultures bumping heads—together?' And then I came up with,

---

From *Cape Cod Times,* 13 July 1996. Reprinted by permission.

'Well, what would be a good vehicle would be a murder mystery that happened in the past.' So we would have a guy—Chris's character, basically—an investigator who takes us into all these different strata of society, kind of like in a Raymond Chandler novel, where the trip is as important as the 'whodunit.'

"But also, because the murder happened in the past, it could take us into the past. This is the first movie I've done, I realized, that has flashbacks in it."

Sayles says he intentionally had scenes involving the present and past blend into each other, often without a cut in the action.

"I didn't want there to be a border, to be a line, between the present and the past, because *Lone Star,* to me, so much is about the burden of history. . . .

"When I started writing it, even though I had done all this research about Texas and Mexico, I was thinking an awful lot about Yugoslavia. I have an Italian friend who's a director who's been helping Yugoslavian refugees get settled in Italy.

"And an awful lot of them are guys who woke up one morning, and somebody put a gun in their hand and said, 'We're all Serbs here and we're gonna go kill your neighbors.' And it was, like, 'Well, wait a minute. You know, I know those guys. I went to high school with them. I don't have anything against them.' And he says, 'No, no, we're gonna kill 'em. This stuff happened two centuries ago, or whenever it was, and we have to kill 'em, because we hate them, and they hate us.'

"And the people that this (director) knew did the antisocial thing, which in this case was to put their gun down and, the minute people turned their backs, flee the country.

"Things are rarely that intense around us, but almost every day we run into something where, if we erased the history part of our brain, whether it's the family history or the social history, we'd act in a totally different way."

Tall (6 feet 4) and athletic-looking, Sayles, 45, wears his short-sleeve shirt with the sleeves rolled up, revealing muscular arms more likely to be found on a laborer than a movie director. Sure enough, when he lived for four years in East Boston in the mid-'70s, he worked as a day laborer.

"I packed sausage over in East Cambridge," he adds. "There are pepperonis still hanging that I had a hand in."

He was born in Schenectady, N.Y., and graduated from Williams College in Williamstown with a degree in psychology. He then worked a series of jobs and wrote—earning an O. Henry Award for the first short story he sold, to *Atlantic Monthly*. He wrote a couple of novels, then began writing screenplays for B-movies like *Piranha, The Lady in Red, Battle Beyond the Stars* and *Alligator.*

*Alligator*?

"I grew up liking horror movies and monsters movies," he says. "*Alligator,* to me, is a lot like *Them* which was a giant-ants movie. I actually just did a (script) polish on a giant-cockroach movie. So I'm at least starting a foray into the insect world."

He made *Secaucus Seven* for $60,000 and earned an Oscar nomination for its screenplay. He's directed nine movies since then, often writing screenplays and working as a script doctor to help finance them.

"My bread job is writing screenplays for other people.... I've written 12 movies for other people in the last two years or so," he says.

In some cases, it has taken him years to get the funding to make films.

"It was 11 years between writing the first draft of *Eight Men Out* and finally getting to make it," he says.

*Eight Men Out,* which came out in 1988, tells the true story of eight players on the 1919 Chicago White Sox—later known as the "Black Sox"—who were accused of throwing the World Series. It was based on a book by Eliot Asinof. Sayles, who occasionally takes small roles, played sportswriter Ring Lardner in it.

"When I was a kid, I heard about the Black Sox, and my first reaction was: How could anybody do that? I was raised Catholic. It was like... 'What a sacrilege! What kind of person could do this?'

"I think Eliot Asinof actually had the same kind of reaction. You know, he was a ballplayer: 'Who were these bums?' But, then, when he started to meet these guys and do the legwork and do the reporting and find out who the different ones were, he found each one did it for a different reason, and that some of the reasons were understandable. Finally, he didn't feel too bad about them selling out—even the fans of Chicago, or (team owner Charles) Comiskey.

"I think, finally, what you get is they sold their fellow players out. And that's the thing you find always, even the guys you were sympathetic with, you hold against them. They didn't tell their fellow players, 'Oh, by the way, guys, we're going for the money on this one. The hell with it if you're competitive or you want to win or you want to make more money.' "

He says the story got under his skin.

"I got to know these characters and I just said, 'Well, this movie, I've got to do this thing.' It was the first movie I wanted to make. It was the first thing I wrote."

He says it was a tough sell, though.

"It's history. It's not like *The Natural,* where, at the end of the book in *The Natural,* the guy strikes out. In the end of the movie, he hits a home run and hits the lights and all that kind of stuff. They figured, 'Hey, who reads books?' But people do know history. You couldn't have the Black Sox at the last minute have a change of heart and win the series."

Also, he says, there was "the ensemble problem."

"We were getting an awful lot of, 'Couldn't you make it "One Man Out"? Or "Two Men Out"? Or "Three Men Out and a Baby"?' "

Despite such thinking, Sayles has persevered, becoming the ultimate independent filmmaker.

"I get away with it because I work harder than most people who are trying to make independent films who have some of the same opportunities, and I'm luckier than people who are trying to make independent films who don't have the same opportunities."

# John Sayles: Filmmaker

DIANE CARSON/1997

DIANE CARSON: *Having just seen the premiere of* Men with Guns*, let's begin by discussing its structure and content. First of all, the film begins unusually, with an indigenous woman talking to her daughter. Were you wanting to invoke a mythological context?*

JOHN SAYLES: I wanted to do a couple things. First, without telling the whole story from *A* perspective, I wanted to suggest another point of view, namely that this isn't the story of us westerners going into an exotic locale. Maybe this is a story seen through the eyes of people of that place, of that way of seeing the world, and the central character, the doctor, is the exotic person.

The first words we hear spoken about him are, "Is he magic? Oh, yeah, he can put his hand on you and he can divine you. Is he some kind of witch doctor?" And at the end, when the people finally show up, since in the beginning we're there with that mother and daughter, we see these other people as extremely badly dressed for the jungle, slogging through the mud. In fact, they ARE the exotic ones. So the mother and daughter introduce to the audience this idea, "Oh, maybe there's another way of looking at this story even though, yes, you are sitting in a movie theater and you're westerners."

The other thing I wanted to get across is this. I read a lot of magical realism when I was learning Spanish. One of the things I noticed about

---

From the Toronto Film Festival 8 September 1997. 

magical realism is even though people may have extraordinary powers, they could never use those powers to improve their lives or escape their fate. They might be able to levitate, they might have some kind of second sight. But if they were poor, they stayed poor. And if they were doomed to be executed by the army, they were executed by the army.

I got to thinking about what that was a metaphor for and about people who have a certain kind of connection to the land, a certain kind of spirituality that most westerners miss, in fact, that we don't really have any more. We have other things, but we don't necessarily have that spirituality any more. That's a very valuable thing, but it doesn't necessarily have a practical application when you run up against a practical world, the world of men with guns. The woman can divine the doctor is coming, can somehow see that he's not going to leave, but she can't divine a land mine five inches in front of her foot, so she steps on it. She's still poor; her daughter is probably going to be without a mother soon, living in this poor community. And she may have an extra healing power and may have a spirituality, but it's not going to have a practical side.

I wanted to introduce that early in the film because spirituality and loss of spirituality and the definition of people's spirituality is something that all the characters have to deal with in some way. In the case of the doctor, he says, "Well, I'm not a religious person. I believe in science. I believe in progress." Well, his belief, as he says, is shaken.

The priest has a certain kind of spirituality and, in his version, one of the reasons he was able to run and did run from the village where he lived is that it's a portable God that he has. The western idea of spirituality is that you have this deal with God. You act a certain way, and it doesn't matter if you're on an airplane, in Chicago, or in the jungle, you carry that with you.

The Indians in this village, their spirituality is absolutely tied to that land. If you leave that land and that way of life, if you stop growing corn, if you stop dressing a certain way, if you stop your customs of marriage and birth and how you address each other and how you respect each other and how you make decisions together, you're not a person any more. You don't have a spirit any more, you don't have a soul any more. It's not portable. And so they can't leave that village without losing much more than their lives. The priest realizes, "If I stay here I'm going to lose my life" and, somewhere in the back of his head, he feels it's crazy to stay. He must feel that "maybe I can still be a Catholic and be good but why do I have to stay? Martyrdom is overrated." He had romantic ideas about it before, but not now.

But it's not martyrdom to these people. It's survival to say [after the men with guns tell them five must die] that five of us have to go. Then five of us have to go. Our survival is the survival of our spirits, the spirits of our children. We're not going to give away our children's future, whereas a westerner would say, "I can't stay here. They'll kill my children or they'll kill me and my children's future will be lost." Well, to them, they're saving their children's future.

DC: *But when all the men with guns are around—the army, the guerrillas—there isn't going to be any end to it. They're caught in the middle. They're doomed if they do and doomed if they don't.*

JS: That's probably the situation that got me thinking about this project in the first place. During the Vietnam War, I wrote a short story called "Tan" about a woman who lived in a village. The only American movie I can think of that resembles it at all is Oliver Stone's movie, *Heaven and Earth*, about the Vietnamese woman. And there's a Bergman movie called *Shame* that reminds me of it. You really don't know what the sides are fighting about, but these people are just caught in the middle. In a war, more civilians are killed than combatants, and very often those civilians don't necessarily have a side or don't necessarily understand anything about the conflict and wish it would just go away.

When I was writing *Men with Guns*, I was thinking not just about the conflicts in Latin America but in the former Soviet Union, in Africa and especially in Bosnia. There is no neutral all of a sudden. I have an Italian friend who has been helping support and smuggle people of various ethnic groups and religious groups from the former Yugoslavia into Italy. And they're basically the guy who said, "I was going to have to shoot my next door neighbor. I was going to have to shoot the guy across the street. And I don't want to shoot that guy. I don't have anything against him. But a gun was put in my hand and I was told, 'You're a Serb. He's a Croat. Shoot him.'"

DC: *The film* Vukovar, Poste Restante *dramatized that.*

JS: Yes, there is no neutral. And if I don't, I'm dead. The story in the barbershop [in *Men with Guns*] was inspired by stories I heard out of Yugoslavia.

There's the doctor and somebody comes to him wounded. And whether it was a wounded guerilla or a wounded army man, if the doctor doesn't treat the man, his buddies are going to shoot him. And if the doctor does treat the wounded man, the other group is eventually going to come back and say, "You collaborated." And they shoot him. That's one of the reasons I gave it a generic title like "Men with Guns" and set it in a generic Latin American country rather than saying, "This is Brazil," or "This is Peru," or "This is Guatemala," or whatever.

DC: *What about the American tourists? Why include them at all. Why not locate the story in a generic country and leave it at that?*

JS: A couple reasons. One thing I wanted was two people coming from a different place taking that journey. And what I said to Mandy Patinkin and Kathryn Grody was, "You're not ugly Americans at all. You're actually pretty nice people. You're better informed, you're very adventurous tourists, you're not just the guys who get on the tour bus and look at things through the tour window and say, 'Do we own this country?' and buy curios and stuff like that. But you are the teflon tourists. You have that first world idea. You feel the world is your theme park. You have a confidence you should not have. You're in places that you probably should not be in in terms of safety, but you're Americans. And so you feel nothing too bad can come to you and you have that ticket out, you have that passport. So if things get too hot, you go to the Embassy, and you're gone."

So they're parallel to Dr. Fuentes, who's taking the same geographical voyage. They're on parallel paths so they keep running into each other farther down the road. Each time we see them together, it changes. The first time, it's very comical. They meet in a diner and Dr. Fuentes is congenial when he says, "Oh, no, I think you have the wrong idea. Things like that don't happen in this country." And he's a little defensive, but it's more, "Oh, come on. Things are exaggerated." The next time he sees them, he's a little angry and says, "No, those kinds of things don't happen here." He's just heard one of his students has been killed. He's just learned something ugly about his own country—he's had his camera stolen. And the tourists are still people who seem ignorant to him. The third time he sees them, they've had their car robbed by a guy who could have shot them. And they don't know how lucky they are that it happened to be who it happened to be. It's just a matter of circumstances that these tourists didn't get shot. But that's just an adventure to tell at home. And there they are, wandering in a very dangerous area, there are guerrillas there, there are snakes, there are all kinds of things happening, and these two are just looking at the archeology.

But Fuentes has changed quite a bit. He's very sad. He listens to things in a much more philosophical way. He's not defensive any more when they're talking about the massacres. He's started to hear his own stories about massacres and see evidence of them. He's found skulls in a human body dump. So each time Fuentes sees them, they're the same—it doesn't affect them. But Fuentes is different.

DC: *They're impervious to it.*
JS: Yeah, so they are a litmus or a thermometer to put up against Fuentes to see how he changed where they didn't have to because they're teflon tourists.

DC: *The terrific Mexican actors that you found—how were they cast?*
JS: [Federico] Luppi who's an Argentinean, the lead [Dr. Fuentes], I had seen him in several movies and always had him in my mind. But I had only seen a few of the other actors before. I had seen Damián Alcázar who plays Padre Portillo, the priest, in a couple of movies. And I had seen Roberto Sosa who plays Bravo, the student, who is found in the market. He was in Alex Cox's film *Highway Patrolmen* and he was in *Cabaza de Vaca*, in which he plays the young Indian kid who takes the bullet out one time and then gets killed later. Roberto's a really good actor.

But the rest of the people were people I had only seen in very, very small parts or we just found there. Probably about a half dozen of them came through Claudia Becker who's the main casting person in Mexico City. They're actors who work fairly often in television mostly, because there aren't that many features. In Mexico, as our first A.D. said, you can watch Mexican television and think you're in Switzerland. They really haven't caught up with the fact that most of their population looks very Indian and are part or all Indian. The rest had never been in a movie or tv show. They were too dark looking, too Indian looking. They'd been in theater, if that, or dance companies or Teatro Campesinos. Dan Rivera González who plays the little boy came to an open call. The woman who plays the mother at the beginning of the movie comes from an island off the coast of Panama, and she's a dancer who happened to be in Chalapa when we had a call. Her language has never been spoken in a movie before.

Lizzie Martinez, our casting director, worked with us doing the extras casting in Eagle Pass in Texas on *Lone Star* and we brought her down. She and her brother canvassed a fairly wide area of a couple of states and then went out to Chiapas and tried to find people there. So they did a lot of that casting, bringing people to me who hadn't necessarily been in movies, who were in theater companies. They put them on tape, and then I would meet them if I could.

DC: *It's refreshing.*

JS: Yes, it's also something we try to do in all our movies, to make a good percentage of the casting, especially smaller parts, local people. They've got the accent. There are good actors everywhere. It's just that everybody doesn't get discovered when they're 13 years old and sent to Hollywood.

DC: *I'd like to connect this with your other films' themes. Your topics are different but your themes are similar, especially your sense of community. Perhaps since I've been studying Asian film, I think of that sense of community as more Asian than Eurocentric and that fierce individualism. What one person does, as in* City of Hope, *affects everything going on which I believe much more than, "I can do whatever I want because it's just me and the hell with everybody else. It won't affect them"—which, of course, it will. Am I on the right track with that sense of community?*

JS: Yeah, or impact. Sometimes there really isn't a community, but there is impact, though people like to think there isn't. I often use the example of a very difficult thing I deal with fairly often. Friends of mine have kids coming out of elementary school now. These friends went to public schools, and they think it's great to have good public schools. But they live in a community where they think the public schools are really terrible and, in some cases, a little bit dangerous. The schools aren't as good as the public schools when they were kids. Now these parents have to decide to send their kids to public schools or private schools. It's an economic decision, but it's also a philosophical and a moral decision. But it's not just your life; it's your kid's life. So some of them, who may have a strong moral resistance to sending their kid to a private school, have to say,

"Well, wait a minute. Am I going to sacrifice my kid's happiness, future, safety in some cases, for my own moral code or my own social learnings? This is his life. But is he old enough to decide, or is she old enough to make her mind up?" It's a tough thing to ask.

Some of what I get into in *City of Hope* is the difficulty in small city politics, especially separating the political from the personal. I know the mayor is a crook, but if he doesn't win, your cousin Louie is going to lose his job with the Parks Department and, you know Louie, he's not going to get another job because he's limited and your cousins aren't going to have bread on the table. So how do you turn against the mayor just because he doesn't like black people and doesn't do anything for them? Are you going to hurt your own family? How can you do that? That's a tough thing, and it gets personal and it gets family and it gets tribal very, very, very often and what is your loyalty?

So YOU have this moral or ethical code. Well, great for you, but I come from a culture where family is everything, where community starts with family, and how can you turn your back on that? The Vietnam War was a good national watershed for the people who just said, "It's our country and, if you're a certain age, you're supposed to either enlist or cooperate with the draft." And other people said, "No, I don't believe in this war. I'm not necessarily even a pacifist, but I don't believe in THIS war, so I'm not going and I don't have to go." There are two ways to look at that. One is that it's heroic. The other is, "Well, you say you have a sense of community and you're not going when the community says you should. What's that? You just do what's good for you when it's convenient for you and then you go to the other side?"

DC: *Tough moral choices.*

JS: Yes. And getting back to *Men with Guns*, it's one of the things I was trying to deal with. Here's somebody who has avoided those tough moral choices by being ignorant on purpose. And in his case, it would take some work to know what was going on. Dr. Fuentes probably lives in a place where the government controls the newspapers, where the official story is not the whole story, not even much of the real story. BUT he could know if he had wanted to. He probably had suspicions, he heard rumors. He even talks about rumors. But he didn't follow up because he didn't really want to. And that can happen in a family. It can be somebody who says,

"No, your father didn't molest you. Come on." "Well, what about that time you found him in bed?" "Oh, come on, that didn't happen. I never found that."

DC: *Yep, it happens all the time.*
JS: All the time because saying the words, admitting it, changes your life forever. I've been thinking about *Short Cuts*, Robert Altman's movie of Ray Carver's stories, and in all those Ray Carver stories, I noticed, when they put them all together, there's this burden of knowledge. If Lily Tomlin's character knew that she had actually killed that little boy when she hit him with her car, the rest of her life she's got to think of herself as the person after that time when she killed that little boy. Now, it's just, "Phew, one time, I hit this kid and he bounced right back. Wasn't that great?" And she can live as a totally different person.

DC: *Denial is powerful.*
JS: And it's not denial in that case. It's ignorance. But ignorance allows you not to carry the burden of that knowledge. Ignorance you can't really find fault with if that knowledge was not available to the person. But if it was and that person turned away from it, or avoided it, then you do have to hold them responsible. And we have to all hold ourselves responsible, and that's a tough thing to do. It's hard to know all that stuff and then act according to it. The world is a complex place.

Certainly the difficulty of our movies, and they are difficult to a certain extent, is that they're complex. And the whole point of most movies is to make things less complex.

DC: *Make it simple and easy?*
JS: Yes, and more dramatic because of that, because you can have those clear good guys and bad guys. Very often the screenwriter's job, my job when I'm writing for other people, is to iron out all those little wrinkles and make a clearer story line. I'm told, "We need a clearer delineation between the good guy and the bad guy." And so you have the bad guy kick a dog or a small child in the first act.

DC: *You still do your script doctoring? You worked on* Mimic, *didn't you?*
JS: Yeah. I make a living as a screenwriter for hire, and I like it. It's a good job, and I get to work with really interesting people, and it pays really well

which helps me make my own films. But I'm glad it's not my only job because that would be very frustrating. No matter what the intention of the movie is, only one out of five lives up even to its own intentions. And that's just the political nature of movie making.

DC: *But you also continue your serious writing, don't you? Short stories and novels and essays?*
JS: Yes, the next fiction I publish, if I can get it published, is a bunch of short stories I'm still working on. I've got about half of them written.

DC: *You work a lot?*
JS: Yeah. I think, if I could, I'd continue to write for other people because I do like it besides making a living at it. But I'd do a little less of that than I do.

DC: *I wish you were still writing some television, like "Shannon's Deal."*
JS: That was tough. Brandon Tartikoff just died, and he's the guy who really got that off the ground. He was very straight with me. He said, "This is difficult for television. It's definitely a 10 o'clock show and what you've handed me here is a lawyer who never goes to court." And after the first mini-season (they only made 13 episodes) he said, "We just did some demographics on this and some testing. Half the people who watch the show don't know he's not a detective." That's the people who watch it! So, complexity and television are strange bedfellows.

DC: *Yeah, I love* Homicide *and* Law and Order, *and I'm always sure, as soon as I start liking a program, it's going off the air.*
JS: Yeah, it's either going off the air or it's going to be hard to keep up that level of interest and quality. It's a big mouth to feed. And I know in Australia and, in some case, in Britain, they can still get away with doing a 13-part episode and that's it. Or something like Helen Mirren's *Prime Suspect*. American television just doesn't limit themselves that way. The cable people are starting to do a little bit, but the whole point of a series is for it to last three to four years at least so it can go into syndication. Then you make a profit. You don't make it on the first three years.

I was very happy with "Shannon's Deal." While it was on, we were allowed to make a good show. And that's all I ask. But it only lasted 13 episodes. Maybe there were only 13 good episodes to be made; maybe there were 20 or more. But it attracted good writers and directors and actors. I was really pleased with the cast. But it's a very hard thing to sustain. The actors get tired and you realize, in a cop show, there are only seven crimes and you've got to recycle those. Then you get into private lives, and it turns into soap opera fairly quickly.

DC: *Do you like acting, since you appear in many of your own films and had a role in "Shannon's Deal" and elsewhere?*

JS: Yes, I like acting but I don't ever want to be an actor. It's a really hard job and it's hard on you psychologically as well as in a career way. It would be fun to do more acting even though I don't necessarily like to look at myself on tv or in movies. I'm not driven to be an actor, but I think it's good for me as a writer. The main thing you do as an actor is think about your point of view. I once had the opportunity to be in two different productions of *Of Mice and Men*. In one I played Lenny who's the big, retarded guy. And in the other I played Candy who's the old guy who's lost his hand. You walk into the same bunkhouse but you see a totally different world. In one, if you're Lenny, you're looking for your dog and you're afraid of everybody. It's kind of confusing and you're tense because George told you not to do this and not to do that. In the other, if you're this old guy, you hear different things and see different things. So it's like a totally different play if you really get into point of view.

As a writer, that's exactly what I try to do. For each character I try to think, "This is a movie about that character. How does this person see the world?" And that's one of the reasons the secondary characters in our movies tend to be a little more primary and come closer to the foreground. They may not have that much screen time, but for the actors I try to listen to that line in the Ronald Reagan movie, *Kings Row,* "Where's the rest of me?" That's the first thing character actors usually say when they get their part is, "Where's the rest of me? What ammunition and evidence do I have for who this person is, not just what his function is." I try to give them those extra couple lines so you have some sense of who the person is as well as just what they're doing in there at that moment in time saying, "Here comes the prince."

DC: *Getting back to this film,* Men with Guns *offers a very archetypal story, this journey. Are you hoping, despite the reticence, especially of American audi-*

*ences to read subtitles, that some of the universality of the archetypes, of the appeal will overcome that resistance, that hurdle?*

JS: What we hope always with all of our movies, which is basically the same story with all of them whether it's *Lone Star* or this one or whatever, is that, whether through reviews or you've built up some kind of audience or the specific subject is interesting enough, you get a critical mass of people to come in the first couple of weeks because we're not ever going to have—and we have never had—the money to advertise on television and open broad, wide. We hope the word of mouth starts moving. Then the movie advertises itself through the people who saw it and that doesn't cost you any money. This movie is the same deal.

Certainly one of the reasons *Lone Star* was more popular was that there were iconic elements familiar to people who don't necessarily or usually go to non-Hollywood movies. There was a badge, a gun, a sheriff, a murder, and that was their way into the picture. So they hung with it a little longer, and some people who had been dragged in or wandered in or didn't know if they were going to like it or not, came back and told their friends, "Hey, check this out." So it was a different group of friends than usually get talked to.

On this picture, there aren't those iconic things. Basically, I just don't consider this movie an American movie. The United States is just ONE of the markets we're going to sell to. In every country in the world, it's going to have some subtitles, so I'm thinking of it as a movie we're selling in the world. It's a story that I think anybody in the world can hook in to if we can get them to the theater. And in English-speaking countries, we hope we'll make some money and some of the people who should see the movie will like it, get something out of it, and will get to see it. But there is no such thing on this one as domestic and foreign. It's all foreign.

DC: *What was your budget?*

JS: It was about two and one half million. We had about six weeks to shoot. We only brought about five people to Mexico, one was the cinematographer who is Polish. We brought a couple of Chicano Americans down to be the casting people and the focus puller. And then the producers and me. The rest of the people we got there, and some of the people we worked with there were free volunteers, but they were local Mexican free volunteers or people getting very little who just wanted to work on a movie and they happened to be in the neighborhood, so we didn't have to put them up.

DC: *What's your next project? You mentioned Alaska at the* Men with Guns *premiere.*

JS: The next project is called *Limbo* and, it's in limbo because I haven't written it or financed it yet. But in a couple of days we're going to go up there and scout. I know what the story is about and right now I'm describing it as a cross between a family drama and a Joseph Conrad kind of tale.

DC: *We'll be watching for it.*

# Lone Director: John Sayles Discusses the Making of *Lone Star*

STEVE GRAVESTOCK/1997

JOHN SAYLES IS EASILY the most respected American independent filmmaker working today. He's managed to create an intriguing, compelling body of work (including the Oscar-nominated *Passion Fish* and the watershed indie hit *The Return of The Secaucus Seven*) without ever compromising himself. His career, however, didn't exactly start off on such a high note. A successful novelist and short story writer, he entered movies as a scriptwriter/script doctor for fabled exploitation filmmaker Roger Corman. His work for Corman generally involved adding wry, deadpan humor—a kind of goofy pragmatism—to cheesy, irredeemable genre films like *The Howling, Alligator* and *Battle Beyond the Stars.*

Ten of his own films and 15 years later, his sense of humor is still intact. When we start talking about his latest, *Lone Star,* which played recently at the Cannes Film Festival, he responds with self-deprecating wit.

"We were lucky," he says of the response, "it was the first movie in the Directors' Fortnight so the audience was able to see it without having seen too many movies."

*Lone Star* is a modern day murder mystery of sorts. The film takes place in Frontera, a Texas border town. The ostensible hero is Sheriff Sam Deeds (Chris Cooper, a member of Sayles's ensemble). Sam has the nightmare job of living up to the reputation of his deceased father, Buddy Deeds. When two off-duty army officers locate a skeleton, it's clear that it belongs to Charley Wade (Kris Kristofferson), Buddy's brutal, corrupt predecessor

From *id Magazine,* 30 November 1997. Reprinted by permission.

Local legend has it that Buddy ran Charley out of town back in the '50s, but to Sam this looks like murder.

"Sam's a guy who's been living a love-hate relationship with his father," explains Sayles, on the phone from Chicago. "As he says, the first 15 years he spent trying to be like him in every way. The next 15 he wanted to give him a heart attack. Sam has purposely gone back to this town to do it. The scene with Frances McDormand [who plays Bunny, Sam's football, Daddy-obsessed ex-wife] is kind of like the Ghost of Christmas Future. If he doesn't get out from under his father's weight, Sam will be wandering around the same room. He has to let Buddy Deeds lie—and leave him there."

Running throughout the film is a sense of compromise, of ideals that have to be acknowledged but also tempered. The characters pursue an uneasy, but adult, peace. Sayles's propensity for mature, ambivalent responses has led many to call his films novelistic.

"There's a sense of complexity about the characters. They aren't just heroic," he comments. "They're like your friends. They do things you don't like, but you still like them. There are a lot of decisions here that are really tough. They're not win-win situations for anybody. You take for example a legend like Buddy Deeds, there are those who just want to put up a plaque and forget about him. And then there's Sam who wants to prove that he was no better than Charley Wade.

"You go back to *Secaucus Seven*; it opens with that kind of heroic music, then there's these mug shots, and then a shot of someone plunging a toilet. There are all these kinds of heroic ideals evoked and then they're living in the real world, and it's about those heroic ideals, but they're dealing with some of life's complexities and some of its realities."

*Lone Star* concludes a chapter in Sayles's career. He made his first two epic visions of American history (*Matewan* and *Eight Men Out*) in the late '80s, then created an epic view of the contemporary American city, *City of Hope,* perhaps the most underrated American film made this decade—and one that compares very favourably to Spike Lee's much-ballyhooed *Do the Right Thing.* Then he switched to more personal, smaller scale films like *Passion Fish* and *The Secret of Roan Inish. Lone Star* marks his return to the epic form.

Though Sam Deed's predicament frequently occupies centre stage in *Lone Star,* it is inaccurate to suggest that he's the film's principal focus. Sayles shuttles between 20-odd characters, including Pilar (Elizabeth Peña),

Sam's high school sweetheart. Years ago Sam's father refused to let them see one another.

"I always wanted [the film] to be about borders and history," says Sayles. "In Texas there are borders between the two or three cultural communities, so you have to talk about history. *City of Hope* is like a snapshot with these people saying this is the American city; *Lone Star* is broader, it shows how we got there. In *City of Hope,* it was a conscious decision not to have cuts or dissolves between the past and the present.

"It's inescapable not to know about it [history]," he adds. "You have to deal with it, but how you deal with it is a different matter. I was thinking quite a bit about Yugoslavia while making it. Yugoslavian refugees are those people who didn't want to murder their neighbours. [They left] because they knew they'd be handed a gun and told they were Croat or Serb and that therefore they had to shoot this person who lives across the street—even if they went to school with them or grew up with them. So their only choice is to get out of town—like Sam and Pilar. It's not your choice. It's about something that happened years ago, but choices are based on history whether you like it or not."

The eerie shifts between past and present create an air of uncertainty, an uncertainty that's reflected in Sayles's portrait of the cultural rifts within the community. People don't fall into stereotyped, predictable roles. Mercedes Cruz (Miriam Colon), Pilar's successful business woman mother, is more contemptuous of illegal immigrants than some of the rednecks. Otis Payne (Ron Canada), a black bar owner, is considered the unofficial mayor of the town's small black community, but he views the political developments with apparent detachment. He's more concerned with trying to convince his estranged son to come back into his life.

Instead of polemics, Sayles creates recognizably human (i.e. conflicted) characters. Everyone has to come to terms with history, sometimes cultural-social, sometimes personal, but usually it's a mix.

"Borders here can be taken as a metaphor, but they vary in terms of how they're defined," he explains. "It's the lines you draw yourself. You may choose to honour some boundaries and not others. In the military, rank is more significant than race. It doesn't matter if a general is black, it matters that he's a general and you better acknowledge that—unless you're a five star general yourself. Off base that might be different—and race may turn out to play a major role.

"You may choose to say that I am a middle-class Mexican American woman and these people [illegal immigrants] have nothing to do with me. If you're her, you may need a way to separate yourself from them. Class is often much more of a barrier than race. Certainly in the entertainment industry it's much more significant if you're a major star like Eddie Murphy than if you're someone who isn't so well known."

Speaking of being well known, Sayles's reputation has been eclipsed by the advent of younger flavour-of-the-month filmmakers like Quentin Tarantino, Roberto Rodriguez, et al. It's a perverse irony, one worthy of a Sayles film, since many of them coast on the reputation of credibility that Sayles and some of his contemporaries (like Victor Nunez and Robert M. Young) laboured long and hard to create—and not by simply re-tooling old genres. Still, it's hardly a sore point with him. Sayles agrees that there's less content in the current crop of independently produced films—"Now it's more a place to show off your skills"—but, he's more concerned with the effects sudden notoriety will have on these filmmakers' careers.

"It [their sudden success] is positive in the sense that it's easier for them to raise the money to make features. It's negative—if there is a negative side—in that for their second film they'll be handed $10–15 million. That's an awful lot of money to have hanging over your head. When Joe [Dante, director of *The Howling, Gremlins*] and Lewis [Teague, director of *Alligator* and *Jewel of the Nile*] and I started, we made three or four movies before we had any serious reviews. We learned our chops and were able to make good movies without that weight on us. Nowadays, the filmmaker tugs in one direction while others tug in another direction—and that price tag is always held against them. The high stakes aspect of it is a double-edged sword."

Then he adds, with typical Sayles-like detachment, "But if the audience goes to the movie, and it didn't star anybody they'd heard of before, that's great. It means they're going beyond the mall."

# Q & A: John Sayles

RILEY WOODFORD/1998

MOVIE-MAKER JOHN SAYLES is an animated conversationalist, but he really lit up halfway through a recent interview.

He'd explained what it is about Southeast Alaska that made him want to spend the summer in Juneau filming *Limbo,* his 12th movie, which tells the story of a land-bound Panhandle fisherman who becomes shipwrecked on an island. He talked about his writing, acting and filmmaking career, and his motivations and insights.

It was the esoterica of putting it all together that made him lean forward and gesture even more expressively than usual. He's a big man, with long arms and large, basketball-palming hands, and he had them working as he explained how sound is synced and how perspectives are unified.

Since he arrived in town in mid-May with producer Maggie Renzi, his partner and long-time professional collaborator, he's been busy. He finished writing a screenplay for Castle Rock, *Gold of Exodus,* as he began pre-production on *Limbo.* Filming begins this week, and he's been getting in shape for the physical demands of shooting, running and swimming and shooting hoops.

After a run, on a hot day at the end of June, he took time to talk about his new movie.

Q: *Did you start writing this 10 years ago, when you first came to Southeast?*
A: I started thinking about setting something here, but not in real specific terms. Then I came back several months ago and saw the differences . . . in Juneau (from) 10 years ago.

---

From *Juneau Empire,* 5 July 1998. Reprinted by permission.

It's kind of a very good and broad metaphor for what's happening in the economy of the United States in general, moving from a manufacturing economy to a service economy. More and more people are being waiters and stewards and selling T-shirts, and fewer and fewer people are cutting down logs and fishing, and working in factories.

One of the interesting things about seeing Southeast . . . it's kind of at the point I'm sure Cape Cod was at 50 years ago, or maybe Fisherman's Wharf in San Francisco was at 40 years ago, where it's just turning from a thing that really did the thing to a thing that says, "Oh, we used to fish here."

Originally, in San Francisco, that *was* a fisherman's wharf, and there were no restaurants there. People would come down and see the Italian fishermen cooking on their boats, and say, "Oh, that smells good. You should open a restaurant!" And eventually, the restaurants took over from the fishermen, and now, fish don't come in there anymore, unless it's on a UPS truck. So it's become a boutique about what used to happen.

Q: *Is this story something you came up with and then chose to set in Alaska, or is Alaska essential to it?*

A: I often think in our movies the location really influences the story; it's like a character. One of the things I've noticed—about a lot of the people who come to Alaska, not necessarily the ones who are born here—it's a place where people reinvent themselves. They're often able to do things younger than elsewhere; they have more responsibility younger, and it's not looked down on to change careers. People often do two or three things or overlapping seasonal things.

That character of the place is very different from a place where there's not much social mobility, where everybody's in their place. One of the things the story is about is the possibility of these people who bring a lot of personal baggage—a lot of negative history from past events and relationships—the possibility of them forming a new family, reinventing themselves as a family. I think that's more possible in a place like Alaska, that has that sense of—if you can stick it out here, you can make something of yourself that didn't exist before.

"People cut people more slack up here than they do in other, more tradition-bound parts of the world or United States, where everything is spoken for and it's very hard to get into the society.

I don't think people here do the pedigree check like they do in some other places.

So one of the reasons for coming up here, aside from the natural beauty and the nature, which is certainly a big part of the story, and kind of is a character in the story, is seeing the society in flux.

And who knows what it's going to turn into? And maybe Southeast will be very different from the rest of Alaska. It's in transition right now from what it used to be to whatever it's turning into.

Q: *Why did you specifically choose Southeast?*

A: I wanted mountains with woods . . . up north the look of the place is more barren, and I wanted a place where there are a lot of nooks and crannies. An important thing about the story is these people are looking for the closest anchorage in a bad storm that came on them suddenly, and they cut around an island that almost nobody cuts around . . . and so they can't just walk out and get picked up when they get stranded there. In Southeast, there are so many islands, and nooks and crannies, by the end of fishing season nobody's going in there. You can get lost here, not too far from civilization.

I also wanted to play with that idea that you see in Southeast, that there's this duality—that nature is kind of like a theme park. There you are on the Princess Cruiser looking at all this stuff, but you're very isolated from it. You don't reach out and touch it. Those big boats are so invulnerable . . . but very quickly, something that is kind of like a theme park exhibit can turn around and kill you.

Nature is big here, and it really doesn't care about you. You're not what's on its mind; it does what it does. It's interesting being in a place where you can go from this incredibly civilized veneer of McDonalds and tourist shops, and pretty much 15 minutes later be in a place you'd better know what you are doing or you could get killed.

Q: *Are you going to be in this movie?*

A: No, I don't learn that much when I act for myself. Unless I'm going to be in a part that's big enough, and that I feel I know how to play, I'd just as soon give the job to somebody who needs it more, a professional actor who can use the gig.

When I act for other people, I actually do learn a lot more 'cause I see how they direct, and I can see how another team does it.

When I act for myself, it's not just to be in a movie, but because I know how to play that part.

In *Eight Men Out,* I play Ring Lardner. When I first wrote it, 11 years before I got to make it, I was too young to play Ring Lardner... but by the time we got to make it, I was really close to his character. I was almost the same age; he's six foot; I'm six-four; he was a writer; I was a writer; I actually look like him a little bit. It just made good casting sense.

Q: *What about the preacher in* Matewan*?*
A: That was kind of the perfect director part. I didn't need to learn other people's lines, I just talked and everyone said "Amen." (Laughing) What more could a director ask for?

Occasionally I'll cast myself just 'cause of my size. For that preacher to be in a very short piece (on screen) and intimidating to the little boy, my size helped.

In *City of Hope* Vincent Spano is six-foot-tall. I wanted the character that he has this physical confrontation with at the end to be somebody who is somewhat threatening to him, so I needed somebody bigger than Vincent.

I'm not into the Alfred Hitchcock thing where I show up in a cameo.

Q: *You were a great alien cop in* Brother From Another Planet.
A: Yeah, that was fun—the original *Men in Black* as we call it.

Q: *Have you considered making something that's more comedic like that again?*
A: You know, it either comes out of the material, or it doesn't. I've written things for other people, comedies, but nothing that I wanted to direct recently.

Q: *You've been doing quite a bit of writing.*
A: Yeah, that's still pretty much how I make a living, as a screenwriter for hire. The last couple of things I did, I adapted a nonfiction book called *Gold of Exodus* for Castle Rock, a book that was just published. I adapted a science fiction book called *Brother Termite* for James Cameron.

I worked on *Apollo 13* and *Mimic*. You don't always get credit; it really depends on how much you change it, not whether or not you make it better.

Q: *Are you still writing fiction?*
A: Yeah, I'm working on a short-story collection that I hope, after this movie, I'll take a break and finish.

Q: *When did you actually write* Limbo*? In the last six months?*
A: Yeah, I think so. Actually once I sit down, I write very fast. So I may think about a script for a couple years, but once I sit down it's really a matter of three or four days, altogether. That depends, I may have to leave and do something else for three or four weeks, and then come back to it. I do a lot of writing on airplanes.

Q: *So do you have a lot of ideas going on?*
A: I have two or three; I don't like to get too far ahead of myself. They may sit around for 10 years or so like this one did before they actually take shape as a real story. I don't have screenplays written, but I have ideas.

Q: *How have you fine-tuned your script since you've been staying here in Southeast?*
A: The main thing I always do for the last draft of the script, and for practical reasons, is talk to the people who really do what you're talking about in the script. In this movie we have gillnetters, charter boats and float planes. You talk to people; say, "OK, what would you use for this job? Where do you fish? When is the opening these days?" The way they work the fishing openings has changed since I was here 10 years ago, and that's something I changed in the script.

We went up in a float plane and landed where we're going to land in the movie. We had the guy fly around a little bit and say, "Well, of the three or four beaches here in this cove; this is the one where I would land, because at low tide it's deep enough; I'm not likely to catch a rock." So you do that kind of thing, both for safety and practicality.

I've gone through and done tide charts for every day we're going to shoot, and I have listings for every shot that's an outside shot near the water, whether it should be a low tide scene or a high tide scene.

Sometimes that's for the aesthetics of the scene. (In the film) when people are out gathering stuff for subsistence food, it's better to do it at low tide, because it's all spread out there.

Later on, there's a point where people are being chased, and I want them to be able to get out of the water and get into the woods fast; and that's easier to do at high tide—there's less beach to cross.

Now you get two low tides a day, and you have to look at what light you prefer. The light in Alaska in the summer is very good for shooting in one way, because you get such a long day. Very often it's overcast, and you can shoot at nine o'clock at night and say that it's six in the morning . . . with one little filter, it looks exactly the same to the audience. So you have that leeway.

I even put a line in the script, because I think a lot of people who haven't been up here and who are going to see this movie don't know that it can be 10 at night and you can see colors and everything perfectly clearly.

So I had a scene earlier where this young girl was having a hard time sleeping 'cause some people are making noise outdoors, and I just changed it. Her mother says, "Why can't you sleep?" and she says, "It doesn't get dark anymore"—she's just moved here. . . . It reminds the audience that just because you can see colors doesn't mean it's not late at night.

Q: *You've been able to make 12 movies now without drifting into more and more commercial work. How have you been able to maintain that?*

A: Well, first of all, I've been interested in maintaining that. The stories that I continue to want to tell have been ones that aren't necessarily appropriate for studios to finance. Another part is that none of our movies have gone platinum, and so studios aren't that interested in hiring me as a director. So it's not like, "Whatever you want to do next, we'll finance."

What basically happens is they have to say, "Well, the public knows what it likes. I don't understand what the hell he's doing, but let's give him 12 million and let him make a movie about whatever he wants."

We've been very fortunate; when we've kind of hit a wall, I've had more than one idea for the next movie. When it became clear I wasn't going to get to make *Eight Men Out* or *Matewan,* I could come up with something I could finance myself from writing screenplays that cost hundreds of thousands of dollars rather than millions of dollars.

None of our movies has lost a lot of money; some of them have made a profit, a lot have broken even. So what that means is nobody is thrilled and excited and thinks that they're going to get rich if they're financing one of our movies.

They're also not going to go to the poorhouse, because we don't go over budget. If you get into financing one of our movies, you have a pretty good idea what you're going to get from the screenplay. I don't change the script at the last minute. We don't promise them stars; sometimes they're pleasantly surprised with what they get.

Q: *So you have credibility.*

A: Maggie Renzi has worked on a lot of the movies and is part of that credibility. And I'm not in an adversarial position with producers; I'm not going to try to get them a little bit pregnant and then tell them it's going to cost twice as much as I said in the beginning. If they say they can give me this much money, then I'll figure out a way to tell the story with that.

Q: *How much of a movie like this one is done with the sound live on camera?*

A: Almost all of the dialogue. Whenever you mix music into it, you start having some things that aren't really making noises. Like we have a couple of scenes on board a boat. We may motor to get ourselves moving, then turn the engine off and drift with the momentum we have while people say five or six lines, so then we'll come back and take the tape-recorded sound of that motor and mix it in, but it'll be consistent from shot to shot.

Just like you do in real life. If you go into a crowded bar, and you really want to hear what the person is saying next to you, you kind of tune it in; you may not even know what the song is that's playing. You do that kind of psychological mixing for people in the movie.

You think of what's eventually going to be heard with what's seen; it's going to be a mix of sound effects, dialogue, and music, and you try to keep those things as unmarried as possible, so later on you can play with the volume.

Q: *You do all the editing, too.*

A: One of the advantages of doing your own editing, and being the writer and director, is that on the day, you're already editing while you're shooting. If you're shooting a master shot, and different angles, and you're doing a three-minute scene, the actors don't necessarily have to ever do it perfectly. They can blow a line every single time, but as long as it's the first part one time and the second part another time, because you've got different angles, I can, as the eventual editor, say, "I've got a great scene here."

I can use the good first part and the good second part, and mix and match. I don't have to keep doing take after take after take, waiting for the perfect performance because it's not theater.

Q: *You put it together.*
A: You're piecing it together. That one reason why somebody has to be in control of the work, to be able to say when we've done enough, or we need more footage of this.

They talk about a director having a vision, and that sounds very grand. To me, it's really that simple. Somebody has to say we've told the story of this scene. We've told this moment. We will be able to put it together in the movie, and it will do what it needs to do.

Very often in movies where there's not one authorial person—where somebody's directing it, but the star has more power than they do, and the studio has more power than the star does, so the director's more of just an employee—those directors are encouraged, and probably rightly so, to shoot a lot more footage, provide a lot more possibilities. So that the people above them who are going to have the final say have more ways to try putting it together. They cover every possible angle, have multiple cameras running.

Whereas what I'm doing is much closer to making a sculpture out of a small piece of clay, and saying it's not going to be any bigger than this piece of clay. The other way of doing it is to shoot this huge block-of-granite worth of footage, and then chisel it away to that same small figure. You can get a good product both ways, it's just that one way is a lot more expensive.

Q: *Shooting begins in early July—What's the first thing you're going to shoot?*
A: With good weather, we're hoping to shoot the big wedding scene that's outside. You try to schedule your outdoor stuff earlier, so if you get bad weather, you still have time in your schedule to go back and get it.

I do weather breakdowns for every scene in the movie, for what could the weather be, does it have to be not raining, can it be raining hard, or raining so softly the camera doesn't see it.

We have about 20 to 24 pages that are supposed to take place in the same four hours of a day. You're not going to be able to shoot all those 24 pages in one day, so the minute you commit to something and, say the day of the wedding is overcast but not raining, the other scenes that are supposed to cut with that exterior have to be overcast and not raining, or a couple hours later so it could've started raining. But some consistency.

So it doesn't have to be a beautiful day for this big wedding scene; it just has to not be raining hard. Alaskans are used to doing things outdoors in the rain.

# INDEX